Advance Praise for
Insurgent Hunter

"I'm partial to AFOSI (Air Force Office of Special Investigations) stories, and this one is terrific! *Insurgent Hunter* is an engrossing memoir that reads like a top-notch thriller. Treadway and Templin are the real deal—and it shows!"

—**Marc Cameron,** *New York Times* bestselling author of *Breakneck* and *Tom Clancy Command and Control*

"I had the privilege of serving with great soldiers, sailors, marines, and airmen in Iraq from 2006–2007—at a time when WIAs and KIAs peaked. This book brought back memories, and I felt like I was reliving the events in those crucial years. Much like 'Dawg's' pursuit of HVTs (high-value targets), special operation forces, acting on tips and intelligence from Iraqis, targeted and killed the terrorist al Zarqawi in June of 2006. It was a good day. I recalled the joy of making a difference and developing others, and when Treadway and Templin describe the explosion that took down Hammer 1, I relived the pain of losing comrades. From Balad to Osan, Treadway and Templin have captured the essence of what it means to live the warrior ethos: always accomplish the mission, never accept defeat, never quit, and never leave a fallen comrade. Despite academic, physical, and professional setbacks, Dawg drives on. God bless our special operators—the quiet professionals. His story is our story."

—**Major General Keith Thurgood,** United States Army (Retired)

"I'm stunned, elated, and grateful to have guys like Jack Treadway making our military and country (and world) a better place to be. *Insurgent Hunter* is one hell of a story. Treadway's background, instinct, and observation of role models helped him to overcome the biggest challenge he'd face in a wartime military—how to motivate others to ultimately succeed in every endeavor they'd face. In war, however, not everything can be controlled. Treadway is the case study of how to move forward and encourage others. Grab your favorite drink, open the book, and be inspired."

—**B. Rudee Schad,** Basic Underwater Demolition SEAL training Class 142, SEAL Delivery Vehicle Team Two, SEAL Team Five, and Schad Commodity, LLC

"One man's compelling journey through this generation's wars—Jack's story covers it all—what life was like coming up through the SEAL Teams as an NCO, transitioning to both the Air Force and the Officer Corps and then his experience as a Special Agent collector outside the wire during Operation Iraqi Freedom. Perhaps most importantly, it tells the story of the often challenging shift to civilian life once the uniform is put away and the memories of lost friends still linger. It was an honor to serve alongside him and the other men and women during the first major conflicts of the twenty-first century."

—**Colonel Chris Church,** OSI, United States Air Force (Retired)

"Jack Treadway and Stephen Templin, the *New York Times* bestselling author of *SEAL Team Six*, have delivered another armrest-gripping, non-fiction, military thriller. Their latest work, *Insurgent Hunter*, describes the incredible exploits of former Navy SEAL and Air Force Office of Special Investigations Special Agent Jack Treadway, an alias because Treadway's real name cannot be revealed.

"*Insurgent Hunter* takes the reader from Treadway's training as a fledgling SEAL, where he is badly injured and nearly killed. After his tenure with SEAL Delivery Vehicle Team 2 and SEAL Team 5, he transitions from enlisted Navy SEAL to Commissioned Air Force officer assigned to the elite Office of Special Investigations. As an OSI Counterinsurgency Agent, Treadway deploys to Iraq and engages in a fierce campaign, along with his fellow OSI agents, to hunt down bloodthirsty Al Qaeda insurgents determined to kill as many Americans as they can.

"The harrowing details of Treadway's day-to-day, life-and-death, experiences as an insurgent hunter in Iraq are described in detail, bringing the reader along on every convoy, interrogation, firefight and IED attack. Templin's own military experience, in addition to his taut, edge-of-seat writing, only adds to Treadway's account, and lends an authenticity few authors of real-life military accounts can offer.

"I was particularly touched by the human aspects of Treadway's saga. His further experiences pursuing stateside sex offenders, and his battle with survival guilt in the wake of returning home from Iraq alive while several of his fellow OSI Agents and closest friends did not, adds an emotional depth to the book not typically found in military non-fiction.

"I cannot recommend *Insurgent Hunter* enough. If you are a fan of gut-wrenching, true-to-life, military literature, this is the book for you."

—**Sean Lynch,** author of *Hold Back the Night*

INSURGENT HUNTER

Memoirs of a Navy SEAL Turned Counterinsurgent Agent in Iraq

JACK TREADWAY &
STEPHEN TEMPLIN

PERMUTED
PRESS

A KNOX PRESS BOOK
An Imprint of Permuted Press
ISBN: 979-8-88845-104-5
ISBN (eBook): 979-8-88845-105-2

Insurgent Hunter:
Memoirs of a Navy SEAL Turned Counterinsurgent Agent in Iraq
© 2024 by Jack Treadway and Stephen Templin
All Rights Reserved

Cover art by Cody Corcoran

Permuted Press, LLC
New York • Nashville
permutedpress.com

Published in the United States of America
1 2 3 4 5 6 7 8 9 10

IN REMEMBRANCE

In memory of Nate, Tom, and Dave—Special Agents who were specifically targeted by the enemy because they were the best at what OSI agents do, bringing the bad to justice.

TABLE OF CONTENTS

Author Note...9

PART I - THE HUNTER

Chapter 1: Downrange..13
Chapter 2: Growing Pains 18
Chapter 3: The Prey...27
Chapter 4: BUD/S..33
Chapter 5: Hell Week...38
Chapter 6: The Reaper's Shadow 46
Chapter 7: SEAL Delivery Vehicle Team Two...............51
Chapter 8: SEAL Team Five 57
Chapter 9: Special Mission Unit..64
Chapter 10: BUD/S Instructor..74
Chapter 11: Jack of Arabia 80
Chapter 12: FLETC..86
Chapter 13: To Catch a Predator 91
Chapter 14: Closing In..95
Chapter 15: The Catch..100

PART II - THE HUNT

Chapter 16: Iraq...111
Chapter 17: Kaiser Soze 118
Chapter 18: IED Planters..124
Chapter 19: Old Man Hajib..132
Chapter 20: Ineffective Fire...136
Chapter 21: The Iraqi Captain 139
Chapter 22: Moped...141
Chapter 23: Hollywood...147
Chapter 24: Best Buddies..153
Chapter 25: Photograph..157
Chapter 26: Hammer One Down 163
Chapter 27: Extract..169
Chapter 28: In Memoriam 176

Chapter 29: Baghdad Bob 185
Chapter 30: The Trial 192
Chapter 31: Psychological 197
Chapter 32: The Choice 205
Chapter 33: Night Crawler 207
Chapter 34: Unbelievable 212
Chapter 35: Old Man Hajib Returns 214
Chapter 36: Justice 219
Chapter 37: FNGs 221
Chapter 38: Goodbye 225

PART III - AFTER THE HUNT

Chapter 39: Homecoming 231
Chapter 40: Rumors of War 236
Chapter 41: Naval Postgraduate School...............................241
Chapter 42: Insurgents in Korea...246
Chapter 43: Backdraft 255
Chapter 44: Unicorns & Rainbows 261

Epilogue 267

AUTHOR NOTE

The events in this book are true—told from my perspective and to the best of my memory. Many of the people in these pages are still hunting bad guys or are at risk of being hunted, so I've used pseudonyms for our names to protect us. The Department of Defense (DoD) requested several revisions to protect sensitive information, which I complied with. Although the DoD approved this book for publication, the views in this book are mine and don't necessarily reflect the official policy or position of the US Navy, US Air Force, Department of Defense, or US Government. Also, dialogue may not be word for word, but it reflects the core of my experiences. This book is one album of photographs of many in my life.

PART I

THE HUNTER

*It is your choices that show what you truly
are, far more than your abilities.*

—JK ROWLING

CHAPTER 1

DOWNRANGE

I FIRST LEARNED TO HUNT men in the SEAL Teams, and it nearly killed me. At SEAL Delivery Vehicle Team Two, an SDV—a covert mini wet submarine—came within inches of slicing and dicing me. At Team Five, I shuffle-stepped through a vomit-spewed C-130 transport plane before I jumped into the snowy mountains of the Korean Peninsula. Then I broke my back in a Special Mission Unit.

Later, I became an Office of Special Investigations (OSI) agent and ran confidential informants in Iraq. One by one, my expeditionary detachment and I removed more than a hundred insurgents from the battlespace. Our most elusive prey was a high-value target on the kill or capture list—a deadly al Qaeda financier codenamed Kaiser Soze. The greatest trick the Devil ever pulled was convincing the world he didn't exist. Then an Iraqi officer, an "ally" who secretly worked for an Iranian backed militia, killed three members of my Expeditionary Detachment (EDet). It was the worst night of my life, and I wanted revenge.

Under a burning sun in the Sunni Triangle, forty miles north of Baghdad, I jocked up and loaded into the second of three Humvees. I was the new operations officer, and my job was to make sure we took down the bad guys and brought our guys home safely. We were agents in the OSI. I climbed into the front passenger seat and switched on the Blue Force Tracker, a computerized terrain map with a GPS system that displayed the positions of good guys around us in blue. It also enabled the Joint Defense Operations Center (JDOC) to follow our mission along with others in our area. If things went south, I wanted to target the bad guys, not the guys in blue. I also had a vehicle radio that I could use to communicate with my convoy, JDOC, medical evacuation, and air weapons teams that included Apache attack helicopters and Black Hawks. Even with the peace of mind that the Blue Force Tracker and the radio provided, operating in the daytime went against everything I had been taught as a frogman.

Hank took the wheel. We didn't use real names. Everyone had a call sign, and his was Hank because with his beard and long hair, he was the spitting image of Hank Williams Junior. And he liked early outlaw country music—the good stuff I grew up listening to with my dad on his 8-tracks in a smoke-filled, jacked-up Dodge power wagon—Waylon Jennings, Merle Haggard, and the other renegade country music singers.

Huey manned the M240B machine gun in the turret. He was the youngest agent and strong as a beast. His youthful way of talking and acting drove our detachment commander crazy, though Huey didn't seem to notice it when he was doing it. One time Huey radioed that he'd somehow locked himself in one of our black armored Chevy Suburbans, and he'd been stuck in the baking sun for an hour. We ran a hundred meters, and when we got to him, we had to press our faces to the smoked glass on the sides or look through the front to see inside. He looked like hell. Even so, we couldn't stop laughing.

One of the agents raised his voice and said, "How'd you lock yourself in the truck?"

Huey sopped the sweat off his forehead with his sleeve. His voice was muffled: "I tried all the electrical, but it isn't working."

"Did you try to open the door manually?" another agent asked.

Huey glowered. "What kind of idiot do you think I am? Of course I tried it!"

"Just try it again."

He did. The door opened, and we laughed our asses off.

Professor was our interpreter. He sat in the back with Huey. He was a first generation Arab American with a PhD from an Ivy League college. Professor smoked and was out of shape, but he was so smart that it was like having another agent with us.

With our different backgrounds and appearances, we looked like a Western posse. I was the only one who wore ripstop desert cammies, leftovers from when I was in the SEAL Teams. Hank wore a sand-colored armor crewman's uniform. Huey liked 501 cargo pants and a sand-colored T-shirt that showed off his bulging biceps. None of us wore rank insignias or nametags.

My team knew a bit about my reputation, and they seemed pumped that I was going out on a mission with them for the first time. We rolled through Balad Air Base, also known as Mortaritaville, because mortars and rockets hit us over forty times a week. Sirens went off so frequently that anyone who'd been there more than a few days stopped running to the bunkers.

The outside temperature pushed above a hundred and ten degrees; inside the Humvee I cooked, especially since I wore twenty-five pounds of Kevlar—a Ranger vest, armor plates, and a helmet. Adding to my gear, I carried an M4 rifle with an EOTECH holographic sight, one magazine of ammo in my rifle and six on my vest, a Sig Sauer P228 compact pistol, a CamelBak hydration pack, a portable radio, and an escape and evasion kit that included money to buy my way out of trouble and a compass to find my way home. The body heat from the four of us increased the temperature inside the vehicle.

We weren't allowed to drive around on base with ammo in our machine gun, so after we left the confines of our base, the wire, we pulled into a designated spot where Huey fed a belt of ammo into the machine gun, the Pig, and test fired it. The two agent gunners in the other vehicles did the same. Then we headed out.

Our three-vehicle convoy hit the hard pack road in a cloud of dust, and we galloped to forty-five miles per hour. We passed holes and craters where IEDs had gone off. In the past year, a thousand and thirty-five of them had been found or had gone off in our area of operations alone. I didn't want to hit one thousand and thirty-six. The road was so narrow here that if we struck an IED and got ambushed, there was no way to turn around; we would have to blow through or back out. Now the heat was the least of my troubles.

We tore past canals and fields that reminded me of the farms in San Joaquin Valley. Much as the San Joaquin River brought life to the valley, the Tigris River brought life here. Despite the homelike beauty of my environment, I looked at my compass and the surrounding area for landmarks in case things got ugly and I had to escape and evade back to base. I kept one eye on my Blue Force Tracker and one on the road for IEDs. I needed more eyes.

Our mission was to contact an asset, one of our informants who'd been giving us intel, but who had recently stopped showing up for his meets. We were out to determine why he'd been laying low. Five miles from Mortaritaville, we rolled past stucco farmhouses with large stretches of fields between them. Our lead vehicle neared a small barn and a tan, two-story house—our spy's home. It seemed to me that the previous operations officer was great at generating paperwork from the agents, but he didn't show them effective tactics to operate in such a deadly environment. When I was going through OSI training, a classmate who had been an undercover cop in a biker gang taught me never to meet a confidential informant at his home or his workplace. If the guy was bad, I'd be on his home turf and probably wouldn't survive a shootout with his gang.

If he was good, the bad guys might see us and wonder what business we had with him. Either way, visiting a source at his home or workplace was a lose-lose situation. I could see that I'd have to make changes to the team's procedures.

We slowed down, left the road, pulled up to the house, and stopped. I dismounted my Humvee. My teammates looked at the building, but none of them set security for potential threats from the outside. Although they were trained and experienced in collecting intelligence, they weren't trained to be soldiers, and without any support here, I was worried for them and myself. My heart rate kicked up a notch, and I took a deep breath to slow it down.

I moved tactically to the house with my M4 at the ready. There was no front door—only a doorway. Orion had exited one of the other vehicles and stacked up first beside the door. He'd been through advanced tactical training developed by an elite Special Forces guy. He was also the wise soul who'd helped Huey in the locked Suburban by suggesting he unlock it manually.

Stacked up behind him was Nate, who was a military brat like me, but he had a law degree. He always had himself under control, and talking and smiling came easily for him. Over six feet tall with dark hair and dark eyes, he caught the attention of the ladies when he walked into a room.

Then came Mac, a quiet, clean-living, easygoing agent who'd graduated from the Citadel, one of the toughest senior military colleges in the country. Nate, Mac, and I had gone through federal law enforcement training together in Glynco, Georgia.

I'd done building entries so many times before that I wasn't concerned about my part, but I was worried about the three guys in front of me and what they were going to do, and I was uneasy about leaving Hank, Huey, Professor, and the others outside with the vehicles.

Orion and Nate entered first. Mac and I followed. There was minimal furniture, so I could move quickly, but I couldn't understand why everyone else was moving so damn slowly. We searched room to room on the first floor. "Clear." No one was on this floor, but we'd taken so much time that if someone was upstairs, they'd had plenty of opportunity to prepare a welcoming party for us.

I gestured that I'd lead us up the stairs. The guys perked up as I passed them to take point. I hustled to the first room on the second floor. Doorways are a death funnel because that's where enemy fire will be focused, so I stepped through it quickly to get out of the kill zone. My footwork was automatic, and I moved as efficiently as possible. Smooth is fast. I turned the corner and pushed off into one side of the room. I popped my muzzle forward, so if anyone stood next to the door, I'd give him a mouthful of steel. I advanced deeper so I wouldn't hold up the train behind me and leave someone stuck in the doorway eating a barrage of enemy bullets. I scanned my sector and cleared my corner. Mac cleared his side.

The Iraqis in this part of the country usually slept on the floor, so there were no beds. "Clear."

We searched the other rooms too. "Clear."

I exhaled, relieved.

I turned to head downstairs, but Orion pointed to the steps leading to the roof, where it was cooler at night and where Iraqis often slept. *Damn.*

I took us up onto the roof. *Nothing.* We were lucky that no one was waiting for us.

We returned downstairs and stepped outside. The agents were relaxed—too relaxed. Commander Mitchell, a stoic leader and the tallest guy in the unit with his black hair and beard cropped short, pointed to a small wooden barn. It was smaller than a room in a house and looked more like an American shed than a barn. It was too small to clear with a rifle or fit a group of agents into.

"I got this," I said.

I slung my rifle, drew my pistol, and entered solo. Inside, sunlight poked through the cracks and down onto a dirt floor. A funky smell hit me. Ahead of me in the dim light, multiple sets of eyes stared at me. Half a dozen chickens sat on wooden nest boxes and perches. They appeared calmer than me.

When I came out, all the agents were watching me. As soon as I indicated that nobody was in the barn, instead of moving tactically, they walked back to the Humvees like they were returning from a fishing trip. *What the—*

I looked at Commander Mitchell, whose face filled with concern. It was like staring into a mirror.

On the ride back to base, I wasn't troubled about the heat or concerned about IEDs—I worried about the next six months of my tour here. *How the hell are we going to survive?*

CHAPTER 2

GROWING PAINS

I KNEW THAT IF I went to Commander Mitchell with complaints and concerns, I better have some possible resolutions for them, or I wouldn't be doing him any good—especially if he already knew that the team lacked proper training for what they were doing. Things would have to be done differently. I was anxious about how the commander and agents who'd been there awhile would feel about me wanting to train them.

We pulled our trucks back into their spots at our compound on base, and we downjocked our team gear and took care of it—the encrypted vehicle and individual radios, crew-served machine guns, extra ammo, medical gear, and so on. We also took care of our own kit, such as rifles and pistols.

Until recently, the agents had an army unit supporting them, but the army had deployed all over Afghanistan and Iraq, and they were strapped for manpower. All OSI detachments in those countries had lost the army tactical security elements assigned to them. Normally, the army would debrief the tactical part of a mission among themselves, and our agents would take their intel to the analysts and debrief the collection side of the mission. Now that the army wasn't with us, there was no tactical debrief. We had to fend for ourselves.

The focus of the mission—the asset—was Hank and Nate's, so they went to the analysts for the intel debrief, which was a whole lot of nothing. The asset wasn't worth the time we wasted and certainly not the danger.

I spotted Commander Mitchell in the hall. Beside him stood Red, a senior non-commissioned officer who was Commander Mitchell's right-hand man and our superintendent. I walked over to them and gave my pitch: "Do you mind if we put ops on hold for a week so I can come up with some training and standard operating procedures for the EDet?"

"Would you?" Commander Mitchell asked.

I nodded. "Yes, sir. I'll ask the guys about the different kinds of missions we carry out, various areas we operate in, times of day, what shooting ranges are available, and what we have for places to practice tactics without being watched by indigenous folks. I'll put something together."

"That would be awesome," Commander Mitchell said.

Red nodded approvingly.

I walked over to the bullpen, an office area the size of a long, narrow classroom and pulled out Orion. He had served in an anti-terrorism specialty team and received some good training. I motioned for him to follow me into my office, which he did, and there I told him what was on my mind. When Hank returned from his intel debrief, I asked him to join us. Hank was one of those guys who could find almost anything you needed and seemed to have connections everywhere. He could access shooting ranges, ammo to train with, and a place to practice with our vehicles.

As we talked, it became clear that there was a bit of a mismatch in the way we viewed the situation. Hank hadn't seen another way to do things, so our conversation was an eye-opener for him. Orion wanted to teach some advanced tactics.

I was somewhere between them. "We need to do better than we're doing, but we don't have a lot of time, so let's keep it simple. We're not going to be able to train these guys to stand there and slug it out with somebody. I think the best thing we can do is teach them some basic patrol tactics, how to clear rooms safely, take care of a downed man, and provide security until we can get the injured out. We should also be able to rescue a Humvee if it gets hit, cover it while we pull our guys out, put them into the other two Humvees, and get out of Dodge."

In a really tough spot, where our losses were too high, making us immobile and unable to break contact, we still had our radios to request medevacs, air weapons teams, and a quick reaction force.

Our differences were quickly resolved when I had them take ownership and be a part of this—Orion would assist with training, and Hank would get us what we needed.

That evening, Orion and I wrote up training for Close Quarters Battle (CQB), doing two-man entries, but we needed a place to do it. I looked outside my office. It was all one floor where we worked, showered, ate, pumped iron, watched videos, and slept—we lived with each other 24/7. Commander Mitchell had his own office and personal room; so did I. Most of the agents were bunked two to a room. We couldn't take a piss without seeing each other. Our building would be the perfect place to practice CQB.

The next day I finished putting together a plan for five days of training, and we started the following day.

On training day one, we did CQB in our own building with empty weapons. We also went over how to communicate, so each guy knew what the other was doing when he did it. In addition, we covered prisoner handling.

Hank had linked up with the Combined Joint Special Operations Task Force, and on day two, we used their shooting ranges across the base. There, I taught the other agents how to shoot, move, and communicate. If an agent's primary weapon went down, he needed to transition to his pistol and let his buddy know, so he could cover until the rifle was back online. We went over stacking up at the door, footwork, and transitioning from rifle to pistol. They already knew some of what I covered, but I helped them become more efficient.

Day three got put on hold—we were hit with an op to go meet a sheikh out in his village. Visiting sheikhs was always a pain in the ass. These elders liked their positions, and they ran the villages. Our job was to collect intel, but a lot of times they simply wanted to chat, and we got nothing. Despite the negatives, we had to maintain contact with them in case something did come up in their area. The sheikhs were the ones who had an ear to the ground. They'd tell us what they wanted or needed in exchange for information.

Once again, we loaded into the Humvees, and I manned the machine gun in the turret. This trip was easier because our destination was closer—I could almost see the village from the base. Also, the sheikh controlled the village, so there was less threat of being attacked. It was more of a hearts-and-minds thing—drink the chai and eat the lamb.

When we arrived, there were kids outside, but their mothers pulled them into their homes and closed the doors and windows. That concerned me. It's one thing when all the adults go inside, but it's another when the kids are pulled in too.

We parked beside a wall with a gate. I manned the machine gun while four agents opened the gate. It was two hundred yards to the sheikh's house, and they walked in a cluster like they were going down to the 7-11. That was a no-go. *We're going to have to work on that.*

A helicopter flew overhead, and gunshots rang out from about a mile behind the sheikh's house. I had no idea what that was about, and I'd heard no reports about it. It was possible US forces were conducting live-fire training, but I didn't know what the hell was going on. I watched windows in the houses, scanning for any that opened or a muzzle that poked out of one.

The four agents were only with the sheikh about thirty or forty minutes before they came back. It was a short meet for a sheikh, but it felt long to me, and I was more than happy to get the hell out of there. The sheikh only wanted to chat, and he told them nothing of significance.

The next morning, we dove into day three of training. Hank had found us a spot near a movie theater and warehouse buildings where we could practice without being seen by Iraqi eyes, including those hired to work on base. There, we practiced basic patrolling. We spread out so we didn't present the enemy with a stinking huge target. The point man covered 180 degrees in front of him. The agent behind him scanned 180 degrees to one side while the next agent covered 180 degrees on the opposite side. Rear security protected 180 degrees to the rear. Now we'd have 360 degrees of double coverage. We practiced in small and large groups in narrow and open spaces. We did contact drills—attacking the enemy and breaking contact.

Day four, we used the same areas but added vehicles to the mix. Each time, I changed up the scenario—a different vehicle going down, agents in different positions, and so on.

For day five, we returned to the firing range, and I ran them through stress courses. A lot of the agents were lifting weights and getting gigabig, but when you come under fire and your heart is pumping piss, that little shot of adrenaline will get you through initial contact. In an extended scenario, it will also sap you, but you still have to react and do your job. Muscular endurance is more important than Atlas muscles. Commander Mitchell had been pushing them to do a more combat-oriented PT, but they wanted to do their own thing.

I showed them why the commander was right. We went out wearing full body armor, did pushups, ran fireman carries, did room entries, and then shot targets that were scored for accuracy. Everything was a competition. After sucking wind, they saw how poorly they shot. They realized that they needed to do more to prepare for battle than lift heavy weights.

Following that fifth day of training, some agents collected intel about a weapons cache in the army's area of operations. Mac, Nate, and Professor went out with our only female agent, call sign Croft, named after Lara Croft in the *Tomb Raider* game and film. Like many other female OSI agents, she was an aggressive investigator, smart, and pretty damn tough. She lived, trained, and hunted with us. The four linked up with a dozen army guys whose unit was across the base. Although the army was busy with their own operations and they couldn't dedicate themselves full time to us, especially for gathering intelligence, they helped us when we needed to act on intelligence.

Their convoy drove into town until they reached an alley that was too narrow to drive through, so they parked the vehicles and moved out on foot. The army guys bopped along like they were hanging out in the streets back home—

they were brave men, but they were from an artillery unit that wasn't primarily infantry. Mac, Nate, and Croft formed a staggered patrol formation, and the army guys followed their lead by falling into the formation.

The cache was where the informant said it would be, but it was explosives instead of weapons. The soldiers stood facing inward toward the cache, but when the agents pointed outward into a perimeter to cover their surroundings, the army soldiers did the same. The agents called in a bomb disposal unit to remove the enemy explosives, and the agents and soldiers held security until they arrived. It's crazy what can be done with only five days of training.

⬦ ⬦ ⬦

After the initial training, we'd knock off at noon on Fridays if we didn't have an urgent mission and continue our training. Our enemies continued to hammer our base with mortars and rockets, and I wanted to put a stop to it. One day, I went into the bullpen. Four agents' grey steel desks were lined up on one wall facing into the room, and three were on the opposite wall facing them. The desktops were green and rubbery; a computer sat on each one with stacks of paper beside it.

One of the previous agents, who'd shipped out before I arrived, had thought he was high speed and impressed a lot of the guys with how many intelligence reports he could write. Out of all the reports he'd written, a few had some decent intel for a target, but he never sounded like he wanted to act on it, and Commander Mitchell had to take charge.

"Look," I told the agents, "I'm not impressed with how many reports you can rope out because unless that intelligence is actionable, you're not affecting the battlespace. We need to take bad guys off the battlespace. We need to take out the dudes that are rocketing and mortaring us forty-four times a week, planting a thousand IEDs out there, and killing our guys."

I asked them to tell me more about our area of operations (AO). They showed me where the Sunni and Shia tribes were. The Sunnis weren't as numerous, but Saddam Hussein was a Sunni, and he'd controlled the country. Now that Saddam was gone, his army was broken up, and his Baathist party was crippled, the Shias grappled for power. The Sunnis were quickly being left out in the cold, and they were indignant, so they tried to tip the scales by joining terrorist groups such as Al-Qaeda. Although the Sunnis and Shias were both Muslim, they hated each other.

A Jordanian jihadist named Abu Musab al-Zarqawi tried to impress the leader of Al-Qaeda—Osama bin Laden—but bin Laden didn't like him. Instead, bin Laden's number two man recommended Zarqawi go to Iraq and start up Al-Qaeda there. A lot of Sunnis joined him. Most of them weren't zealots like Zarqawi, but they were irate, and they wanted to regain power.

We marked off areas for each of us on the map. Then I said, "If something happens in your part of the AO, like a mortar going off or a soldier getting killed, I'm going to say, 'hey, man, that came out of your area. You're responsible to get on it and shut it down.' Your primary job is to protect this base.

"We have a CRAM system for detecting and destroying incoming rockets and mortars before they strike." (This was the Counter Rocket, Artillery, and Mortar system.) "I want to put it to more effective use. We receive advance warning when rockets or mortars are incoming, but I want to destroy the bad guys who're doing it. CRAM gives us the point of origin, and if rockets or mortars come from your area, you're responsible for shutting them down."

I could see the light bulbs going on in the agents' heads—they were beginning to see what I could see.

Our mission was tactically oriented, meaning we were focused on the security of our base and the immediate surrounding area to about a dozen miles out. There are more strategically oriented units, focused on targets that could affect the course of the war. OSI agents also were involved with units at this level, but our unit was at a less sensitive level, and protecting the base was our primary mission.

Now that the agents had a purpose for gathering intel, they met with their assets more often.

Croft and Orion, who were partners, learned of a farmer who was willing to meet with them. Because we had to provide our own security element for the patrol and meet, our whole EDet of ten agents had to go out. Emptying an EDet of all its agents for every meet not only meant fewer reports being produced, but it also meant that if one Humvee were hit by an IED, we'd lose a third of our EDet. We were considered "Low Density High Demand;" there weren't many OSI agents, but units all over the world needed us. Losing a third of an EDet on one op would be devastating.

For Croft and Orion's meeting place, we chose a site that took the farmer's safety and ours into consideration. The site was far enough off the beaten path that the farmer wouldn't be followed or spotted by insurgents, but the location was safe enough for the ten of us to secure a perimeter and break contact with enemies and get out if we were attacked. We also put a Quick Reaction Force patrol and aircraft on standby to come to our rescue, if needed.

The night of the meet, Nate led the patrol as driver in the front Humvee. He could study maps and terrain like nobody else and had a keen sense of direction. On our drive out from the base, he went straight when he was supposed to go straight and turned where he was supposed to turn. In a war zone, a wrong turn can be a son of a bitch because it can expose you to curious eyes and increase the probability of hitting an IED. Nate was the perfect point man. In his truck, Orion kept his eyes on the Blue Force Tracker while monitoring the convoy communications, and Red manned the machine gun in the turret while monitoring comms with the base JDOC.

Commander Mitchell wanted me in the middle vehicle so I could make tactical calls under fire, especially in the event of a downed vehicle. I helped navigate for our trio of Humvees while Hank drove and Huey handled the big gun.

I, in turn, wanted Commander Mitchell in the rear vehicle. In the SEAL Teams, if you had a good boss, you protected him from anything from a bar fight to a fire fight. It was a habit I didn't want to break. In the back with him was his gunner, Gator, a guy built like the Hulk who'd formerly worked as a park ranger. I had to work out consistently my whole life to maintain a bench press over 350 pounds, but guys like him, country strong, can walk right in without ever working out and toss up 350 or more on their worst day. *Genetics.* Next to Commander Mitchell sat our interpreter (terp) Shaky, who was from one of the war-torn countries in the Middle East but had become an American citizen. To look at his belly and white beard and to be around his jolly demeanor, you'd think he belonged in a mall playing Santa Claus for the kids, but he did everything asked of him, even if it scared the hell out of him. In front of Commander Mitchell and Shaky, Mac drove, and Croft sat in the navigator's seat—if our convoy got turned around, they would lead us out.

Nate turned off the asphalt and led us onto a back country dirt road. My truck and Commander Mitchell's followed. I hated this route, but the asset didn't have a car, and this was the best area for him to walk to at night. Soon we reached the last leg, which paralleled a canal to our left. Several soldiers had drowned in a similar canal when their Humvee rolled into it and sank upside down.

The high dirt berm and trees to our right prevented us from escaping that way. As a SEAL, this was the kind of place I was trained to set an ambush. Hit the front truck first so the convoy can't drive forward. Then hit the rear truck, so they can't back out. Once they're bottled up, open fire on the center. My breathing sped up, and my pulse pounded.

I wondered if my fellow agents were as nervous as I was. I kept my worries to myself and vowed to figure out a better place to meet this farmer next time.

On a positive note, we'd arrived early and were driving on the opposite side of the canal from where our meet was supposed to take place. We drove past the site. It looked clear.

Nate turned left. We followed him over a massive pipe that took us over the canal. Then we turned left again and rode on a dirt path that doubled back on the site side of the canal. *No ambush—yet.*

We shut off our lights, and our gunners and others switched to night vision goggles. I chose not to wear the NVGs and went old-school by letting my cones adapt to the darkness. I looked around for vehicles or people nearby, which would definitely be out of place considering the secluded area we were in. We slipped the Humvees in between and around dirt berms and trees, giving our turret gunners their best vantage points for high ground and avenues of approach.

Some of us dismounted the Humvees while others remained inside. I opened the door of my armored truck—it sounded so damn loud out here in the middle of nowhere. No matter how gently I tried to close it, the noise neared unbearable. Forgetting something in the truck and opening and closing it again would make matters worse. Everyone had to have their shit together.

Quietly, I slipped into my sector, becoming part of the bushes. I only took my eyes off my field of fire long enough to ensure that the gunner nearest me and the agents to my left and right knew where I was—the biggest reason being that I didn't want one of them to mistake me for a bad guy and shoot me. There'd been plenty of mishaps in the Teams during live night-fire drills. Seeing tracers going over your head and hearing the zip and sonic crack of nearby rounds is a good way to learn you're under fire, and you never want it to happen again.

I screwed a suppressor on my weapon. Other agents thought it was to silence my shot, but it was more to suppress the visible flash of my muzzle at night. I had also taken out the tracers from my ammo before loading my magazines. I only liked using tracers with machine guns because it could help mark a target for helo gunships like the AH-64 Apache.

We sent out our welcoming party on foot with Nate watching for the farmer. I stayed back with the others to protect our perimeter.

In the distance, a human silhouette materialized on the road.

Nate and Hank moved forward with Shaky, who told Farmer, "Turn away and put your hands up!" In Nate's truck, Red aimed his machine gun at Farmer. Mac and Hank walked up and searched him. When they found he was unarmed, they brought him back inside the perimeter to see the familiar, friendlier faces of Croft and Orion.

Their meet with Farmer seemed to take much too long. I didn't like being in one spot for this amount of time. The booger-eaters were known to set up IEDs for us on our way out. I heard movement immediately to my left about fifty yards out.

"Take cover," Red said.

Orion, Croft, and Farmer hurried to the nearest Humvee and used it as a shield.

The sound came closer.

I switched the selector on my M4 rifle from *safe* to *fire*. The noise sounded like only one person, but it could have been two. *Who would be crazy enough to advance this close to us? They gotta know they're outgunned.*

There'd been intel traffic about foreign fighters in the area, the only zealots crazy enough to enter our perimeter and attack us with suicide vests. Even so, our gunners and others with their night vision weren't reporting anyone.

I aimed my EOTECH sight at the thicket where the noise was coming from. *Okay, this is going to be a quick recognition and shoot problem.* I felt pretty good about my advantages: good cover and concealment on this berm and the superior firepower of my detachment and me against one booger-eater. The thicket moved. My trigger finger was ready. Then the target came into my sights—a baby donkey.

What the hell?

Somebody chuckled behind me.

My trigger finger relaxed, and I lowered my rifle muzzle.

We finished the meet. The intel was worth the wait. Farmer not only passed us information about the location of a nearby farm where there was a weapons cache with mortars and ammo used to attack our base on a regular basis, but he also gave us the identities and locations of four insurgents responsible for the mortaring. We were going to need assistance to take down all of these targets.

CHAPTER 3

THE PREY

THE NEXT DAY, IN THE scorching heat, we loaded up in our three-Humvee convoy and patrolled five miles to Forward Operating Base Orion, which housed a company of soldiers from the Third Infantry Division. They had the resources we needed to go after the four insurgents and the weapons cache that Farmer had reported.

Inside the gates of FOB Orion, we met with the commanding officer, a major in his thirties, who looked at us with our various uniforms, beards, and long hair like we were aliens.

Commander Mitchell introduced himself and said, "We have targets for you, Major."

"You had my curiosity, but now you have my attention," the major said.

"Croft here will brief you," Commander Mitchell said.

Croft didn't miss a beat. "We have intel on a nearby weapons cache, the names of the insurgents who are using it to mortar our base, and where those insurgents live."

"Really?"

Croft showed him a map and pointed to a place near the Tigris River.

The major rubbed his chin. "Yeah, I know that area."

Croft and Orion shared photos and our other intel with him.

"We'll probably need help from EOD," Orion said, referring to an Explosive Ordnance Disposal unit.

The major pointed two fingers at the map like two pistols. "We can run two ops simultaneously—hit the weapons cache and the mortar men at the same time."

My posse and I smiled.

"I've got indigenous troops from the 203rd Iraqi National Guard Battalion that we can use too," the major said.

I didn't know how much an Iraqi unit would be infiltrated by spies, so I was concerned.

The major must've read it on my face because he added, "I won't let the Iraqis know where we're going or what we're doing until we get there. And I'll take away their cell phones prior to the op."

It sounded sensible. "Good."

"Who are you guys again?" the major asked.

"Air Force Office of Special Investigations," Commander Mitchell said.

His quizzical stare made me think he still didn't get who we were.

We finished our meeting, and the major got his men ready while we went back to our base and prepared for battle.

Early the next morning, before the heat cranked up again, my EDet and I loaded up into the three Humvees. This time a different terp joined us—an Iraqi-American marine interpreter named Ibrahim, who sat in the back of my vehicle. Beside him sat Farmer, who would help identify the insurgents who were mortaring our base.

The sun broke the horizon as we ventured out of the wire. All of us were fired up because we were going to action some intel. Behind us were the days of writing inconsequential reports.

Nate steered us out to FOB Orion, where our little convoy slipped into the middle of an army convoy of Armored Personnel Carriers (APCs) and Humvees led by a weird contraption at the front. It was a Husky VMMD (vehicle-mounted mine detection), which can survive the blast of an IED.

The army guys and my posse headed out. A Kiowa helicopter flew overhead to serve as a forward observer. A black "beach ball" sat on top of the rotors of the little chopper. It contained one system to capture video, another to collect thermal imaging, and a laser that measured distances and designated targets. Two Apache attack helicopters joined us. The birds were great to have, but the villagers would be able to hear them before we arrived.

We kicked up dust through several miles of flat farmland before the terrain became hilly and the Husky brought us to a halt. I fidgeted while we sat, worrying that our suspects might flee into the tree line.

"Why is that John Deere tractor-looking contraption stopping?" I asked.

"Looks like the Husky detected an IED," Hank said.

"Oh." Now waiting seemed like a better idea than getting blown up.

Apparently, the Husky raised a false alarm, and after a few minutes, we resumed our trek and soon arrived at the village. The buildings were multi-storied. Beyond them stood palm trees and thick vegetation that hugged the Tigris River.

As we approached our target village, we gave Farmer a black hood with eye holes in it, and he put it on so he couldn't be identified. Our convoy stopped on a road that circled the village. Soldiers exited the lead vehicles and penetrated deep into the town while troops from the tail of the convoy hopped out and breached the buildings close by. The agents and I helped protect the vehicles' perimeter, some of us facing the village and some of us scanning the surrounding fields. Farmer sat hidden in the middle, ready to identify any insurgents our soldiers captured.

The soldiers brought three cuffed and black-hooded suspects close to where Orion and I were posted.

"We got more squirters running into the palms," one of the soldiers said.

Orion and I grabbed the three prisoners, and I told the soldier, "Go get 'em." The soldiers dashed off.

We marched the three prisoners in front of Farmer's Humvee.

Outside of the vehicle, I couldn't see Farmer's lips or hear his voice, but I heard over the radio, "Positive ID on all three—they're the mortarmen—verifying IDs."

The situation was too electric for Orion and me to be tied up with the three prisoners, so we took them to the APCs and loaded them in there until the army's intelligence team back on base could verify. Then we returned to our positions on the perimeter.

"I've got movement," Orion said.

I turned around.

Orion aimed his rifle up at the second story of a house that was fifty yards away. "Saw someone looking out that window."

There were troops several yards away from the house on the opposite side. If the moving guy had a weapon, he could aim down at the soldiers and open up on them. I radioed to a senior army guy and said, "Hey, you didn't clear one here. We got a guy running around in his house. Can you call some guys back here to clear this one?"

He radioed back to me. "Look, I got men hitting the weapons cache and human targets, and now we're chasing squirters into the grove too—can you guys clear it?"

I didn't want to pull all my guys off the perimeter. "Can you at least send me one guy?" I asked.

He sent me one soldier.

Orion and I took the soldier and Gator to the door of the building where Orion had spotted the movement. Ibrahim trailed close behind us.

I told the soldier, "You're on point—there's the front door."

He opened the door, but there was an iron gate inside. He tried to open it, but it made a loud noise and didn't budge.

"I'll find another entry point," Gator said before peeling off from our train and looking around the corner.

"He's in the first-floor window here," Orion said, "trying to peek at us without showing himself." Then Orion yelled at the window: "Hey, man, you better open this door or we're going to blow it off and break your windows!"

Ibrahim translated.

A voice came from inside the house shouting anxiously in Arabic. "Don't hurt my house! don't hurt my house!"

Ibrahim yelled back at him in Arabic. They shouted back and forth at each other for a couple minutes.

Finally, a little dude wearing a dirty, white man-dress—an ankle-length robe with long sleeves called a dishdasha—came to the door and unlocked it.

I grabbed him, pulled him out, and smashed him against the outside wall of his house. I told Ibrahim, "Ask him how many guys are in there."

Ibrahim spoke to the man in Arabic, and he replied. "There's nobody else in the house."

Gator returned.

"Gator, hold this guy," I said.

He did.

We still treated the house like there were people inside. Without Gator, we were a three-man entry team. Orion held the door open, and I motioned for the soldier to go first. He went through the door and straight into the middle of the room. *What the hell are you doing?* Then he turned around and looked right back at us with another open door behind him. If bad guys came out shooting, the soldier was going to catch a back full of bullets.

I rushed in with Orion. Inside, we looked at each other from the corners of our eyes: *Is this soldier shitting us?*

"Where we going next?" the soldier asked.

"What?" Orion said.

"I'm an intel analyst," the soldier said. "What do we do now?"

When the army sent me a guy to help clear the house, I thought they'd sent me someone tactical. I noticed his first lieutenant rank—not only was he an intel analyst but an officer to boot. I calmly pointed behind us. "We got it man, go ahead and get in the back of the train."

I stacked up at point next to a doorway. Orion squeezed me on the shoulder—the signal that he and the soldier were ready. I entered the room tactically, and we cleared it. After we cleared the first floor, I took us upstairs and then to the roof.

I radioed back to the army leader: "One prisoner and the house is clear."

The tone of his reply was upbeat: "Roger."

We returned to our convoy, prisoner in tow, and radioed the analysts back at the base for identification. The little guy in the man-dress was a nobody.

The army must've been impressed with us clearing that house because they asked us to help them clear another in the southeast corner of the village.

We moved swiftly over there. Inside the house, we found a big Iraqi dude— at least six foot four with a honking nose and a Saddam Hussein moustache. He also wore a dishdasha. He stood there with his wife, and they played innocent. Ibrahim translated.

"I don't know anything," he said. "I'm not a part of anything."

"If that's the case," I said, "let us search your house."

"No, I can't let you search my house."

"Then you're going to come with us 'til we find out who you are," I said.

His wife got excited. "Don't take him away. Don't you take him away!"

I went to cuff him, and he eyed me like he wanted to get froggy with me, but he looked around at the rest of us and wisely decided that that was probably not a good idea. Then we bagged his head.

His wife yelled at us.

"Hey," I said, "if he really has nothing to hide, we'll bring him back before the end of the day."

We cleared the rest of the house before we escorted Big Man out the door. His wife screamed.

We took Big Man to the convoy. Farmer identified him as the ringleader of the mortar three, and we stuck him in an APC too. Then we radioed our analysts, who verified all four of their identities. *Jackpot.*

One of the army soldiers called in. "We found the cache—mortar tubes and mortar rounds and other weapons and ammo."

Minutes later, another voice came over the radio. "EOD preparing to blow the cache." There was a pause. "Beginning countdown. 3, 2, 1...fire in the hole."

An explosion quaked the earth.

Hearing the M112 blocks of plastic explosives—C4—eliminate the cache was music to my ears. It was a momentous mission. We proved that we weren't just a package that the army had to protect; we were a resource that could fill gaps when the army wasn't able to fill them.

The army guys escorted us and our prisoners all the way back to Balad Air Base. Then they split off with the insurgents while we went to the analysts and briefed them.

Our EDet returned to our compound where we waited to hear what would happen with the prisoners we'd grabbed. There was a program called The Sons of Iraq that had been started in another province. The purpose was to encourage disenfranchised Sunnis to come back over to the good side and take some ownership in securing their own country. These Sunnis received jobs working on roadblocks to stop people from bringing in and planting IEDs, and initially the US military paid them. Later tribal sheikhs took over. Whether the mortarmen we'd captured were part of that program or not, all four of our prisoners were released.

What the hell? What if they go out and kill one or more of our guys? We couldn't believe it.

Huey was especially pissed. "I want to give the CO a piece of my mind," he said about the battalion commanding officer, who was in charge of the JDOC and the battalion that patrolled and secured the immediate area around the base.

I told Huey, "Look, man, you're not a colonel, and you're not going to tell the colonel what to do."

Huey was still upset. We all were.

Two days later, a Predator recorded some insurgent activity, and I was invited to view it. On the video, three men drove out to a farm area. Two stepped out and pulled a mortar tube and mortar rounds out of the trunk of the car. They set up the tube in a field and fired the mortar. Then they threw the tube back in their trunk and drove off. As they headed along the canal, the Predator fired a Hellfire rocket down through the roof—blowing all three of them to bits. Villagers came out to see what happened. Two male villagers popped open the trunk, grabbed the mortar tube and chucked it in the canal, where it sank out of sight. They didn't like these outsider insurgents disrupting their way of life.

The three dead insurgents were the same three mortarmen we'd captured in the village. We never saw or heard from Big Man again. It wasn't quite the ending I expected, but they were removed from our battlespace.

Just days later, a higher value target appeared on our horizon. He was on the kill or capture list—wanted dead or alive. He'd prove to be the most elusive and deadly, testing us to the bone. We codenamed him Kaiser Soze.

CHAPTER 4

BUD/S

WHY WOULD ANYONE IN THEIR right mind want to attempt some of the toughest military training in the world? Both my grandfathers served in the military during World War II. One was an army airborne paratrooper. The other joined the army's infantry, and he often sang the old patriotic song "Over There." My father was a navy veteran, having retired after twenty years. Everyone who joins the military has his reasons, but for me, it was in my blood.

I played football in high school, and I loved the physicality of it. As an offensive running back and a defensive corner, I liked to hit people and get hit back. One of my coaches also coached at a nearby junior college, and he seemed to think I was going to go there and play.

I earned good grades up until my junior year. Then I started going to a lot of keg parties at different friends' houses. When we didn't have a house, we went to an old oak tree on the outskirts of town and partied there. I didn't tell my parents where I was going, and my dad was pissed.

I got into several fights. Once, a friend and I were in a park, and three drugged-up skateboarders came at us like madmen. One of them hit my friend in the ribs with a skateboard, and he went down hard. I took on all three of them and beat one so badly that he couldn't get back on his feet. Someone called an ambulance and the police. The downed skateboarder was rushed to the hospital. The police questioned me. Fortunately, witnesses said that I acted in self-defense.

In an attempt to keep me out of trouble, my father made me get a part-time job that lasted from after football practice to eleven at night. I worked weekends too.

When the football season ended, I once again found time for mischief. One day my friends and I went up into the mountains, where we fished for trout and dove off cliffs. We drank beer, and in the evening, we shot our empty cans off logs with .22 pistols.

My buddy and I returned to my house the next day, and we walked through the garage where my dad was working with my uncle on his motorcycle. My uncle stared at me, and I realized he was looking at the pistol handle sticking out of my pocket. I went inside to the fridge, grabbed a beer, and headed to my room. I drank a few sips before I set the beer on my dresser. Then I sat down, pulled out my pistol, and cleaned it like my father had taught me.

My dad walked in, looked at the beer on my dresser and then the pistol. He pointed at me. "I don't care what branch of service you choose, but you better pick one because after you graduate, your dinner plate is broken."

"Yes, sir," I said. I didn't want any more school anyways.

I did some soul searching. I'd always enjoyed watching war movies with my dad and was impressed with heroes of the past and the things they did. I was a fan of the John Wayne movie *The Green Berets*. The men in that film were both intellects and men of action. Sylvester Stallone's *First Blood* was epic too. The main character, Rambo, was some kind of mysterious super-soldier. The summer after my junior year, I visited an army recruiter. "I want to be a Green Beret."

"Special Forces," the recruiter said. "That's the official name. To do that, you'll first have to go to Airborne School and jump out of airplanes."

"Great, my grandfather did that."

"Then you'll have to go to Ranger School," the recruiter said. "If you pass that, you'll serve as a Ranger until you make E-5, then you can try out for Special Forces." (Now the army has a more direct pipeline to Special Forces, but in those days that was the sequence.)

"Sign me up," I said.

So he did.

I filled out the paperwork and took the Armed Services Vocational Aptitude Battery (ASVAB). The test covered science, math, English, and some other things. I passed. Then I went home and told my dad. I thought he'd be pretty happy with me for finding direction.

"Boy," he said, "don't you know the baddest men on the face of the earth are Navy UDT/SEALs?"

"Who are they?" I asked.

"Why don't you look into it?"

I did, but I struggled to come up with anything. There was no internet back then, and I found nothing in the city library except an old black-and-white picture of a WWII frogman. I went to the navy recruiter, and all he had was a thin pamphlet about the qualifications and a paragraph about what they did. UDT is an acronym for Underwater Demolition Team—frogmen. Around the time of the Vietnam War, UDTs evolved into SEALs, an acronym for the areas they now operated in: Sea, Air, and Land. SEALs conducted small-unit special operations. "It's similar to Special Forces," the recruiter said, "but there're fewer of them. They're stationed near Coronado, California, or Virginia Beach, Virginia."

I was thrilled. "Either way I go, I'll get to live next to the beach. That's for me."

I went back and told my dad.

"You know," he said, "when I was on recruiting duty, fifteen men applied, and I had guys who were so physically prepared that I thought for sure they were going to make it. But it was the one guy I didn't suspect—a short Mexican kid—who was the only one to make it."

My father had served as a quartermaster on submarines, navigating and using the periscope. He reminisced: "On the submarine, we have a compartment that's called an escape trunk. One time a group of SEALs used it to exit. On the periscope, I watched them boogie off on their rubber raiding craft. After a while, there was a gigantic explosion. It lit up the sky. Then they came back."

The way my old man held them in such high regard made me think that if I became a SEAL, I could earn some of his respect too. I'd filled out and signed paperwork for the army, but I hadn't signed a final contract yet. That same summer after my junior year, I returned to the navy recruiter and filled out their paperwork. My ASVAB scores were high enough for the SEALS, and I signed up. I was proud.

I told a couple of my good friends. They told two friends who in turn told two friends, and soon it seemed like everyone knew. I wasn't pleased. Now the pressure was on. I couldn't fail. I didn't want to bring it up or talk about it anymore.

I saw Chuck Norris's *Delta Force*. *SEALs probably do that kind of work too.* Then I saw a *Soldier of Fortune* magazine article about SEALs in the US invasion of Grenada, codenamed Operation Urgent Fury. There were photos of abnormous dudes wearing cammies and scuba gear and carrying submachine guns. *That's what I'm talking about!*

I put a calendar on my wall and planned out how I was going to pass the physical screening test (PST)—a five-hundred-yard swim, followed by push-ups, sit-ups, pull-ups, and a one-and-a-half-mile run. (Some of the standards have changed since then, but it's still tough.) Doing each separately isn't nearly as challenging as doing each one back-to-back with only about two minutes in between.

My dad had shown me how to do the sidestroke, so I knew how to do the swim portion. I did my own PST to see how I stacked up. I didn't do too badly, but I didn't simply want to meet the minimums. I marked off tasks on my calendar to reach my goals and beyond. My recruiter also gave me a sheet that showed the requirements to get through each phase of SEAL training, so I squeezed some longer runs and longer swims into my calendar. I wanted to beat the four-mile timed run for third phase—the end of training.

I worked out daily. Every other morning, I woke up an hour earlier to run four miles before going to school. I began my start time from the digital clock on the microwave in my kitchen and rushed out the door. In the early morning darkness, I ran a route through my city behind some railroad tracks. Halfway into my run, there was a clock on a bank, and I used it for my split time, to see if my pace was on target. When I reached home, I hurried inside the house and looked at the clock on the microwave.

Once a month, I took my own PST to see how much I'd improved. When I reached my running goal, I put weights in a backpack to challenge myself further. On Sunday mornings I threw part of a telephone pole in the back of my truck and went out to the cross-country trail behind my high school's football field and ran with the log across my shoulders with both arms over it. I'd be embarrassed to be seen, so the nastier the weather, the better—no one would be out and see me. As it turned out, no one was there even in clear weather.

We had a school pool, but it was always busy with classes and the swim team, so I couldn't use it. Instead, I swam at a nearby lake. But once a month, I'd hop the fence to swim my PST, then do my pull-ups, push-ups, and sit-ups near the football locker room. Then I headed to the track to knock out the run.

After graduation, as part of the class of 1986, I went to navy boot camp at San Diego. At that time, they had no special program for recruits in the SEAL pipeline, so I actually got out of shape in the two weeks before the PST. I volunteered for the nightly training given to screwups, but my company commander thought I was being a smartass and told me no. Instead, he gave me extra workouts from time to time. I'd finish with a pool of sweat beneath me. I liked how it sucked.

The SEALs held the PST, and my company commander let me go try out while the other recruits did busy work at the barracks. A lot of recruits didn't know what SEALs were and just showed up, and they made for irritating obstacles in the pool. I hoped they didn't prevent me from passing. About twenty-five of us entered the water.

"Ready, go!" a SEAL said.

We swam, and it was chaos. Some didn't finish. About a dozen of us passed. In the locker room, a couple of SEALs weeded out the guys whose ASVAB scores were too low. Half a dozen of us proceeded outside, where we did the push-ups and sit-ups. Only two of us remained for the pull-up bar. I passed and the other guy didn't. Wearing a T-shirt, dungaree pants, and ankle-high steel toe boots called *boondockers*, I did the run by myself and finished the first mile in well under six minutes. The SEAL chief in charge was impressed.

In my group, I was the only one to make it this far. I'd qualified to attend Basic Underwater Demolition/SEAL (BUD/S) Training. I was excited to have made it this far, and I was determined to attempt the rest of the challenge.

Every sailor had to attend an "A" School for their job specialty. Before I could go to BUD/S, I had to study at Sonar Tech School, which lasted twelve weeks. During boot camp, I tried to have my orders changed to Boatswain's Mate school, which only lasted four weeks or so, but the navy wouldn't do it.

Boot camp ended, and I went to Sonar Tech School. To stay in shape, I joined the boxing team. I did my time and graduated.

Then I drove to Coronado, California, for BUD/S and a rude awakening.

CHAPTER 5

HELL WEEK

BUD/S OPENED MY EYES. So many guys were taller than me. A couple were triathletes. One had played Division One college football. One had passed the Olympic trials in swimming. There was an Army Ranger who'd seen combat in Grenada. Others seemed to have muscles on their ears.

A SEAL instructor stood on a podium and said, "Look around—80 percent of you won't be standing here when we're done."

It felt like an apple was in my throat. I tried to swallow it, but it didn't go down. I was still a teenager and hadn't even started shaving yet. They shaved all our heads, and I felt like a baby. *Oh shit, I've bitten off more than I can chew. I'm going to embarrass myself. What's my dad going to think of me? What's everyone at home going to think of me?*

BUD/S began with three weeks of Indoctrination (INDOC), a preliminary ass-kicking. After that came three phases. First phase was seven weeks of Basic Conditioning, the real ass-kicking. Second came seven weeks of Land Warfare—more ass-kicking. In the third phase, Combat Diving, we'd get our asses kicked again. (In future classes, Land Warfare and Combat Diving swapped places.) All in all, BUD/S was one long, hard kick in the ass.

During INDOC, we learned tadpole skills such as first aid and small boat handling. The instructors tested us on some of the classwork—standards for passing written tests were higher for officers than for enlisted men like me. We did beach runs, pool and ocean swims, and the obstacle course—all of which were timed at some point, and each week the cutoffs became tougher. There was a ship's bell in the compound, and all anyone had to do to quit was ring the bell three times.

In our barracks, we lived four to a room. One of my roommates had served on a ship.

"How was it on a ship?" I asked.

He groaned. "I started out chipping off old paint from the bulkheads—sanding and repainting. That sucked. Then for several months I cleaned dishes in the galley. That sucked too."

From our window, we could see a ship's lights out at sea. My roommate used his flashlight to signal out our window.

A light flashed back at us.

"What'd he say?" I asked.

"He said he's tired of sitting on that ship watching other people have fun on the beach."

"I never want to get stuck sitting on a damn ship," I said.

The next day, we earned our frogman gear—including our wetsuits, during what was affectionately called *Wetsuit Appreciation Day*. Instructor Taft put a thermometer in the San Diego Bay and checked the temperature. I overheard him quietly say, "Forty-eight degrees."

"Oh shit," another instructor muttered.

Instructor Lark turned to our class and announced, "It's a toasty warm fifty-eight degrees!"

Wait, that's not what the other instructor said.

"Hooyah, toasty warm fifty-eight degrees!" our class shouted.

We entered the water wearing our UDT swim shorts, inflatable life jackets with emergency flares attached, and our newly acquired fins.

We stepped into the water, and the cold snatched my breath away. I was in the top third of the class when we swam without fins, but with fins, I dropped to the bottom third. I tried to swim with my arms when I should've let my legs do most of the work.

I was in a three-man swim team with my swim buddy Brian and a Southerner named Randy Clendening. Instructors rode around in boats to monitor us. The water sapped the heat out of our bodies. We'd hardly reached halfway in our swim when flares started going off—some red, some white. The instructors steered all over the bay pulling swimmers out of the water.

My fingers were so cold that I could hardly hold them together. Water passed through them like a sieve. I shivered so violently that I struggled to swim a straight line. Brian shook intensely too. Then he stopped shivering and smiled. He corkscrewed down until he disappeared under the water.

"What's wrong with Brian?" I asked.

Randy glared at me. "He's hyping out, you idiot." Brian had succumbed to severe hypothermia. "We have to rescue him."

"Shit!"

Randy and I swam down and pulled him up. I popped the CO_2 cartridge on Brian's life vest so he would float, and Randy snapped open a red flare. The instructors motored over to us and helped us into the boat.

"You guys don't look too good either," one instructor said. "Get in."

We climbed into the boat.

The other instructor faced Brian and asked, "What's your name?"

Brian looked at him like he was speaking a foreign language.

"How many fingers am I holding up?" the instructor asked.

Brian started to climb out of the boat, but we pulled him back in.

The instructors sped to shore. Then they put Brian in an olive-drab ambulance. The ambulance was heated, and they had heating blankets and warm intravenous fluids on hand.

The ambulance shuttled students from San Diego Bay to sick bay nonstop.

Brian recovered, and later that day they brought him back.

We double-timed to the chow hall and ate. Everywhere we went during training, we double-timed. It was a mile to the chow hall and one mile back—three meals a day, you can do the math. Afterwards, we returned to San Diego Bay and redid the swim. Two guys near me rang the bell.

What have I gotten myself into?

We transitioned from INDOC to First Phase, where the standards were stricter. Three weeks later, Hell Week broke out: five and a half days on a total of four hours of sleep to do more than twenty hours of PT each day, run over two hundred miles over the course of the week, and experience hypothermia day and night.

Hell Week started Sunday night. Twenty-four hours later, we crossed the Naval Amphibious Base in seven-man crews carrying our black rubber boats—IBSs (Inflatable Boat, Small)—on our heads. The boat pounded my skull from above, and the asphalt shocked my legs from below—the opposing forces battled each other in my knees. The instructors stopped us on Turner Field next to San Diego Bay.

"We're going to do a heartwarming tradition that we call Lyon's Lope," Instructor Ledet announced. It was named in honor of Vietnam veteran SEAL, Ted Lyon. The instructor explained what we were to do. He finished with, "This is a race, and it pays to be a winner." Only one boat crew would win. The losers would have to do some torturous exercise while the winning team caught their breath.

We ran from one end of the base to the other without the boats. Next, we picked up our boats and raced with them—once again the boat jackhammered my head, and the asphalt pounded my knees. Then we hopped in our boats in the bay and paddled out to a buoy. We practiced "dump boat," flipping our boats over to expel water, which meant that we had to jump in the frigid water to do it. After my crew and I righted our boat, we paddled our hearts out to the shore. Then we got in the water again and formed a human centipede by wrapping our legs around the man in front and hand-paddled backwards, parallel to the beach. It was tough enough to swim in the cold ocean in full uniform and puffed-out kapok life vests, but swimming in this way while under sleep deprivation seemed next to impossible and greatly increased our exposure to the icy water.

Finally, we staggered onto land.

We were one of the losing boat crews, so Instructor Ledet made us do exercises with our boat, pushing it up over our head multiple times. Then we lowered our boat to the ground, put our feet on it and did incline pushups until our arms became slushy.

The cold rattled my teeth and shook every bone. I had difficulty thinking and controlling my body. All of us experienced hypothermia.

"I feel really bad for you guys who lost, so I'm going to give you a second chance to beat the winners," Instructor Ledet said. "Prepare to do this exercise again. Except this time, instead of paddling your boat, you get to swim with your boat, so leave your paddles. Ready, go!"

Some guys rang the bell and left their crews undermanned. The instructors didn't care. We raced to put our boats in the water and swam our boats out.

We circled the buoy and returned as fast as we could, but my boat crew lost again. We paid the piper. My extreme shivering made it hard to control my arms to lift the boat. When we did incline pushups, some guys kept landing head-first on the ground.

"Well, that was such a hoot, let's do it again!" Instructor Ledet said.

I couldn't comprehend how I could survive Lyon's Lope again, let alone the whole Week, but I lined up with my boat crew anyway.

Guys ran to the bell and rang it—"three alarm fires" we called them— they rang it so many times and so loud it sounded like the whole base was burning down.

Instructor Ledet waited for the ringing to stop. "Sing 'Happy Trails' to your buddies."

I didn't know what the hell that meant, but those of us who remained sang to our classmates who'd rung out. I mimicked what the others were singing: "Happy trails to you...."

When we finished the song, Instructor Ledet said, "Prepare to do Lyon's Lope again—ready."

This was impossible, but I readied myself.

"I changed my mind," Instructor Ledet said. "I'm bored with this."

The men who'd just rung out seemed deflated. One of them, a guy who was overly confident and didn't think much of me, made eye contact. His expression seemed to say, *What the hell—you didn't quit?*

I couldn't help but flash a cocky grin at him, but my teeth were chattering.

We picked up our boats and left San Diego Bay.

During the day, the sun never poked out of the clouds. It rained, and our boats became so full and heavy that when we stopped, we dumped them to lighten the load.

Tuesday night we ran over to the steel piers where the navy ties up its small boats, and we jumped in the bay. We practiced water survival. Our Ranger combat vet hyped out in the frosty water and went under. An instructor jumped in and rescued him. Another instructor helped carry our classmate to an ambulance. The Ranger's head flopped, and he looked dead. Medical staff restored his core body temperature, and the instructors tried to return him to Hell Week, but his body temperature dropped again, and he was pulled. He'd be rolled back to train with the class behind us.

Researchers from Duke University had been studying us, and now they observed us in horror. A chaplain came out, but then he disappeared. I think he was crying.

Wednesday night, I realized that a triathlete, the D1 college football player, a Ranger combat vet, and several others weren't around anymore—and I was still here. I'd always been mean, and now my meanness helped to keep me warm. At first, I didn't want the other guys to go, but now I felt like nothing could be done about it. *Let them go.*

On the beach, I was called into an ambulance. I climbed into the back of it and stood face-to-face with an instructor who looked like Mr. McGoo—except this McGoo was a bad ass in the Vietnam War—Master Chief Rogers. He sipped hot cocoa, and a wool blanket covered his lap. He spoke calmly like Mr. Rogers. My brain was too numb to know what he was talking about. I simply nodded in agreement. Then I heard the word *quitting.*

"Hell no!" I shouted.

He looked at me like he couldn't believe I'd shouted a four-letter word in his presence. "Get this man the hell out of here!"

Another instructor tossed me out, and I landed on my stomach out on the sand. I hurried to regroup with the rest of the guys.

The night became colder, and it felt as if it would never end. We ran on the beach—well, zombie-shuffled. We sniffled and coughed, and our spirits were low. We needed cadence, a military call-and-response work song, to pick us up. The guys who normally called cadence had become so hoarse that they couldn't do it anymore. Until now, I'd tried to keep my mouth shut and my head down to stay off the instructors' radar.

"Somebody better step up and show some motivation, or your asses are going in the drink!" Instructor Taft said.

I popped out like I was bigger and older than I was and called the cadence. The guys repeated after each line:

> C-130 rollin' down the strip;
> SEAL Team froggy gonna take a little trip.
> Mission top secret, destination unknown;
> I don't know if I'm comin' home.
> Stand up, hook up, shuffle to the door;
> Jump right out and count to four.
> A one one-thousand two one-thousand three one-thousand four,
> If my main don't open wide,
> I've got a reserve by my side,
> And if that one should fail me too,
> Get outta my way, cause I'm comin' through.
> Singin' hoo-yah hey,
> Runnin' day.
> Singin' hoo-yah hey,
> Just another easy day.

The cadence took our minds off the cold. It put spring in our step, and we didn't sniffle and cough as much. Our raspy voices filled with hope.

Instructors ran by to see who was leading the cadence. Instructor Taft reached the middle of our class and spotted me calling cadence. He stared at me as if he was surprised. There was a twinkle in his eye, and he gave me a nod.

I'd survived to that point, and I still had gas in my tank. Whether the others realized it or not, they did too. The recognition from one of the more respected instructors filled me with the idea that I was going to finish Hell Week.

Wednesday of Hell Week, medical staff set up tents where they checked us out. Over half of us had walking pneumonia, but we acted as if we were fine. The doc squeezed my leg, and I'd retained so much saltwater that it oozed out of my skin. It was the same for all of us. I didn't want to be pulled out of Hell Week. I wanted to finish.

On the last day of Hell Week, Friday afternoon, with the physical overload and lack of sleep, we were *The Walking Dead*. We stood near the obstacle course, which was close to the ocean. We'd done something bass-ackwards—again.

"You're going to carry your boats through the obstacle course," an instructor said. "Then you'll race your boats in the water from here to Imperial Beach—without paddles." That was seven-and-a-half miles one way.

Holy shit.

"And you guys are such screw-ups, we're considering extending Hell Week another day."

I was afraid. I saw the fear in my classmates' faces too.

"I can't do this. I can't do this," someone mumbled.

"I'm done," said another.

We ran with our boats. Dave and "O" had dysentery, and they shit themselves. There was no way they could survive this with their bloody diarrhea. They were tough as nails, but medically, they were shot.

They headed toward the instructors and the bell.

The instructors yelled at them: "No, you stay with the class! You get your asses out there!"

Dave and O returned to their boat crews, and we encouraged them.

In my boat crew, Don said, "There's no way. There's no way I can do this."

Then I realized something, and I spoke up: "Every evolution we've done during Hell Week, they've always had ambulances following us around. There's no ambulance. The instructors are bluffing."

Someone pointed at me and said, "Did you hear Treadway? We're not going to do it."

Others spread the word. "There's no ambulance. We're not going to do it."

They cheered me. "Yeah, all right!"

An instructor shouted, "Drop down!"

Oh shit, they're watching us.

We dropped down into the incline pushup position with our feet on the boats.

An ambulance pulled around the corner.

All my classmates swore at me. "Asshole, there's the ambulance! Bastard!"

Don cried. "There's no way I'm going to do this—I'm done!"

"Shut up, shut up," I said. "They're going to hear us."

The instructors made us do incline pushups.

After they finished hammering us, the lead instructor said, "Like we told you, you won't need your paddles, so put them in the ambulance. Now!"

All our officers had quit, so our highest-ranking enlisted man, Mike, was our class leader. He ordered us with his scratchy New York accent, "Hurry up, get your paddles in there!"

I grabbed my paddle and ran with my boat crew and the others to the ambulance. Someone threw open the door, and we tossed our paddles in there. We were too incoherent to be concerned with the details.

"You dumbasses!" an instructor shouted. "You just beat up the skipper with the paddles—he's in the back of that ambulance!"

Oh shit.

Mike shouted, "Get the paddles off him, get the paddles off!"

We hurried to take our paddles off of Captain Larry Bailey, the commanding officer at BUD/S. He was sitting in the ambulance.

Captain Bailey hopped out of the vehicle, and we snapped to attention in slow motion in front of him. Our bodies were shot.

"Captain Bailey!" Mike shouted.

"Hooyah, Captain Bailey!" we shouted.

Captain Bailey said, "Hey, guys, it was a rough week. You earned a teaspoon of respect from the Team guys." He gave us a congratulatory speech. Finally, he said, "Hell Week is secured."

I looked around. Twenty-five of us remained. We'd lost over two-thirds of our class. I was surprised to see tough guys crying. Others hugged each other. I was so proud that I made it I thought I'd burst.

CHAPTER 6

THE REAPER'S SHADOW

THE REAPER'S SHADOW CREPT CLOSER. After recovering from Hell Week, we ended Phase One by learning hydrographic reconnaissance and some other SEAL skills. Immediately afterward, Phase Two kicked off—Land Warfare. We navigated on land, rappelled, patrolled, and practiced small-unit tactics, some of it out in Mount Laguna. We also shot a lot—with pistol and rifle—until our fingers bled. The learning pace picked up, and the required times for our swims and runs shortened.

For the last five weeks of Land Warfare, we flew out to San Clemente Island to practice demolitions and put together all that we'd learned. We worked more hours and slept less. Lieutenant John Koenig, a legend in the SEAL community, led us. His rank was O-3, equivalent to a captain in the other military branches. Before he became an officer, he was an enlisted man. During his career he ran classified ops in Vietnam, served as a Military Group advisor in El Salvador, rescued Governor General Paul Scoon's family from house arrest in Grenada, and conducted an operation in Panama to help capture Dictator Manuel Noriega.

One night, he made us paddle our boats out into the fathomless Pacific and insert on boulders on the coast—rock portage. We wore UDT life vests over our olive drab uniforms and carried our weapons and other gear. We paddled our IBS out of the surf zone and followed the coastline until we reached our objective. Then we sent in two swimmer scouts.

The waves were so epic that we couldn't see the beach. The swimmer scouts returned, and we helped them into the boat. They appeared half-drowned, and they puked saltwater.

The older swimmer shook his head.

"We're going to die," the younger swimmer, Don, said. "We can't go through there. We're going to die."

"That's it, we're not going to do it," Mike, our class leader, said. "I'm making a decision."

In my boat was Billy Johnson, a Golden Gloves boxer from Seattle. He carried our M-60 machine gun. He was sharp, but he talked as if he'd been punched in the head a few times too many. "Mike, you stupid son of a bitch, you're going to get us in trouble. We can't go back."

"Shut up," Mike said, "I'm in charge."

We paddled back to the training compound and landed on the beach.

Lieutenant Koenig stood there. I couldn't tell if he was happy or angry. The man was an enigma.

"See, Mike, you stupid son of a bitch, I told you we were going to get in trouble," Billy said.

"Shut up," Mike said.

Lieutenant Koenig spoke in his Mississippi drawl, "Why'd you boys come back here?"

"My swim scout told me it wasn't a good insertion point, sir," Mike said.

"Who's that?" Lieutenant Koenig asked.

"Me, sir," Don said.

Lieutenant Koenig stared at him for an awkward moment. "Boy, what's wrong with you? Did you think you were going to die?"

"Yes, sir," Don said.

"Did you think you were going to see God?"

"Yes, sir."

Lieutenant Koenig flashed a bitter smile. "Good, boy, because you're going to go back and do it again."

We paddled back out again. This time we were quiet.

I glanced behind. Lieutenant Koenig stood on shore watching us.

"See, Mike, I told you," Billy said.

Once more, we paddled along the coast, outside of the surf zone. Then we lined up with our insertion point. Somehow the muzzle of Billy's M-60 had poked a hole in our boat. One guy held his hand on the hole while another pressed the foot pump to prevent us from going flat.

The whites of Don's eyes expanded like egg whites in a frying pan.

This is not good.

"This is too dangerous," Mike said. "I'm making a command decision."

"Screw you, Mike," Billy said. "I'll walk on the bottom if I have to. I ain't going to get hammered by Lieutenant Koenig."

"We can't let him down," Don's swim buddy said.

The waves clapped so hard that it sounded like an explosion.

Oh shit.

We pointed our bow at the shore and went for it. The first whale of a wave sucked the oxygen out of our boat.

"Paddle, paddle, paddle!" Mike shouted.

We paddled our asses off.

"Water!" Mike shouted.

I turned around to see a wall of water rise behind our stern. Mike jumped off the back of the boat.

"Mike, you chickenshit!" someone yelled.

The wave slammed us, and bodies flew everywhere. The ocean pulled me down so hard and so deep that I wondered if it'd ever release me. It seemed so far to the surface. Eventually, I floated back up.

Another wave picked me up, and it seemed the jagged boulders on shore came rushing at me. Out of the corner of my eye I saw a pristine beach, but that wasn't where I was going. *If I land on those rocks, I am not going back into the water to drown or get slammed into the rocks repeatedly.*

I flew up onto the rocks and bounced. It knocked the wind out of me, but I bear-hugged one. The ocean tried to drag me off of it, but I hung on for dear life. I was banged up, and the saltwater stung my abrasions, but little cuts and bruises had become routine. I was happy to be alive.

I looked up and spotted Lieutenant Koenig standing several rocks higher than me. "Someone get this man off these rocks."

Cool.

I glanced to the left, and our boat floated upside down. Billy sat on top like Winnie the Pooh carrying an M-60. The wave spit the boat onto the beach, and Billy glided over the sand as if he was on a hovercraft.

Boat crews that had arrived before mine helped me off the rocks. My crew was too scattered and too exhausted, and they received help as well.

"See?" Lieutenant Koenig said. "That wasn't so bad, was it?"

If we said it was bad, he'd make us do it again. If we said it was good, he'd make us do it again. We kept our mouths shut. Luckily, we didn't have to do it again.

Before each meal, we had to do chin-ups. Every other day, we'd have to sprint a quarter mile up a hill within the time limit to eat a hot meal. Randy couldn't do his minimum chin-ups, and Billy couldn't meet the run times, so they both had to eat cold military rations, Meals-Ready-to-Eat (MREs) while sitting in the cold ocean. Frequently, I snuck warm food out to them. The instructors ignored me for the most part, but one day they kicked my ass for it.

Randy was a Southerner like Lieutenant Koenig. "Boy," Lieutenant Koenig said, "how is the South ever going to rise again if you can't pull yourself up?"

⊕   ⊕   ⊕

We finished Second Phase and returned to Coronado for Third Phase, Diving, which came pretty easy for me—and that was the beginning of my problems.

We studied dive physics and did combat scuba, using both open and closed-circuit types. I passed each test in the water and in the classroom the first time. Our SEAL instructor proctor told me, "I'm holding an unscheduled class tonight, but I need someone to stand watch on the quarterdeck tonight with a student from another class. Since you're doing so well, I thought you could skip my class and stand the watch. You good with that?"

I said, "Sure."

I missed the class and stood watch. The next day, we had a pool competency test, and for the first time, I was lost. Instructors were in the pool with us, and they messed with our scuba gear and tied knots in the hoses and so on. We also had to exhale water at the bottom of the pool before ascending—"blow and go"—and I was told that I ascended too early.

I had to redo the competency test, and I would only be given this second chance to pass. Earlier in training, I must've riled the buddy of one of the instructors because neither one of them seemed to like me. I retook my test. This time when I did my blow and go, my inflatable life jacket had been tied to my tanks by the instructor who didn't like me. I couldn't ascend. I tried to untie my lifejacket but couldn't work the knot out, so I ditched my life jacket under my weight belt.

When I surfaced, one instructor passed me, but the one who didn't gave a thumb down. "You failed," he said. "You never ditch your life jacket at sea."

I was dumbfounded—and pissed. *I was cheated.*

The instructors rolled me out of my class and put me in the upcoming class that'd just finished Phase Two. I'd repeat Phase Three with them while they went through it for the first time. When pool comp came again, I placed myself at the front of the line to get this monkey off my back. I passed the first time with no problem. The master chief said, "Get out of the water, Treadway. You should've graduated weeks ago." He was one of the veteran SEALs who'd fought in Grenada, and I was proud to have his approval.

I sat alone beside the pool waiting for my classmates in my new class to finish.

Several weeks later, I graduated BUD/S. Originally, I had orders to join Team Five in my home state of California, but the pool comp fiasco switched my orders to SEAL Team Delivery Vehicle Team Two in Virginia. It stunk to have my orders switched and to have to leave my home state, but I was happy to graduate BUD/S.

Before becoming an official SEAL, I went through three months of SEAL Delivery Vehicle training in San Diego and three weeks of army Airborne School at Fort Benning, Georgia.

During our first parachute jump, I stood at the front of the line to go out the starboard side of the plane. I wasn't afraid, but I looked around, and some people seemed scared. First in line on the opposite side of the plane was a female University of Maryland Army ROTC cadet who appeared as calm as if she'd done this a hundred times. I gave her a thumbs up and she gave me an uninterested look as if to say, "Whatever." She jumped—and I went out about the same time. At first, I lost track of the plane and the ground, and there seemed to be sky everywhere, but I stabilized and caught my bearings. My chute opened without incident, and I checked to make sure it opened fully—it did. I exhaled long and hard. I enjoyed flying through the air like a bird. I wished my flight had been longer, but the earth interrupted my experience. I landed the same way the instructors had taught us—a parachute landing fall (PLF). I held my knees together, and when my feet touched the ground, I allowed my body to buckle to absorb the shock. I turned and struck the dirt with the side of my calf and then thigh and butt. I rolled around onto my back. I wanted to go again.

During the week, I got my wish. We did three more day jumps and one night jump. Several of us made friends with the ROTC gals, but the uninterested one remained uninterested, and she didn't hang out with us. *Oh well.*

At our airborne graduation, our guest speaker was a full-bird colonel in the air force who wore a SEAL trident on his chest—a prior enlisted frogman. At the time, I didn't think twice about it.

After I earned my jump wings, I went through six months of SEAL Tactical Training. Then I was assigned to my first SEAL Team platoon at Virginia Beach, Virginia—only a hop-skip-and-a-jump away from the University of Maryland—and a hop away from the Reaper.

CHAPTER 7

SEAL DELIVERY VEHICLE TEAM TWO

I WAS ONE OF THE newest guys at SEAL Delivery Vehicle Team Two (SDVT 2), and I almost died. In the Teams, it's said that your first platoon makes you. For some, it breaks you—especially if your platoon rejects you as a dumbass or a jackass. I was the only member of my platoon not old enough to legally enter a bar. I was fortunate to be surrounded by awesome guys that treated me like a little brother, but man, I took my lumps like a little brother. Our officers in charge—Bondo and G-man, Platoon Chief Dave LaConte, and Leading Petty Officer Mule—understood, tolerated, and mentored me. For our more experienced operators, such as Chief LaConte, we dropped their call signs and used their rank and last names as an added measure of respect. At that time, the Teams were relatively small, and preserving our tradition and culture seemed almost as important as being a competent operator. Other guys such as Rudy were like a big brother to me. (I would later serve with Rudy in Team Five, where he was still a big brother, and he continues to be my big brother today).

The Naval Special Warfare insignia is the largest insignia in the navy, and it's gold colored. Normally, gold insignias are only worn by officers, but enlisted SEALS wore this one too. Both officers and enlisted men sweated, froze, and bled for it—side-by-side. Only after a guy proved his competence in a platoon was he awarded his trident. There was no shake-take-and-salute ceremony. Chief LaConte ensured that the Team tradition was upheld.

The full Team stood in ranks behind half a dozen of us new guys. At my side was another new guy, Tiny, a tough little surfer dude from the central California coast who was used to cold waves and loved jazz and too much coffee.

SDV Team Two Commander Stephens faced us and pinned our tridents on our uniforms.

That's peculiar, I thought. *He only put the backing on one of the three pins sticking out of the back of the trident. He must be doing this for time's sake. After all, there are several of us.*

The guys behind us clapped and cheered. Commander Stephens kept his speech simple.

This isn't so bad. I like simple.

The master chief called the Team to attention.

Now what?

Commander Stephens grinned. "Platoon Leaders take charge and carry out the plan of the day."

I did an about face to fall out of formation, but as I faced the Team, I saw grins and hands filled with riggers tape, zip ties, spray paint, and grease guns. Chief LaConte's grin seemed the biggest. *Oh shit!* Tiny and I jetted in different directions. Tiny was so fast that he got away—for the moment.

I bolted straight through the same door that the commander and master chief were exiting. They both turned around and stopped me dead in my tracks just long enough for my teammates to body snatch me and give me a proper welcome to the brotherhood.

Guys collapsed me from behind. They taped me up and pounded on the trident pin, punching tiny, bloody holes in my chest. They used rigger's tape to give me a happy hat, taping my hair up into a point. They used the tape as a blindfold, too, and taped my hands in front of me. After they bound my legs with tape, I must've looked like a mummy. It felt like they greased me with a grease gun, and I heard a spray paint can spraying. Then they picked me up and dumped me in an ice-cold dip tank. Finally, they carried me and the other new guys into the classroom and stacked us up in the back like cords of wood.

The Team guys sat in the classroom, and the commander came in and stood in front of them. He did a commander's call, talking about up-and-coming events, and there was some discussion. I didn't care.

I figured everyone was watching the commander in the front, and nobody was paying attention to me in the back, so I chewed on the tape binding my hands until it loosened up a bit. I gnawed on the tape on my arms, freeing them too. The tape around my eyes came undone, and I could see.

The commander stared down the center of the classroom at me. He broke midsentence. "Somebody secure that man."

They turned around and pounced on me. This time they taped me up even worse. Then I heard them sit back down and continue with the commander's call.

Later, they played with us some more.

"Who's the dumbass that gave them a knife?" an older voice said.

Then came the sound of footsteps scattering away.

Little by little, I shed my mummy wraps. The other new guys did too. I spotted a knife on the deck that the Team guys must've mercifully left to help us cut our way out, but I couldn't reach it. The Team guys peeked around corners as if they were checking to make sure we'd calmed down and weren't going to stab anyone. Then they came and helped us take off the tape.

The other new guys and I changed into our cammies and put our tridents on our chests—with backings this time. It was a proud moment. We went out and celebrated. It was obvious to any Team guys that we were new SEALs.

Pinning on my trident wasn't what almost killed me, though. Similar to myself, SDVs were new too. The SDV was a manned submersible developed for long-distance maritime infiltrations. It was cold, cramped, and dark, like being buried in a little black coffin under water. Because of the dangers involved with them and the lack of real-world missions, more guys were dying in training accidents than combat ops.

A teammate of mine, Johnny Lancaster, expressed his frustrations: "All training and no action makes Johnny a dull boy." He was a crazy large, imposing guy and mentally solid. I didn't talk with him much because he was older, more experienced, and in another platoon, but once he told me, "I'm going to get out and go to college—earn a business degree."

Others talked about starting a business or becoming federal agents.

"That sounds cool," I said. "I think I'll get out and do something like that too."

My teammates laughed.

"What's so funny?" I asked.

"You'll never leave the military. You're a lifer, man."

Johnny helped experiment with changing breathing apparatuses while riding in an SDV. During one dive, when he switched breathing apparatuses, an ocean current pulled him out of his seat and into the SDV's five-foot-wide propeller, killing him. I realized that if it could happen to a stud like Johnny, it could happen to me—no matter how hard I trained.

Several weeks after his death, at the navy base in Little Creek, Virginia, we tested an experimental SDV platform. I jammed myself into the SDV pilot seat, and Chief LaConte sat in the co-pilot's seat to navigate. Tiny sat between us as a mission specialist.

A Sea Fox—a small, high-speed, twin-engine boat—towed us on a sled out into Chesapeake Bay. Unexpectedly, the sled dove straight down, taking our SDV and us with it. The wake from the Sea Fox and the sled swept the chief and me aft and under the SDV. None of us had finished donning all of our dive gear yet, so we were in for one hell of a breath hold.

From my waist down, I was pinned between the sled and the SDV. I struggled to free myself but couldn't. I looked up—it was thirty feet to the surface. My body craved oxygen. Suddenly, in front of me, the SDV's propeller started spinning at full tilt. Tiny must've throttled it, trying to surface. The propeller neared me—or I neared it—either way, it wasn't going to end well. I put my hands across my chest and thought, "Well God, if this is how I'm supposed to go, I guess this is it for me."

Just then, I burst free, and the force of the water shot me face-first at the propeller. I closed my eyes. Then another force, as if a missile was tied to my ass, shot me at a different angle. I rocketed to the surface. The upper half of my body rose out of the water.

The nose of the SDV breached the surface with Tiny's head sticking out. He breathed from his scuba tank, and his hand held the SDV throttle.

Where's chief?

I looked around. He still hadn't surfaced. Then, ten yards behind me, Chief LaConte's head surfaced. His big eyes stared at me. I never saw him scared like that before. *This shit is dangerous.*

The safety boat pulled up beside us carrying the officer in charge, the safety officer, and a hospital corpsman. They hauled the three of us in. The chief, Tiny, and I removed the few items of gear we'd had time to put on before the accident.

The officer in charge said, "Jock up and do it again." In the Teams, I learned that whenever a training mission went to shit, we had to do it again.

Still shaken and catching my breath, I tried to hide my fear and appear professional. I put my gear back on. The safety officer checked me out and gave me the thumbs up. I was young and wanted to impress the other frogmen by showing that I wasn't fazed and was ready to get back to work. I entered the water first.

Then it dawned on me. *Shit. I forgot my dive mask.*

The chief was still in the boat jocking up. He looked down at me and smiled. His face seemed to say, *It's all right, kid, I'm a little rattled too.*

I learned that near-death experiences can unnerve a person, and that can interfere with the next op, so it's best to double check oneself and one's teammates.

✛ ✛ ✛

One day, the seasoned guys didn't think I was around, but I overheard one ask, "What do we call the new guy?"

"Dawg," a senior enlisted guy said.

"Why?"

"He's loyal," the senior enlisted guy said.

Others piped in: "If one of us gets in trouble, he'll jump in and defend us." "He's aggressive." "He volunteers for the tough stuff." "He licks his balls."

They laughed.

"Dawg it is," the senior guy said.

I never heard my real name again. On the PA system that broadcasted over the compound, it was always, "Dawg, your presence is requested on the quarterdeck." They put it on my locker: Dawg. Even the team commander and master chief called me Dawg.

In addition to our work with the SDVs, our platoon did several weeks of land warfare training. Near the end of the training, evaluators graded us on our readiness to deploy. During one of our final missions in the exercise, our point man wandered around like a blind man, causing us to hump for a longer time. The chances of reaching our objective within the allotted time slipped further and further away.

"Put Dawg on point," Chief LaConte said. "He's got a good nose, and he'll get us there quicker."

I made up for lost time, but while I was doing so, I realized that I had to slow down a bit for our slowest frogmen who were carrying more gear than me.

Although I was a new guy, I appreciated Chief LaConte putting so much faith in me. Years later, he retired as a senior chief and worked as a contractor in Afghanistan, where he was killed by an IED. He's buried at Arlington National Cemetery.

While I was at SDV Team Two, I flew across the country to take courses out on the West Coast, such as the one to become a diving supervisor. I had teammates there, and my California roots ran deep. My compass kept pointing me there.

When my four-year enlistment contract neared its end, I had choices to make. The navy offered me a reenlistment bonus. My commander promised me a dive supervisor job in Sardinia, Italy, to oversee divers who inspected the hulls of ships. After that, the navy would send me to the Defense Language Institute in Monterey, California, to learn Spanish, and I'd report to SEAL Team Four in Virginia Beach, Virginia.

The bonus, language school, and Team Four appealed to me, but I wasn't excited about being in Sardinia alone watching dudes inspect ship hulls. Also, the whole purpose of being a SEAL is engaging in unconventional warfare—my teammates and I were eager to fight for our country. Except for the brief invasion of Panama, most of us weren't seeing any battles, and I didn't expect that to change any time soon.

I'd kept in touch with a college football coach who'd tried to recruit me out of high school. I mentioned that I was nearing the end of my enlistment. Now he was at Sacramento State University, and he called me every two weeks to come out and play defensive back. If I did that, I could earn my four-year degree and a commission as an officer in the navy.

I took the coach's offer. I went full time to Sacramento State University and served part-time as a SEAL in the navy reserves—until everything changed.

CHAPTER 8

SEAL TEAM FIVE

ON AUGUST 2, 1990, IRAQ's dictator Saddam Hussein invaded its neighboring country, Kuwait, and the US formed a coalition to eject him. The Gulf War had begun. Before my first game as defensive back at Sacramento State University, I was recalled into the navy.

The navy sent me to Coronado, California, to join SEAL Team Five, which was putting together a platoon to relieve SEALs in the Gulf. It was a crack platoon, and some of their guys had served in a Special Mission Unit.

"Hey, Dawg, you want to join our platoon?" they asked.

"Hell, yeah!" I said.

"You'll have to reenlist," they said. In other words, I could no longer be a part-time SEAL. I'd have to leave Sacramento State and return full time to the navy to be a part of this platoon going to Iraq. It's what I'd trained for.

"Sure," I said.

I called up my coach at Sacramento State and told him.

"Hey, you're a good man," coach said. "We'll leave your gear in your locker for when this is all over. When you come back, you still have a spot on the team."

I tried to explain that I wouldn't be returning to Sacramento State any time soon, but he didn't seem to understand.

After I reenlisted, what I didn't realize was that the war would end so quickly. The ground war began on February 24 and ended in less than four days. The Iraqi army surrendered, and Kuwait was liberated. My platoon and I never even made it to the Gulf.

Instead, I lugged around a machine gun and trained. Later, Team Five sent me nearby to Naval Special Warfare Group One's new Scout/Sniper Course. My sniper partner was a hairy guy we called Wookie. He grew up in Nebraska, shooting a little .22 rifle at prairie dogs when they poked their heads up out of their holes. Before becoming a SEAL, he drove a Pepsi delivery truck for a living. While in the Teams, he married a Filipina.

Wookie and I excelled at sniper school. One of our instructors was a civilian woman who wasn't even five feet tall. She'd won the Wimbledon Cup at a 1,000-yard match in a national competition at Camp Perry, Ohio. She'd beaten out the top civilian law enforcement officers and military marksmen. She taught us how to judge the wind's effects on our shots and how to communicate it to our sniping partner. I was better than Wookie at calling windage, but he was a better shot. Targeting a human silhouette from a distance, I'd shoot groups within the circumference of a hand on a chest. Other sniper students would say, "Ooh" and "Ahh," but then Wookie's shots would touch each other on the chest, and it was "Wow!"

As snipers, Wookie and I reunited with the same platoon. Our focus shifted from desert warfare to winter warfare. We switched from desert cammies to overwhite snow camo uniforms. Each of us carried less water and more survival gear. Instead of training in the California deserts, we flew out to the snowy mountains of Colorado and Montana.

We patrolled on telemark skis and carried seventy-pound rucks. Our platoon conducted live-fire breaking contact drills—shooting and moving on skis—and patrolling through the continental divide for several days while being tracked by two SEAL winter warfare experts. I thought we were high speed until army Green Berets from the Tenth Special Forces Group parachuted in with snowmobiles—*smarter not harder*.

My platoon deployed to Busan, Korea. There we helped train Republic of Korea (ROK) frogmen and conducted other operations, such as surveillance on a port to identify incoming and outgoing ships.

On another mission, my squad of eight guys, had to parachute with a squad of ROK frogmen into the snow-covered Korean mountains, take out enemy radar, and mark targets for our jet bombers to strike—a training op.

In addition to the seventy-pound Berghaus ruck and combat jump equipment we all humped, Wookie carried the beastly barrel of a Macmillan .50 caliber sniper rifle. I packed the receiver. Dressed in our overwhites, we boarded a Korean C-130 transport plane. On aircraft such as this, we referred to our squads as "chalks." The ROK chalk sat on the jump seats on the port side of the plane, and my chalk sat on the starboard side. Although it was freezing outside, the aircraft's interior was heated to the point of feeling stuffy.

The platoon officer in charge, Bomber, operated with us. He told the aircrew, "Make sure we do low-level navigation." Because the Korean peninsula was so mountainous, we'd be flying up and down a lot to remain close to the earth—like a roller coaster.

I remembered that Bomber became seasick easily. In a previous op with Team Five, we exfiltrated through the cold night on a small boat. We were piled on top of each other, and he threw up on the back of my neck.

Bomber tried to wipe it off. "Sorry, Dawg."

"Don't worry, sir. That's the warmest thing I've felt all night."

Heavy rain washed it off, anyway.

Another time, we had to give ourselves our own immunization shots. I gave myself my shots, but Bomber didn't like needles. He turned to a guy in our platoon and asked, "Can you give me my shot?"

"Happy to." The guy stuck the needle in Bomber's arm and injected him.

Bomber looked away.

The guy left the needle in.

The rest of us chuckled.

"What?" Bomber looked down at the needle poked in his arm and the syringe hanging freely. He passed out and hit the deck like a sack of shit.

We rushed to make sure he hadn't broken the needle off in his arm. He was okay.

Now he was acting stoic on our Korean plane.

"Sir, you're going to get sick," I said. "Not to mention the rest of us."

Soon after, Bomber opened a bag and puked in it. Other guys opened their bags too. Those without bags or who couldn't open theirs in time, vomited in the piss tubes or on the deck. I wasn't too bothered by the changes in altitude, but the hot, stuffy cabin stank of vomit. I was about to contribute to the barf-fest.

The ramp aft of the plane lowered and morning light rushed in with a burst of cold air. It felt like rolling down the window after being carsick. The air was crisp and fresh. I took a breath of life.

The jumpmaster called out and showed us ten fingers: "Ten minutes!"

We passed the word on to each other and made sure we were ready to jump.

The jumpmaster showed five fingers. "Five minutes!"

"Stand up!" the jumpmaster said. "Check equipment!"

We did. My hook was secured to the static line. When I jumped, my chute would open automatically. Well, I hoped it would, anyway.

The jump light turned green.

The jumpmaster held his hand out flat. "Go!"

I shuffled behind two guys, trying not to slip in a pool of chunky goo with what looked like pieces of corn in it. The stench was unbearable, and I held my breath and tried not to gag. I'd never been so eager to jump off a plane.

The two in front of me exited the aircraft.

Then it was my turn. I leaped to freedom.

As planned, our altitude was low—fifteen hundred feet. On the positive side, there wouldn't be enough time to become cold in the frigid air before we landed. On the negative side, if my parachute had any problems, there wouldn't be much time to fix it. I looked up and examined my chute. It had opened clean—no problems.

I lowered my gaze. Below was a valley, and we were supposed to land in it; however, Siberian winds blew us into the side of a mountain. I steered hard to prevent myself from smashing into a cliff. We weren't using the MT1X parachutes that maneuvered like sports cars—these were the MC1-1 Bravos, and they turned slowly like Cadillacs. Winds in the basin swirled, making it more difficult to maneuver. I tried to follow the guys so I'd land with them and we could rally up together quickly, but I didn't want to be so close that I'd crash into someone. One guy smacked into a tree. *Ouch!*

I descended below a hundred feet. The wind drove me toward the trees on the mountainside, and I pulled my toggle away from them. The ground seemed to rise at me faster. The gear in my rucksack was connected to me with a descent line, and I was supposed to release the ruck, but a shack on the mountain was coming at me, and I couldn't drop my ruck without snagging it on the building, causing me to do a gnarly face plant. On the other hand, landing with all that extra weight was going to pound me into the frozen earth.

I lowered my ruck to the tip of my boots. I passed over the shack. The moment I cleared the roof, I released my ruck—just in time. I bent my legs and tucked my chin. The balls of my feet hit first, and I tossed myself sideways to even out the force of the landing. Next, the outside of my calf and thigh struck the ground, then my ass. I rolled onto my back. I'd done so many of these—some so hard that I'd banged my head close to knocking myself out—that now the parachute landing fall was automatic. I was fine.

Another guy wasn't fine. He injured his shoulder, but he'd gut it out and continue with us. The guy who hit the tree broke his leg. We called in a medical evacuation for him.

We stuffed our chutes into parabags and left them to be picked up later by an administrative team. The guy with the broken leg stayed there with a teammate and waited for the medevac. The rest of us moved out.

The ROKs led us up the side of the mountain, cutting through fresh snow. The white stuff was only a foot-and-a-half high. My Sorel snow boots were good, and I didn't need snowshoes. Glacier goggles guarded my eyes from the rising sun and its glare reflecting off the snow. Hiking in my polypropylene thermal underwear kept me warm.

We crossed over the first mountain and then another. A couple hours had passed since we landed. We worked our way around a third mountain until we reached a vantage point that was high enough to see our objective but not at the summit where it would silhouette us against the sky.

Down in the valley, about a thousand yards away, was a line of half a dozen mock-up enemy tanks, a radar dish mounted on a block, and a red and white checkered box with the dish's electronics inside. Bomber and his comms man had to mark the tanks with a laser designator, and they separated from us to find the best view. Two ROKs patrolled with them as security.

Wookie and I slipped into a thicket—a natural sniper hide. Two ROKs hid themselves nearby as security for us.

Wookie unpacked the barrel of the sniper rifle, and I took out the receiver and handed it to him. He put them together and attached a twelve-power Leopold scope and peeked through it.

I removed the spotter scope from my pack and spied the valley below. The satellite dish, its electronics box, and the tanks appeared twelve times larger. Wind kicked up ice crystals and drove them sideways at a speed of about ten miles an hour. "Ten-minute wind left to right," I whispered. Although the gusts in the valley blew in different directions, it was common practice to compensate for the wind closest to the target.

Wookie adjusted the windage knob on his scope.

Bomber's voice came into my receiver: "Fast movers inbound." Our jet bombers were coming.

"Ten minutes out," Bomber said. "Prepare to execute."

Showtime. We had to destroy the enemy radar before it picked up our incoming jets. Wookie loaded a .50 Cal Raufoss Mk 211 armor-piercing round with an RDX high-explosive tip in his rifle.

I observed the checkered box that looked like the branding for Purina dog chow.

Minutes later, Bomber said, "Execute, execute."

Bang! Wookie's arm jolted.

A brief flash appeared when the round hit the top corner of a white square. "Hit," I said.

One was enough, but Wookie tickled his froggy bone and loaded a new round before he followed up with another shot.

"Hit," I said.

Then he squeezed off another for the hell of it—three holes in the satellite.

"Nice," I said.

"Laser designators coming online," Bomber said. He and his radioman would paint the tanks with their laser designator, and Wookie and I shielded our eyes so any splash from the laser wouldn't damage them.

A jet rumbled in the distance. Then it screamed overhead, and its munitions whistled on their way to the ground. An explosion thundered from deep in the valley. I opened my eyes and saw the fiery aftermath. The first tank was no more, and the one behind it was aflame. The jet continued to screech as it departed.

More jets flew in and busted more tanks.

The sun faded behind the mountains, and Bomber called us to return to our nearby layup. He and the others met us there. The building wasn't spacious enough for all of us to enter, so we used it to shield ourselves from the wind.

"What are we going to do about the rest of the targets in the valley?" I asked.

"Tonight at 02:00, an F-117 Nighthawk is going to strike some of them," Bomber said.

The stealth ground-attack plane was used in the Gulf War, but I hadn't experienced one yet. "What are we going to do to laze targets for them?" I asked.

"They don't need us," Bomber said.

"What?" I asked.

"They've got smart munitions that don't need a laser designator."

"I've got to see this." I set my G-Shock watch alarm for 01:30.

Wookie and I found a spot on one side of the building next to some cinder blocks. Each of us slept in a Wiggy bag that was rated to forty degrees below zero. I was toasty and couldn't help but think about how tough those guys were who fought here during the Korean War without this Gucci gear—back when ships were made of wood and men were made of steel.

My alarm went off, and I poked my head out of my sleeping bag. It was too dark to see anything in the sky. As the time neared the F-117's arrival, I couldn't hear the usual scream of a jet turbine. I couldn't hear anything. Abruptly, there was a high-pitched zip followed by *boom, boom, boom*. I hadn't heard the zip of the engine until it was practically over my head—then it was gone. A soldier on the ground wouldn't have had a chance. The F-117 was out of this world, and I was glad it was ours.

After several days of taking potshots in the valley, observing battle damage, and reporting, my polypro thermals stank. My teammates were ripe too. Early on our last morning, we humped back over the mountain pass and patrolled an hour to a flat area where helicopters could land to extract us.

The helos didn't arrive, so we hoofed it two hours to the nearest road, and the air force picked us up in trucks. This happened much too often.

My polypro stank so bad by that point, I'd have to throw it away.

Later, a one-star admiral wrote both Wookie and me letters of commendation for our sniping work.

After we'd finished our deployment and returned to the States, I was back in the gym doing bench presses.

Wookie joined me and said, "Well, Dawg, I called my old boss, and I got my old job back."

"Which Team?" I asked.

"Naw, I'm leaving the Teams. Boss is giving me back my old Pepsi delivery route. I'm getting my Pepsi blues back, and I'm going home."

I thought he was joking, but he was dead serious. We'd joined to serve in combat with the best, but five years of training without a war was long enough for Wookie. He returned to Nebraska with his Filipino wife, and he delivered Pepsis.

CHAPTER 9

SPECIAL MISSION UNIT

WE CAME CLOSE TO BEING spun up for real world ops, but we never went—always a bridesmaid, never a bride. Instead, we trained. One day, while we practiced clearing rooms, the new Team Five executive officer watched my platoon. He walked on the catwalk above as we moved through each room. He'd done this before, and I had a feeling he was watching me. Even so, what we were doing was dangerous; I had to focus and not shoot a buddy or step out at the wrong time and catch a bullet myself.

After we finished a round, the XO asked, "Can I jump in your shooting train?"

It made me a bit nervous to be talking with the new number two man in charge of Team Five. "Of course, sir."

"It's been a while since I've done this, so watch out for me," he said.

Now I worried even more. Once we entered the building, my nerves simmered down. We came up on a corner where the XO was supposed to turn and shoot low while the guy behind him was supposed to turn and shoot high. The XO looked like he was about to stand and get shot in the head, so I put a hand on his shoulder and stopped him.

After we cleared the kill house, the XO smiled at me. "Thanks. You guys are doing killer work."

Later, he suggested to my platoon officer in charge and my platoon chief that I screen to become part of a Special Mission Unit (SMU). He'd commanded a team in that unit.

I put in my application papers, and I took a psychological evaluation. One psych test asked a lot of crazy questions such as, "Do you think of your sister as more of a dog or a flower?" "Do you ever feel like a woman trapped inside a man's body?" Another asked, "Do you sometimes feel the urge to destroy things?"

64

Later, some of the Team guys in charge of the SMU and the psychologist interviewed me. "Why do you sometimes feel the urge to destroy things?" the shrink asked.

"I don't know—sometimes it feels good," I said.

"You have anger issues," the shrink said.

Destroying things was the nature of the job, so I smiled.

The shrink turned red and yelled at me. "You have anger issues!"

I laughed. *Dude*, you've *got anger issues*.

The shrink stood up, but a SEAL on the panel put a hand on his shoulder. Another whispered to him.

The shrink sat down.

I heard that the shrink angrily asked another candidate, "Why do you feel like a woman trapped in a man's body?"

"Gender preference I suppose," the candidate answered.

"What?" the psychologist shouted.

The SEALs on the panel seemed concerned.

"I'm a lesbian trapped in a man's body," the candidate said.

The shrink lit off. "Are you joking!"

The SEALs on the panel couldn't help but snicker.

I didn't hear the results right away, so I didn't think much more about it.

I enjoyed being home in California. I had orders to become an instructor at BUD/S, still in southern California, to teach in their diving phase. In addition, I would instruct students in a new hand-to-hand combat class called the Special Combat Aggressive Reactionary System (SCARS), so I took the course. It was thirty days straight, eight to twelve hours a day, with no weekends off. The training was so intense that guys sometimes broke knuckles, ribs, and orbital bones around the eye. I loved it. What I didn't like was hitting the ground so many times. My body ached from so many hard landings. It was like playing football.

Near the end of the thirty-day SCARS course, the lead instructor, who'd served in the same SMU that my new XO had, asked if I knew the command master chief of the SMU.

"I know of him," I said.

"He's on the phone, and he wants to talk with you."

I went and answered the phone.

"Congratulations." the command master chief said, "You've been accepted for training at our unit."

I was relatively young and hadn't seriously considered it. I enjoyed my life here, so I said, "Can I have some time to think about it?"

"Sure."

After I hung up, I felt like Lou Brown in the movie *Major League*. He's managing a tire shop when he receives a call to go coach a major league baseball team. He says, "I don't know. Let me think it over, will you, Charlie? I've got a guy on the other line about some whitewalls. I'll talk to you later."

I think it's harder for guys on the West Coast to leave. For guys on the East Coast, they get to stick around because the SMU is closer to where they already live.

The next morning, I went to work early. I still didn't know what the hell I was going to do. I walked into the building. The only other person there before me was the operations officer, and I asked him if he knew the command master chief who'd called me.

"Yeah, we go way back. Why?" the ops officer asked. "Does he want you to go out there?"

"Yeah, I think so," I said.

"Let me get him on the phone right now." The ops officer made a call. Then the two of them had a conversation. The ops officer said on the phone, "Yeah, he's done well here. Love to send him out there. You're getting a great guy." There was a pause. "Yeah, sure, we can do that." There was another moment of silence. "Okay, brilliant. Bye." He hung up the phone, turned to me, and said, "Congratulations."

"What?" I asked.

"Yeah, he wants you to take a language test first. Wants you to learn Spanish at DLI before you go." The Defense Language Institute was up north in Monterey, California.

"What?"

"You got it. That's awesome."

I walked out of the door in a daze. My plans for the next several years had changed in a matter of minutes.

◈ ◈ ◈

I left my five-plus years at SEAL Team Five on the West Coast and, after Spanish school, ventured out to the SMU on the East Coast. The initial training was a selection course, and almost everything we did was timed and graded—swimming, parachuting, running, shooting, and so on. We took our Sea, Air, Land namesake to extremes. It was dangerous too. I loved it.

One night after work, I went out with the guys to a bar. We were playing pool when someone behind me bumped my pool stick. I put my stick on the table and turned around to see who did it.

I had a thing for blondes with green eyes, and this was Sharon Stone 2.0. Beauty blazoned or not, she was messing with my game, so I picked her up and put her on a stool. Then I grabbed my pool cue and resumed my shot.

My teammate came over and said, "She looks impressed at how you picked her up so easily. You need to talk to her."

"Naw, I'm playing pool," I said.

"Talk to her, Dawg."

I brushed him off.

He kept bugging me.

As the bar neared closing time, she and I gravitated toward each other, two planets about to collide, and I talked to her. The attentive way she looked at me and the way she engaged in conversation made her seem pretty dialed in, and as we left the bar, she gave me her phone number. Even so, her friends and my friends seemed far away—in different universes.

We separated and went to our cars.

My buddy caught up with me. "Well?" he asked.

"Well what?"

"Did you get her number?"

"Of course."

"That's what I'm talking about."

I didn't call her.

On another evening, I told my buddies, "I'm staying home tonight. When you need a designated driver, call me."

Later, my buddy called, but when I arrived, he and the others were still sitting around, laughing and talking and drinking—nowhere near ready to go.

"What's up?" I asked.

"Join the party," my buddy said.

"No. I thought you guys needed a ride home."

"We need you to join the party."

"No," I said.

"Come on."

"I'm not feeling it," I said.

I leaned against a post, waiting for them to finish.

Sharon Stone 2.0 appeared, and we talked. We made each other laugh, and I liked the way she looked at me—like she thought a lot about me, and she wasn't going to let me down.

"Sorry, I lost your phone number," I said.

She gave it to me again.

I put it in my wallet.

A few days later, I went riding with my buddies on our Harley-Davidson motorcycles. Unlike the Japanese crotch rockets that take off fast and wear a rider out almost as quickly, the American Harleys are peerless for cruising. Mine was a 1990 FXSTC Softail Custom with a lot of chrome. The Softail appeared to have the rigid frame of the older Easy Riders, but its hidden suspension springs made for a smoother journey. I leaned back and stretched my legs forward on pegs, as if I was riding a chopper, but it wasn't a chopper.

We stopped out in the country at one of my teammate's houses. The same guy-talk bored me, and I started thinking about her, so I pulled her phone number out and called.

"Would you like to go do something?" I asked.

"Yeah, I'll go do something with you," she said.

"Pick you up in an hour?"

"Sure." She gave me directions to her house.

An hour later, I pulled up to her place wearing jeans, a tank top, and a leather jacket. I looked like I'd been riding for a while and smelled like exhaust. I cut off the engine.

She came out wearing a nice skirt and a Levi's jacket. She looked at the motorcycle and then at me. "Oh, no. I'm not getting on that thing." She rushed back in and shut the door.

That didn't turn out so well. I sat there for a moment trying to process. Then I started my Harley.

Suddenly, she came back out wearing jeans.

"What changed your mind?" I asked.

"My friend said that if I didn't come out here and get on that motorcycle with you, she was going to."

I smiled.

"All right, where you want to go?" she asked.

"Wherever you want," I said.

"Don't scare me on that thing." She hopped on the back.

I twisted the throttle and took her to the bar where we first met. There I ordered drinks.

I'd only taken one sip of beer when she said, "You seem kind of bored."

"What?" I asked. "We just got here."

She smiled.

"You like riding the motorcycle," I said.

"Yeah."

We went out and jumped back on. I grabbed the throttle with the ease of shaking a friendly hand. The Harley engine vibrated, and the exhaust growled loudly enough to let me know I was on a beast but not enough to wake the dead. Sharon wrapped her arms around me, I pushed at gravity with my biceps, and we rolled. The motor had so much muscle that it effortlessly spirited us north through Virginia Beach.

A tugboat's engine clack-clacked in the distance and blew its horn goodbye. We cruised past the ships lined up on the piers at Naval Station Norfolk. Gulls called out and flew high into the setting sun reflected on the bay.

The sounds of the tugboat and the gulls disappeared with the setting sun as we entered Hampton Roads Bridge–Tunnel. The Harley's rumbling echoed, and Sharon held me tighter. After three-and-a-half miles, we came out of the tunnel, and the natural light returned. We passed through Hampton and continued northwest on the interstate.

"Let's go to Busch Gardens," she said.

I was happy to take her to the theme park. "Sure."

We traveled an hour, but when we arrived in Williamsburg, Busch Gardens was closed.

"We can stay in a hotel and go first thing in the morning," I said.

She paused for a moment. "Well, okay. I don't usually do this."

This was simpler than I thought it'd be. We checked into a hotel room.

She grabbed a movie menu and sat down on the bed. "Let's watch something."

"Which movie?" I asked.

She studied the menu. "*Ace Ventura: Pet Detective.*"

I picked up the remote control and ordered the movie. "Are you hungry?" I asked.

"Pizza would be good."

I called for pizza.

While we waited for it to arrive, she fell asleep. When the delivery guy came, she was still asleep, so I sat alone eating a full pizza while watching *Ace Ventura: Pet Detective*.

What the hell?

The next day, I found out she was serious about Busch Gardens. I hated roller coaster rides. Each one she took me on gave me a headache, and then we rode them again. She had a grand old time, but for me, it sucked. In spite of the roller coasters, I enjoyed being with her.

In the following weeks, Sharon and I saw more and more of each other. When I went out with her, I had to be on my A-game—there were always other guys wanting to step in to replace me.

Our family backgrounds were similar. Her mom cut hair for a living, and mine did too. Her dad started out in the military, and my dad had been in the military too. When I visited her family, it was comfortable. Soon, we became an exclusive couple.

She knew I was a SEAL from my Team friends, but I didn't tell her where I was working, and she didn't ask. One night she called me and said, "We need to talk."

"What happened?" I asked.

"I went to a party with some of my friends, and there were some SEALs there. My friend told them that you're a SEAL. They asked what team you're in. I told them I didn't know. Then they asked what base you were at. I told them I didn't know that either. When they asked why I didn't know, I said we never talk about it. I was so embarrassed," she said. "They laughed at me as if you're not for real."

I chuckled. "No Team guys are at Oceana."

"It's not funny," she said.

I told her two words to say to other SEALs—the government prefers I not print them here.

After she used the magic words, they treated her well.

Motorcyclists are thirty times more likely to die in a crash than people in a car. However, when a biker pushes the limits like I did, that number probably jumps to sixty. One weekend, a friend and I went out riding. Although my hog weighed seven hundred and thirty-six pounds, my buddy's Ninja crotch rocket was only about half that weight. Our ride escalated into a race through winding country roads. He bent into a blind curve in front of me, and I cranked the throttle to catch up. A panel station wagon came at me from the opposite direction and swerved into my lane.

I had two choices: go through his window like a missile or take my chances with the ditch and trees to my right. I chose the latter and veered off the road. I strained to keep myself upright, but the mud grabbed my wheels and wouldn't release them. My bike stopped, but I kept going.

Before I could tuck and minimize the impact of the landing, my lower body struck a tree. It changed the direction of my flight, and I bounced like a rag doll. I crash-landed on the road and tumbled. My helmet bounced several times off the asphalt.

My buddy had already turned around and pulled up next to me to block any oncoming cars. "Dude, you all right?"

"I'm good," I said. "How's my bike?" I turned and spotted my Harley in the ditch, fifteen yards behind. I struggled to my feet and took a step in its direction. My leg buckled, and I fell. "Shit!"

My friend fetched a nearby Team guy, and they drove me and my bike in his truck to my house. Sharon happened to be there, and she drove me to the Naval Clinic. There were only two doctors who had clearance to work with my unit, and one of them checked me out.

"I'm fine," I said.

He shook his head. I wasn't fooling him. "You won the trifecta for knees—your MCL, meniscus, and ACL are completely torn off one end of the bone. You're going to need reconstructive surgery."

"And if I refuse?" I asked.

"Then you'll be out of the SEAL Teams, especially the unit you're training in now."

Frogmen aren't scared of much—except for getting kicked out of the fraternity. "Get me on the cutting table. Now," I said.

Within a week, the surgeon cut part of my patellar tendon from the front part of my knee to replace the ACL.

When it was all over and I came off the anesthetics, Sharon and a physical therapist were at my side.

"You're the last SEAL the surgeon will ever operate on," the physical therapist said.

"Why's that?" I asked.

"You woke up during surgery and let out a monstrous yell, and you wanted off the table."

"I don't remember," I said.

"Scared the hell out of the doc and his assistants. They had to administer more anesthetics and strap you down."

The doc had put a tube in my knee, and now I couldn't walk on it.

Sharon drove me home. My knee was a mess, but she took care of me.

Normally, a trainee won't recover well enough and is removed from the SMU for two reasons. First, in the time it takes an injured man to recover, a healthy new candidate could begin training while meeting the contingency requirements. Second, our work is fast, physical, and dangerous—one slip could get an injured man killed, or worse, his teammate. Even so, the command took a chance on me, gave me some time to recover, and allowed me to continue in the next class.

While I recovered, Sharon and I became more serious. "What do you want out of the future?" she asked.

"I want a family," I said. "How about you?" I asked.

She thought for a moment. "I want to be a stay-at-home mom. I know it's not popular, but I've wanted to be a mother for as long as I can remember."

"I'd like to provide enough so that my wife can be a stay-at-home mom."

She nodded. "When both parents have to work, kids get in trouble or suffer."

"Yeah, I got in the most trouble after school, when both of my parents were still working," I said.

"Me too."

One day, I popped the question, and she said yes. We didn't want to spend a lot of our family's money that could be better spent on something like a down payment for a home. We didn't want a big party either. We both had friends who'd had big, expensive weddings and were divorced soon after. Instead, we planned an intimate wedding at the beach for us and her family—her sister, parents, and grandmother.

I was going to wear my Service Dress uniform—the navy crackerjack; however, that morning, I bought a suit instead. I had to wait for the tailor to finish it, and I was late for the wedding. As I approached the turnoff street for the wedding, I noticed Sharon's dad on his way out to search for me. He was a big veteran-turned-fireman with a lot of guns, and I didn't want to be on his bad side.

Nervously, I parked the car and took my place on the beach as fast as I could. The clear blue sky above was beautiful, but it was nowhere near as gorgeous as she was. Her white dress fit her body perfectly, and her mom had done up her hair in baby's breath flowers. She looked so flawless and pure that my nervousness left me and confirmed that she was the one. A light wind tugged at me. The air smelled familiar—fresh and salty. We made our promises, and her sister cried. The rest of us smiled. Sharon and I were now husband and wife.

Later, my friends were upset with me for not inviting them to the wedding, but I was happy with our simple wedding. Soon after, Sharon became pregnant with my son.

⊕ ⊕ ⊕

I returned to training, but things were different. Before, when work was over, I took care of my gear, PTd to make myself faster or stronger, practiced shooting, or hung out with the guys out in town. Now I had other responsibilities. *Let me get my shit done, so I can spend as much time with my wife and son before I have to leave again.* No longer was I the guy who wanted to stay at E-5 or E-6 rank and be an operator in the Teams my whole life.

I'd returned to training too soon, though, and once again, I was in a lot of pain. One evening when I stripped off my clothes, I discovered that my knee was changing colors. Each night, I took Motrin to reduce the pain and swelling and washed it down with beer.

The next day in training, we did a monster mash. We swam to the insertion point, ran to the target building, cleared rooms, climbed up two or three stories of stairs, and slid down a pole outside the window. When it was my turn, I grabbed the pole. It was wet from the guy before me, and I fell. More pain shot through my knee than ever before, and now my back hurt too.

I tried to hide my agony, but I limped noticeably for the next few days. Despite my best efforts, it became clear that I couldn't continue. I was offered a slot at BUD/S as an instructor. I wouldn't have to serve a full three years there, only long enough to heal and return. I took the deal.

While I was at BUD/S, doctors checked me out and discovered that in addition to my knee troubles, I had a broken back. There had been so much focus on my knee that my back missed everyone's radar. I had a lot of healing to do.

CHAPTER 10

BUD/S INSTRUCTOR

BUD/S TRAINING WAS OFTEN PERILOUS, and one of the hazards was doing free ascents, which took place in a sixty-foot dive tower. A trainee enters through a chamber at the bottom of the tower, such as a SEAL might do when locking out of a submerged submarine. Then the student must "blow and go"—constantly exhaling air while calmly swimming to the surface. If the trainee fails to blow out enough air or ascends too quickly, the expanding air in the lungs will burst through, leak into the veins, return to the heart, and stop the flow of oxygen-filled blood to the brain—causing an air embolism. This lack of oxygen to the brain causes death.

Before students began their free ascent training, instructors would sometimes dive from the surface and see how long they could hold their breath at the bottom. On January 10, 1997, Instructor Keith Kimura, who taught Class 210, dove down and held his breath. Unconsciousness can happen without warning. Minutes passed, and when someone noticed that something was wrong, the instructors attempted to rescue Keith, but it was too late—he'd drowned. The dive tower was shut down.

The dive tower remained shut down until I became the Dive Phase Leading Petty Officer, in charge of roughly a dozen instructors. A couple instructors were Air Force Combat Controllers, one was an army Green Beret, and the rest were SEALs. I was impressed by all of them.

The SEAL Dive Phase Officer in Charge approached me one day. "We need to reopen the dive tower. I'm thinking Flipper would be good to run your free ascent and trunk operations," he said, referring to another SEAL.

"I don't know if he's the best choice," I said.

"Who do you think would be better?" the OIC asked.

"The army guy," I said, referring to the Green Beret, on loan to us.

"No."

I didn't buy into the old rivalries between services thing; I wanted the best man for the job. "He has experience operating the army dive tower in Key West," I said. "I've been working with him on a lot of our dive ops here, and he knows his shit."

"You gotta be kidding me."

I dug my claws in. "He's the best guy for the job."

"All right, I'll take your word for it."

Our command sent the Green Beret out to the East Coast for training, and he returned and got our tower back on line. He had a devastating sense of humor, but one time when we entered the tower, the Team guys were gabbing, and the Green Beret said, "Shut the hell up, I'm the only one talking right now! This is serious."

He ran the dive tower like clockwork.

After we ran some ops in the tower, the OIC approached me and said, "Hey, man, I'm glad you talked me into selecting him."

I taught from classes 215 to about 230. There was an author writing a book about BUD/S, and Discovery Channel did a documentary, but my dive phase chief and my other bosses thought I was planning to return to the Special Mission Unit after healing up, so without my having to ask, they shielded me from the book and documentary spotlights—no interviews, no pictures, nothing. I didn't like that kind of limelight anyway.

There was pressure on us to produce more SEALs, but the other instructors and I vowed only to graduate the best. We weren't going to send anyone to the platoons who could hurt or embarrass them.

During the beginning of a winter Hell Week, the students stood ragged, soaked, and cold on the beach, but this night, about sixteen of them quit. I spotted an officer who fell behind on a low crawl event. He seemed on the edge of quitting, too, so I focused on him.

I wasn't a yeller. I crouched down next to him. "Hey, sir, what was your job before you came here?"

His face was full of doubt. "Admin."

"Huh. Bet you were pretty good at it, or you wouldn't have been able to come here."

"Hooyah," the officer said.

"I'll bet you were a lot warmer there, right?"

He slowed down. "Hooyah."

"I can see you're thinking about what you're doing here, and I can have you back in that toasty warm office within a week."

The officer stopped crawling.

"I need a quitter!" another instructor yelled. "We're not going to stop crawling on this sand until I get another quitter."

The officer rose to his feet and ran to the bell.

The SEAL Officer in Charge was under pressure to graduate more SEALs, and he looked at me as if to say, "What the hell did you say to him?"

Later, we did log PT, and I scanned for another target. Each boat crew of about seven men lifted a hundred-and-fifty-pound log onto their shoulders. To my cadence, they hoisted the log over their heads and lowered it on the opposite shoulders. I continued this until their arms weakened. Then I had them do squats with the logs on their shoulders. Next, each boat crew curled the logs like a giant barbell for multiple reps. When their biceps were blown, I ordered them to do sit-ups with the logs. Finally, they raced to see which team could roll their log across the sand the fastest. I noticed a slipknot who was pretending to help his boat crew but was actually putting in little to no effort. Slipknot dragged his whole boat crew behind, causing extra attention from the other instructors and me—causing his teammates to suffer.

I told the boat crews, "I want you to take my logs up over the berm, rinse them off in the ocean, and bring them back. The boat crew that gets here last gets to use Old Misery for the next evolution." Old Misery was an extra thick, extra heavy log that was still there from when I was a trainee. I never saw a boat crew pick it up.

Slipknot looked like he'd already given up.

"Ready, go," I said.

The boat crews raced up and over the berm, carrying their logs. Then they returned over the hill with their rinsed logs. Slipknot's crew was last over the hill. Slipknot dropped to his knees and stayed on the berm. His boat crew tried hard to make up the distance between them and the other crews, but they came in last.

"Down log," I said.

The boat crews lowered their logs.

"Stand by," I said.

I walked toward Slipknot on the berm. "Get over there and help your team out!"

"I want to ring the bell!" Slipknot said.

The SEAL instructor OIC put his hands on his hips and shook his head.

"Then do it!" I shouted.

Slipknot ran over and rang the bell.

"Anyone else want to join him?" I asked the boat crews.

No one stepped forward. Slipknot was alone.

"Prepare to up log," I said.

The boat crews prepared to hoist the logs. The losing crew readied themselves beside Old Misery.

I pointed to the losing boat crew. "Go get a different log."

They seemed confused for a moment. Then they left Old Misery's side and stood next to a regular-sized log.

I got what I wanted—the guys that were ready to do the work. There was no way I would have made them PT with Old Misery—someone would get hurt.

Slipknot turned away.

✧　✧　✧

I put trainee Marcus Luttrell, of Class 228, through dive phase. He was never on the chopping block for anything. The instructors never had to talk to him about stepping up his game. He was one of the top swimmers. Later, he'd go on to a legendary career in the Teams and write his memoir, *Lone Survivor*.

The students wrote evaluations of the instructors, and they consistently rated me as a hard ass but fair. I didn't give anyone extra attention who didn't need it. I'd much rather train and advance them than hammer them.

We instructors were there for different reasons. Some guys were transitioning out of the military. Some, like me, were broken and were there to get strong again and train some good frogmen to go out and help our brothers in the platoons. All of us except for one instructor were taking college classes too.

I studied Criminal Justice at National University in San Diego. My college professors had various law enforcement backgrounds. They included police officers, detectives, NCIS agents, an IRS criminal investigator, and other federal agents. One was a judge. Several professors mentioned working with agents in the Air Force Office of Special Investigations (OSI). These OSI agents worked many of the federal law enforcement jobs that other federal agents did. They shared the same first phase of law enforcement training with most of the other federal agents too. OSI employed both civilian and military agents. On top of that, OSI did counterintelligence work, which appealed to me even more.

At BUD/S, one of our Air Force Combat Controllers, "DJ," had deployed with an army Special Operations Command unit to Iraq during the first Gulf War, hunting Scud missile launchers. Enemy soldiers discovered the Americans and attacked. The assault lasted hours, and DJ called in a dozen aircraft sorties, saving them. He was awarded the Bronze Star with Valor.

Some other instructors and I finished a dive and walked into our office area, where DJ sat working at his desk.

"What you working on?" I asked.

He held up some paperwork. "I'm putting in a package for Air Force Officer Training School—OTS. You guys ought to do it too. Shit, you have the same training as me; you might as well copy my package and throw it in."

I'd considered going to the navy's Officer Candidate School (OCS) to become an officer. Two SEALs I knew had applied, but both were the same age as me and were rejected for being too old. Even if I were to become a naval officer, I worried that my body was now too broken to lead SEALs. *Maybe I can become an officer in the air force and an agent in OSI*, I thought.

I felt torn about leaving my SEAL brothers. I knew it would upset some of them. As part of the application process, I asked for letters of recommendations to the Air Force's Officer Training School from some of my old commanders. One commander almost talked me into abandoning my plan to go work for him. I stewed on it for days.

In the time since I'd become a BUD/S instructor, my daughter was born, and now I had two children. One day, my wife and I took the kids with us grocery shopping. In the dairy section, my wife put cheese in the basket. Above it was a sign that said WIC. Then she picked up a dozen eggs, and I saw the WIC sign again. When she reached for the milk, it was there too.

"What does WIC stand for?" I asked.

"Women, infants, and children," my wife said. "It's for, well, low-income women and their children under five years old."

It felt like someone had punched me in the gut.

When we stood in the checkout line and my wife took out her WIC vouchers, I felt eyes staring at us. My uneasiness increased, and for the first time in my life, I felt inadequate. I never knew we were poor. I was embarrassed.

The next day, in the training compound, I bumped into SEAL Commander John Koenig, my former BUD/S Land Warfare Phase instructor. He was in civilian clothes. He'd always had an air of mystery about him—I didn't know if he was retired and doing some contract work or if he was still active and involved in some special program.

"Afternoon, sir," I said.

"What you up to?" he asked.

"Just finished dive ops."

His eyes narrowed. "You look like something's on your mind."

"I'm thinking about leaving the Teams and becoming an officer in the air force."

"Oh? You got a wife?"

This was getting personal, and it made me nervous, but he had an invisible way of pulling me in. "Yes, sir."

"Kids?"

"Two."

Commander Koenig seemed to relax. "Boy, I know you're struggling with leaving, but you have to do what's best for your family because when this is all over, your family will be all you have. Don't worry about letting your brothers here down. Someone will replace you as soon as you're gone. A husband and father can't be replaced."

His words weighed heavy on me. "Thank you."

I wanted to become an Air Force OSI officer, but the background check would take six months to a year, and I couldn't go without a job for that long—I had a family to support. The air force notified the Special Forces instructor and me that they had an immediate slot for us in Officer Training School to become Security Forces officers. It seemed like a no-brainer to me, combining soldiering and police work as an air force officer.

From my group of Third Phase instructors, the air force picked up one Combat Controller, one Green Beret, and three SEALs, including me. All of us were accepted for OTS. My OIC wasn't too happy. We'd jumped boat in the middle of the ocean and left him with all our paddles.

Our jump boat was a microcosm of the mass exodus that was occurring throughout the Teams. Within a few years after 9/11, Congress would pass a bill to extend the navy's officer commissioning age to thirty-five years old for prior enlisted SEALs with degrees, and to entice enlisted men to remain, the navy more than doubled reenlistment bonuses.

CHAPTER 11

JACK OF ARABIA

PEOPLE PAY MONEY TO WATCH war movies and read books about war—Team guys wanted the real deal. It's ironic that during the years I served in the SEAL Teams, I didn't see a warzone, but after I left, I got my wish. I breezed through the Air Force Officer Training School and became a second lieutenant. I was excited that I became an officer, and the extra pay helped my family.

I didn't have time to feel nervous about it because I quickly attended Phoenix Raven School, where I trained to be an air marshal for the air force. After graduation, I flew to Afghanistan.

As an air marshal, I shuttled high value terrorists from the battlefields to Guantanamo Bay Naval Base—Gitmo. There, the terrorists were held as prisoners and interrogated. In total, Air Force Security Forces transported a hundred terrorists. While in Afghanistan, I saw OSI work counterintelligence and counterterrorism missions. An OSI commander explained the work they were doing this way: "In the States, investigators put a drug case together and track the main supplier—then get a SWAT team to assist in serving the warrant. Here, we hunt insurgents and terrorists and use a military unit to hit doors and crack heads. Your Security Forces experience now and your previous SEAL Team experiences would be a natural fit with us."

What the commander said made sense.

I knew what intel commanders needed to protect a base and what intel a military team required to action a target—I just needed to learn how to investigate and track. My hunger to join OSI grew.

While I waited for OSI to finish my background check, the Iraq War heated up, and I received orders to become part of a five-man team going to Tabuk Air Base in the northwest corner of Saudi Arabia, near Jordan.

One of my guys said, "You've got to take me with you, sir."

He was a hard worker, eager and smart. I smiled. "Okay, I will."

I told another airman, my best communications guy, "I want you to go with me."

"Lieutenant, my wife's pregnant, and I don't want to miss the baby being born," he said.

"If you deploy with us, I'll do everything I can to get you home in time to be part of that. I can't guarantee it, but if I can, I will."

"Okay, sir, I'll go."

I wanted to go straight to Iraq, but although my guys knew their jobs well, they weren't like Team guys itching for a gunfight.

A captain, two ranks above me, complained: "You're taking all the best guys with you. It's not right."

"Why not?" I asked.

"Last time I deployed, I had to take some slipknots with me. That's just the way it's done."

"Man, that's your fault," I said.

Our lieutenant colonel, who was two ranks above the captain, studied us. We looked at him.

"I'm in agreement with the lieutenant," the colonel said, "that is your fault." For the most part, I took the guys I wanted.

In March 2003, the day after we invaded Iraq, I arrived in Tabuk, Saudi Arabia. My headquarters was in Qatar.

In April, the last of the twenty-four F-15Cs flew their missions, and the 485th Air Expeditionary Wing began to close shop here in Tabuk. By May, only a fraction of the fighters and forty-six C-130H Hercules airlift aircraft remained. More than two-thirds of the 3,500 personnel had returned stateside. The personnel who stuck around lived in tent cities surrounded by concertina wire and a handful of Jersey barriers. I was in charge of ground defense force and communications personnel in a sector of the air base. We did patrols of our perimeter, but we had to leave the outside patrols to the Saudis. Occasionally, when it was dark, a terrorist would take potshots at us. Because of that, one of our officers refused to enter my sector.

I scoped out where the shooting was coming from—a couple of tall buildings under construction outside of our wire. I remembered nights when I provided sniper overwatch for SEAL platoons assaulting ships. Bright lights shining toward my field of vision washed out my scope. I requested that, instead of our lights facing inward and highlighting us as targets, they be raised and aimed outward. My request was granted. The shooting dropped off to nothing.

In the desert, sandstorms were brutal—a giant oncoming tan wall, like something out of the movie The Mummy. I wore an olive drab cravat over my nose and mouth like a bank robber in a Western. My sinuses would still blow up from all the sand that I inhaled. One guy told me to take DayQuil, which cleared up my sinuses for a day.

In order for my men to effectively protect the base, I sought out the wisdom of intelligence experts. OSI agents reported intel of an al Qaeda terrorist who had been conducting video surveillance outside of our base. The terrorist was captured and interrogated. He gave up the name of another terrorist, who worked on our base for a British defense contractor. Suddenly, the terrorist who worked on base stopped showing up for his day job.

One of the OSI agents on our base was a skilled interrogator who now goes by the pseudonym Matthew Alexander. He was always armed, sometimes rode in a helicopter, and went off base a lot doing interesting things. During one of my periodic visits to him, he told me, "Nineteen al Qaeda terrorists are planning attacks on Westerners in Saudi Arabia. One of al Qaeda's targets is your base here. They plan to hit opposite sides. The first strike will be with a vehicle-borne IED, drawing your forces and attention to that side of the base. Then they'll hit the other end with a vehicle-borne IED, opening a gap for a truckload of heavily armed terrorists, who'll pour into the base and shoot everyone on sight. Then a third VBIED will drive onto the base and strike where the most Americans are."

"That must've been one helluva interrogation," I said.

Agent Alexander nodded. "In another incident, Saudi Arabian troops got into a shootout with local terrorists and wrapped up a handful of the nineteen planners. The Saudis discovered that a compound in Riyadh was one of the targets and confirmed that our base was a target too."

I was impressed with how specific the agent's intel was. Although he made me want to be an OSI agent even more, I had to focus on the here and now: survival.

We shared the information with our commander. Soon, a lot of the leadership packed up and left. The officer who wouldn't enter my sector while we were taking potshots from terrorists was one of the first to go. Others followed suit. The base commander was unable to take a military flight out, so he finagled a civilian flight out and got in trouble for it.

At an informal gathering after lunch, my boss said to his chief, "We have to get out of here."

"Who're we going to leave in charge?" his chief asked.

My boss looked at me and said, "Lieutenant Treadway has this."

I turned to my master sergeant and smiled.

Master Sergeant wasn't smiling. In 1996, he was stationed at Khobar Towers in Saudi Arabia. It housed members of an air force fighter squadron. Air Force Security Forces and OSI warned the leadership about surveillance being conducted outside the perimeter, but Saudi authorities didn't allow them to investigate. Hezbollah terrorists, backed by Iran, bombed the towers, and nineteen Americans were killed. Master Sergeant was fortunate to have survived. Ultimately, air force leadership was held responsible, and careers were ended. This was *Groundhog Day* all over again, but master sergeant remained by my side.

My boss and his chief wrote themselves up for Bronze Stars and skedaddled. The only remaining ranking officer was a civil engineering lieutenant colonel, who was in charge of the final tearing down of the base.

Headquarters, in Qatar, called me on my cell phone: "What force protection condition are you in?"

"You've heard our recent intel, haven't you?" I asked.

"Yes."

"What force protection condition do you suggest I put myself in?" I asked.

"Oh, no. We're not going to control that. That's up to you." They knew we were about to be hit, and it seemed they were setting me up to be the fall guy for it.

"With the intel I have, if you're leaving it up to me, we're going full on— Force Protection Condition Delta."

I had my men tighten ID and vehicle checks and increase patrols. We pulled in additional military personnel for guard duties. We caused interruptions and delays to daily routines and cancelled missions—whatever it took to secure our base. The downside was that we could only maintain this high state of readiness for a limited time.

The civil engineering lieutenant colonel, Agent Alexander, Master Sergeant, and I got together and planned security for the base. I had some smart noncommissioned officers with experience from Korea in air base defense and setting up barriers, so I tapped into their expertise.

Qatar HQ redeployed people to other bases throughout the Middle East and sent some home, decreasing the number of targets for the terrorists. Agent Alexander sent his agents back home to the States, but he stayed with us. Also, we moved our tent city closer to the flight line, putting more distance between us and the entrance. This also gave us better visibility of our perimeter.

We were able to send some of our Security Forces home, including my communications expert with the pregnant wife.

One guy told me his grandmother was dying and asked me to send him home too.

"I'm sorry," I said, "She's not immediate family, and I can't send you now."
Others tried to find reasons to return to the States.

I looked at the entrances to our base. We had one, and the Saudis we shared
the base with had several. I wanted the Saudis to limit their entrances and
increase their patrols outside of the base. In the evening, I went and met with
the Saudi colonel. We sat down and talked about family while eating dates and
drinking chai tea. It was so time consuming that I didn't even reach my request
during the first meeting. On the second evening, I brought it up.

"That is not problem," he said. "It is not concern. Come have another
meeting with me."

I really don't have time for this bullshit.

We mounted .50 caliber machine guns and M240B machine guns on our
Humvees and increased their patrols. Al Qaeda would see our defenses and
know that we meant business. We kept our entrance in the same spot. We
had our military working dogs sniff incoming vehicles for bombs and so on.
Terrorists would have to drive a quarter mile before they reached the bulk of our
population, so at the end of that road, I posted a stationary machine gunner and
a machine gunner on a Humvee to take down any terrorists before they reached
us. The insider terrorist who'd scoped out our base had seen the old version.
This was the Real Muther. If an al Qaeda martyr was wanting to see Allah, we
would oblige him to go it alone.

I changed my working hours to noon until midnight so I could cover
two shifts and see as many of my defenders as possible. Daytime temperatures
reached over a hundred, but evenings cooled off into the seventies. On May 12,
after my second shift ended, I went to sleep.

Sirens woke me. I stumbled out of my tent to find Saudi patrol cars circling
our perimeter. *What the hell?*

The Saudi colonel, who was the wing commander of his base, ran up to me
in his flip flops, a milky white flowing thobe, and a white turban. "Lieutenant,
lieutenant, I cannot believe it! They killed Muslims. Muslims killed Muslims."

I rubbed my eyes. "What're you talking about?"

His voice shook. "They attacked Riyadh, and thirty-nine people died.
Muslims killed Muslims."

I realized then that the whole reason he hadn't been willing to help me
tighten security was because he thought he and his Muslim buddies were safe,
and he didn't care that Westerners like me were in danger. Now we were in this
together. "Really?"

"Whatever you want," he said, "I will do it."

"Yeah. Close all your entry points except one, and please increase your patrols."

"Yes, yes, I will do it right now. Thank you, thank you," he said. "Anything else?"

"That's all for now," I said.

"Thank you, thank you." He hurried away.

The intel passed to me by Agent Alexander that facilitated our heightened defense posture was spot on. After action reports on the attack in Riyadh correlated with the method of the terrorist operations he had briefed us on. We dodged a bomb—several, in fact. Soon after, I was promoted to first lieutenant.

CHAPTER 12

FLETC

THE NUMBER ONE REQUESTED JOB by officers in the air force is pilot. Number two is agent in OSI. Two years after Saudi Arabia, I pinned on the rank of captain and was accepted to OSI. About ninety other officers were rejected. I made it all the way to the Federal Law Enforcement Training Center (FLETC) in Glynco, Georgia.

Nearly a hundred other federal law enforcement agencies trained at FLETC—NCIS, US Marshalls, ATF, ICE, DOJ, and the rest of the alphabet soup. We trained in two phases. Every agent took the first phase, which consisted of around three months of learning about federal law. That included a lot about the Fourth Amendment; search and seizure rights, such as arrest warrants and phone tapping; and training in the basics of being a federal investigator. The second phase was specific to each agency—that is, OSI training in second phase was different from US Marshall training in second phase, for example.

The chow hall and dorms were familiar structures of the military to me. Fortunately, I didn't have to march from Point A to Point B. I was eager to do PT, shoot, and drive, but I knew I'd have to study hard. It helped that I was interested in law enforcement and counterintelligence.

My classmates were a mix of air force personnel and civilians. Most were training to become OSI agents, but in the first phase, there was a sprinkling of other agencies mixed in with us. Each of the OSI agents seemed to have a specific talent such as foreign languages, computer science, forensics, or military tactics.

In the evenings, I worked out at the gym, where I bumped into one of my classmates, Mac. He was a quiet black guy, married and with strong Christian values. We chatted, and he mentioned that he was a graduate from the Citadel. I told him about a well-respected Team guy who'd graduated from the same tough military college in South Carolina. Back at the dorm, Mac's room was a bit down the hall and around the corner.

Nate, the charismatic and aggressive law school grad, lived in the dorm room next to mine. He and I left our doors open a lot, and we talked with each other between studies. He drank wine more often than beer, and I wondered if it was a law school thing. Because our rooms shared a wall, I heard when he had visitors. One was a short, athletic, Irish redhead training to become an ATF agent. Sometimes they went off campus together. About halfway into our training, she must've graduated because she stopped coming around. With her absence came a taller gal, also athletic, with auburn hair.

Later, Nate told me he'd overheard an instructor mention that I was a SEAL. The instructor must've read my personnel folder. Nate mentioned that his father was a special operator in the air force's Combat Control Teams, and he'd worked with SEALs. Nate had an inquisitive mind, and he asked me about the Teams. Although he was about ten years younger than me, he carried himself well, and we hit it off. I figured that he got his law degree because his father wanted him to, but deep down he wanted to be where the action was, which is why he was training to become an OSI agent.

On the other side of Nate's dorm room was Baker, who liked to throw parties. One evening it was raining, and Baker had a walloping shindig, inviting both male and female classmates. One of them, a Ranger who was training to become an agent for the Department of Justice, got tanked. He grabbed Baker's expensive mountain bike and proclaimed, "I'm going to ride this down the stairs."

"Why don't we wrestle instead," Baker said.

"I'll wrestle you downstairs." The Ranger drove the bike down several flights of stairs and crashed at the bottom.

Mac, Nate, Baker, and I laughed.

"Let's go!" the Ranger called up.

"You look too serious," Baker said. "I don't want to die; I only want to wrestle."

"I don't know how not to kill you!" the Ranger said.

"Well," Baker said, "I guess that's all I need to know. I'm not going down there."

In his free time, Baker biked and ran avidly. During training, he usually came in first on the runs. My knee was shot, and the other was worn out, too, so I held back and paced myself to come in third or fourth place. Then an instructor, a former navy corpsman, outed me. "Hey, frogman, you're not going to let these air force guys beat you, are you?"

Son of a bitch. I passed two guys. My knees hurt, but I passed Baker too. I won. After the run, Baker looked pissed. "Where did that come from?" he asked. "Man, he dimed me out," I said. "I had to."

On the class list, Harley's name was close to mine, and the instructors usually paired us up together. He was a 280-pound beast who'd played football at an NCAA Division I university and became an undercover cop in a biker gang. For the operation, his department loaned him a half pan-head, half shovel-head piece-of-shit Harley Davidson motorcycle. He'd just finished his operation, cleaned up, and testified in court against the biker gang before he joined us at FLETC.

During hand-to-hand training, the instructors showed us some jujitsu moves down on the mat, and they told Harley to get on top of me. He did.

"Harley, what do you think about this?" I asked.

He smiled down at me like I was his new girlfriend. "I think you know what I think."

"If a dude as big as you ever gets on top of me like this, it's already over for me," I said.

During another part of training, we had to do a source meet. The scenario was that we would rendezvous with our confidential informant (CI) at his place of business. I wore civilian clothes with a training badge clipped to my pocket and my pistol exposed on my hip. Harley geared up similarly.

Harley asked the instructor. "Is there any way we can meet the CI anyplace other than his workplace or home? I ran CIs before, and this is no good."

The instructor looked at him for a moment. "Wait one." He went back and talked with one of the controllers. When he returned, he said, "You're right, but we want you to do it anyway."

Harley shrugged his shoulders. "Okay."

The scenario required us to pull up in a vehicle, so we hopped in our car and drove ten yards before we parked behind a truck next to the building where the CI worked. A man fitting his description came out, and Harley walked over and talked with him. I watched the perimeter.

Another car pulled up. "Get down," Harley said as he pushed our CI to the ground, hiding him from the other vehicle's view.

The man in the car asked, "Hey, is Billy here?"

"I don't know who you're talking about," Harley said.

I shook my head. Then I spotted a gun on the man's dashboard, so I called out, "Gun!" and put my hand on my pistol grip but kept it holstered. With my free hand, I pointed at the man and said, "Hey, you need to leave."

"But I need to talk to Billy," the man in the car insisted.

"No, you need to get out of here," I said.

The man backed out and drove off.

I watched to see if he came back. He didn't.

The instructors gave us kudos for how Harley and I handled the scenario.

In another simulation, a building needed to be cleared. Harley and I took it down by ourselves. One of the play-actors hadn't been included in the intel brief earlier, so I didn't know whether he was friend or foe. He was uncooperative. "I got this," I said. I swept his feet and put him on his face.

Afterwards, the instructor said, "The only advice I'd give you two is that you're pretty aggressive, and you might need to tone it down a little bit."

My aggression was normal by SEAL standards, but I was new to law enforcement, and I wasn't sure whether I should tone it down or not. I turned to Harley and said, "Too aggressive? Really?"

"Phht—man what do you think?" Harley said. "That's the only way to do it."

Mac was intensely focused and strong like a defensive back. Smart too. Nate picked up the tactics quickly and was athletic. Mac and Nate worked well together as partners and became close buddies.

I scored high on the PT tests, and the instructors asked my permission to put my name up on the wall. "Sure," I said. I won shooting and driving awards too.

Friday evenings, I drove my Dodge Ram three hundred and eighty-nine miles one way to Eglin Air Force Base where my wife and kids were. Then Sunday night, I drove the five and a half hours back to FLETC.

My wife and her folks came for graduation. I wasn't the most academically gifted there, but I really busted my ass on studying, especially during the OSI phase. Up at the graduation podium they were about to announce the Director's Academic award. Mac, Nate, Baker, and Harley talked about who they thought had won. Others did too. I didn't hear my name mentioned at all. Maybe I was too much of a knuckle dragger—even to my own posse.

The commandant called my name.

"What?" several agents said.

I walked up to the podium and received my award. The victory tasted sweet. Even better, the commandant awarded me FLETC Honor graduate.

We had a big bash off campus. When the off-campus party places closed, we decided to take the party back to FLETC. Somehow, we ended up short a vehicle with too many people.

My wife smiled. "I'll ride in the trunk."

"Me too," one of the female agents said.

"You sure?" I asked.

They both nodded.

An agent popped the trunk, and Sharon and the female agent crawled in laughing. Back at FLETC, we let them out and continued our party. When the party ended, Sharon and I caught a ride from another agent, who took us to a hotel in town where we had a room.

CHAPTER 13

To Catch a Predator

I WANTED TO WORK COUNTERINTELLIGENCE somewhere like Iraq or Afghanistan, but first I had to cut my teeth as an investigator of general crimes. I had no idea I'd stumble onto a case that would receive national attention.

After graduating from OSI, I was assigned to Detachment 309 in Hurlburt Field, Florida. I only had to move my wife and kids twelve miles away. Similar to other dets, there had to be an on-call agent. A lot of the calls would be about a victim in the base hospital. Because it was only a few blocks from where my family and I lived, I'd receive calls at home to go to the hospital, even when I wasn't on call.

On Friday morning, March 24, 2006, my phone rang. I woke up and glanced at the clock—it was a little after 03:00. I was on duty, so I couldn't ignore it. I answered the phone.

"We have a sexual assault victim in the emergency room who we need you to interview," an agent's voice said.

"I'm on my way," I said.

I threw on my suit and gun, grabbed my badge, and hurried over to the emergency room, where I checked in at the desk. Then I hurried down the hall. When I entered the exam room, I was surprised to find a six-foot tall, muscular guy slouched on the exam table. *How in the hell? Do I have the right person? How could something like this happen to you?* I fought back all my preconceived notions of a rape victim. He didn't appear or smell drunk, but he didn't look right either. He was shaking.

A nurse finished taking his medical history.

I went into Special Agent mode and treated him with the utmost empathy. "I'm sorry this happened to you. I'm an OSI agent, and I'm here to help."

He sized me up and down. "Thank you."

I didn't want to be too intrusive, but I asked, "What happened?"

"I regained consciousness in someone's house, and I didn't know where I was. I was restrained, and two guys took turns doing things to me. They laughed. I told them, 'Hey, I'm a federal agent,' but they laughed harder and did more things to me." Then he went into detail about the forcible sodomy and other sexual horrors they inflicted on him like a pair of hyenas.

"If it's okay," I said, "I'll need to take some pictures, and the hospital has to do an exam, so we can gather DNA evidence. It will help us figure out who did this to you and what they did."

His eyes had a far-off look. "Okay."

Another agent from my det, Agent White, arrived, and I updated him while the nurse took the victim's blood and urine samples. She laid down a sheet of paper and motioned for the victim to step onto it. "We use this to gather any trace evidence that might fall. You can ask questions or stop this at any time."

He stepped onto the paper.

"Please take off your clothes," the nurse said.

The federal agent's hands shook as he stripped naked.

The nurse gathered each garment and sealed it separately in a plastic bag.

I took pictures of the wounds on his genitals and other parts of his body. "What's your connection with the air force?" I asked.

He still had the shakes. "I'm an officer in the Air Force Reserves here on temporary duty."

Agent White took notes.

The nurse scraped the victim's fingernails for DNA.

"Do you remember any more about the house you woke up in?" I asked.

"I don't think it was very far from here," the victim said.

"Do you remember where you were before you ended up in the house?" I asked.

"I went to a couple bars," he said, "but I don't remember the name of the last one. And I don't remember drinking that much."

"What do you remember about the last bar?"

"A guy bought me a shot, and it made me so sick that I wanted to throw up. I got dizzy."

"Do you remember anything more about him?" I asked.

"He was in his thirties and had red hair. And an English accent."

The nurse combed the victim's dark head hair and pubic hair. She swabbed his pale lips, cheeks, thighs, buttocks, rectum, and genitals—collecting any saliva, blood, or semen. She sealed everything and had me sign for it. The whole process took hours. I felt bad for him.

He changed into a hospital gown.

I gave him my business card. "I know this has been tough for you. If you ever want to talk or hear an update on this case, call me."

He took the card. "Thanks." Then he called his buddies to come get him, and I interviewed his friends who were with him that night. They gave me the names of the first two places they went but said the agent went off on his own after that. The bars they went to were nearby in Destin and Fort Walton Beach.

"He might've been experimenting," an acquaintance said, "but I don't know him that well."

Silently, I disagreed. The agent was too messed up by the experience for it to simply have been an experiment.

Agent White and I went back to our offices and worked on the case.

Later, when the bars opened, we went to the first one where the victim and his friends said they had been. I displayed my badge to the broad-shouldered man with no neck who met us at the door—the bouncer.

Agent White showed him a picture of the victim and asked, "Have you seen this man in here before?"

The bouncer shook his head.

We asked him some more questions—nothing.

"Is the manager here?" I asked.

"I'll get him for you," the bouncer said.

The manager came out, Agent White showed him the picture, and we asked him the same questions.

I noticed the bar had a video surveillance camera, and I asked, "Can I see the footage?"

"Sure."

The manager took us back into a small, dimly lit room and showed us, but we couldn't see the victim or anyone who stood out as the suspect.

"Thanks," I said.

We left and visited a couple other places with no luck. There were a lot of bars to cover in Destin and Fort Walton Beach.

The next day back at the office, Agent Kelly McPherson approached me. She was an Irish redhead who'd graduated from the US Air Force Academy, where she was the team captain for the cross-country and track and field teams. Like me, she was a distinguished graduate from FLETC, but she was senior to me and had already proved herself in the field as a tenacious investigator. Today, she has her own law firm and represents women in divorces and goes after deadbeat dads. Trust me, you don't want to be on the opposite side from her.

"I'm bringing in someone who says he has information about the rape suspect," she said.

"Super." I sat in on the interview with her and the informant.

Afterwards, I told her, "The informant didn't match the victim's description. The perpetrator we're looking for has red hair and is in his thirties."

She frowned. "I'm going to follow this lead."

"Go ahead, but it's not the same guy."

That night, in the office, I prepared to go out again, and Agent White said, "We're not going to find anything."

"I don't think he was raped," another agent said.

Agent White and others nodded in agreement.

I still believed the victim.

I dragged Agent White out, and we visited every bar we had time for, working our way back towards the base, but we came up goose eggs again.

The next night, Agent White shook his head. "Not again. This case is dead—if it's even a case at all."

Other agents told me *no* or avoided me.

Then Agent Westwood said, "I'll go with you." I didn't know him well, but I was grateful for his assistance.

CHAPTER 14

Closing In

Agent Westwood and I ventured out to the bars and spoke with bartenders. We didn't tell anyone about the crime. Finally, one female bartender pointed to our picture of the dark-haired victim. "Yeah, I saw this guy. He seemed fine. Then he went to the bathroom. A red-haired guy with a British accent ordered him a shot. When the dark-haired guy came out of the restroom, he drank his shot, and suddenly he looked like he'd fall off the barstool at any moment. The red-haired man grabbed him and said, 'I got this. I'll give him a ride home.' Then they left."

"How'd the red-haired guy pay for the drinks?" I asked.

The bartender wiped the counter. "Credit card."

"Could you find the stub for us?" Agent Westwood asked.

"I'll take a look." Minutes later, she brought us the receipt.

We looked at the name on it: Devery Lane Taylor.

The next day at the office, Agent Westwood and I ran the name through Florida's Department of Motor Vehicles database. A picture of a red-haired male popped up on the monitor, and below it was his age—thirty-eight—address and other information.

"That's him!" I said.

Agent White looked over my shoulder. "No way."

"Tomorrow let's go interview him," I said.

"He's probably a civilian. Out of our jurisdiction," Agent White said.

"We can get civilian law enforcement to help us out."

"We can," Agent White said. "Man, he's weird looking." After a pause, he asked, "Can I have a digital copy of that photo?"

"Yeah." I gave it to him.

The following morning, the screensaver on a civilian agent's desk showed Devery Taylor's picture. It surprised me until I realized that Agent White was probably behind the prank—targeting the agent because he was a civilian or he'd left his computer vulnerable.

When the civilian agent showed up for work, I watched for his reaction to the strange face on his computer monitor.

"Who put Taylor's picture on my computer?" the civilian agent asked.

Agent White came out of hiding. "You know this guy?"

"Yeah, I went to ASBC with him," he said, referring to the Air and Space Basic Course required for air force second lieutenants. Some of our civilian agents were sent to the course too.

"He's air force?"

"I think so," the civilian agent said.

This case is very much alive. I typed the suspect's name into the air force's global email address book and got a hit. I read the bio that came up, then said, "Devery Taylor is an active-duty captain and chief of patient administration at the base hospital. The same one where we interviewed the victim."

"No way," Agent White said.

"Yes way," I said.

"We'll need warrants from a civilian judge if we try to arrest him off base or search his house," Agent White said.

I did some background work on Taylor and found that he'd worked with the FBI before. Here, at the hospital, he'd been selected as company grade officer of the year. He seemed to have an ego. I considered this information as I wrote the first warrants of my career.

Agent White researched different drugs. "Sounds like our victim was drugged with GHB." Gamma-hydroxybutyrate was more commonly known as a date rape drug. "Taylor has a buddy working in the pharmacy. We'll need to make sure he's not giving him anesthetics."

My det commander, Chris Jameson, saw what I was doing and said, "Aren't you going on leave tomorrow?"

"Yes, sir."

"You can't get those warrants signed today anyway," Commander Jameson said.

I understood his concern. Agents have a habit of not knowing when to put a case down once they start it. He was looking out for me by not letting the job bleed into my approved time off with my family. However, never tell a frogman they *can't* because it'll make them want to do it even more. "Thanks for looking out for me, sir."

I wrote the warrants the best I could. Then I went off base to Fort Walton Police Department and visited Detective Oakley, whom I'd been working with on other cases. He looked at the warrants. "These are good to go. I know a judge we can walk in and talk to right now."

He took me to the judge. I presented the warrants to her. She read them and without any questions or hesitation, she signed them. I was stoked.

We left the judge's office. "I'd like to be involved in this case too," Detective Oakley said.

"Okay," I said. "You want to do the interrogation with me?"

"Yeah!"

As information arose during the investigation, I thought about how I'd interview the suspect. Now that I had the arrest warrant, I spent a couple hours reviewing the case and looking for what I could use to get to the truth.

In order to interrogate Taylor, we had to give him both his civilian Miranda rights and the military's warning rights under Article 31 of the Uniform Code of Military Justice. "Maybe we should game plan this before we question him. You have to get through the civilian rights, and I have to give the military rights."

"Whatever," Detective Oakley said. "We'll be fine."

I called Taylor to be interviewed at the Fort Walton Police Department, and he agreed to come in voluntarily.

While Taylor waited in the police department's interview room, other agents went out to his house to execute the search warrant.

I entered the video observation room. On the monitor, the whole interview could be observed while audio came through on a speaker. Two air force lawyers from the Judge Advocate General sat in the observation room to make sure we properly gave Taylor his rights. A lead detective from Fort Walton PD was seated, too, along with a senior OSI agent. Kelly and her partner came in last.

Normally, only two agents are present for questioning, so I asked if they wanted to join us.

They shook their heads and said, "You got this."

I guessed that with JAG lawyers, a civilian lead detective, and a senior agent present, they didn't want to be scrutinized.

Detective Oakley walked into the room and said, "Let's go."

We went into the interview room and sat down across from Taylor. The detective was old school and gave Taylor his Miranda rights straight. I tried to weave the military's warning rights into conversation. I wanted to work off of his ego. I played the good cop.

"I need to get a drink of water," I said. Then I asked Taylor, "Would you like a drink?"

"Sure," he said.

I left the interrogation room and returned to the observation room. "Are we good on rights advisement," I asked.

The JAGs gave me a thumbs-up, and the lead detective nodded.

"Super." I grabbed a glass of water for myself and one for Taylor and returned to the interrogation room. I gave Taylor his drink.

"Thank you," he said.

I sat down across from him.

Detective Oakley leaned forward and said, "You raped a federal agent, didn't you?"

"No," Taylor said.

"A lot of agents think you did this," I said, "but I don't think you have anything to worry about. Obviously, you're a good officer. You were selected Company Grader of the Year."

"I didn't rape anyone," Taylor said. "I don't even know who this federal agent you're talking about is."

Detective Oakley slammed his hands on the table "You know who he is because you raped him!"

I took a drink. "Again, you're an intelligent guy and held in high regard by your commander, and I don't think you have anything to worry about, but what if I told you that we have footage from the bar of you putting this federal agent in your vehicle?" We didn't have footage, but I gave him the what-if scenario to motivate him.

The wheels spun in his mind. Then he bit. "Yes, I put him in my car."

"I understand," I said. "You took him to your house. Nothing can be held against you if it's consensual."

His eyes darted as if he was looking for an exit, and he bit again. "Yes, the federal agent and I agreed to go back to my house, but he kept passing out on me."

Now I knew we had him. I pressed for more. "Well, he's saying it wasn't consensual."

"I don't know why he would say that when it was consensual."

"Okay," I said. "He also said there was another man in the house."

Taylor crossed his arms and bit his lip.

"Well, who was he?" I asked.

Taylor rocked in his chair.

I waited for an answer.

Taylor looked at his watch and continued to rock in his chair. "I want a lawyer."

I couldn't talk to him anymore without his lawyer present. Besides, I had vacation plans at Disneyworld with my family. I left the room.

The interrogation had lasted over three hours, and my suit was musty. I entered the video observation room. The JAGs and the civilian lead detective smiled at me—confirmation that I nailed it. "Yes!"

The senior OSI agent teased me about playing the good cop routine so convincingly. While I was outside the interrogation room, Devery kept asking, "Where's my lawyer?"

Now the other two agents wanted to get in on the action. They joined detective Oakley, who was still asking questions. They demanded answers too.

Taylor's nostrils flared, and he glared at them.

Meanwhile, about fifty pieces of evidence were seized from his home.

I went on vacation.

When I came back, I found out that Detective Oakley got in trouble because Lane had asked for a lawyer, but he continued to question him without Lane's lawyer present. Even so, Lane revealed nothing to the detective. Oakley's supervisor went so far as to make him watch the video of the interview—pointing to me as an example of what to do.

Agent White told me, "After all the work you did to track this creep down, then the warrants and the awesome interview, Commander Jameson gave your case to Kelly."

"Well," I said, "I'm the rookie, and she's senior to me and all."

Agent Westwood saw us talking and came over. "Dude, they robbed you. That case was yours."

"It ain't fair," Agent White added.

I smiled. "Thanks, but I'm okay. I've got other cases to work on."

The other dozen or so agents in our det seemed upset too.

"Well, it's less paperwork I got to do," I said. I didn't know any better. I was happy with the work I'd been able to do, and it didn't keep me awake at night. I just figured the case needed to continue being worked while I was gone.

CHAPTER 15

THE CATCH

LATER, I OVERHEARD AGENT WHITE and other agents talking about a previous case where an active-duty helicopter mechanic stationed on our base had reported being raped by a European man he met at a bar in Fort Walton Beach. The agents didn't take him seriously.

"What?" I asked.

"You think this guy could be related?" Agent White asked.

"Why wouldn't we ask him?" I said.

"No way," someone said.

"Dude admitted to being an alcoholic," Agent White said. "He checked into rehab. He's unstable."

I always had an inquisitive mind and an attitude to take things a step further. It didn't always lead to success, but I left it all out on the field. I made sure. "I want his information."

Even my commander was reluctant, but they showed me the case files.

I read the report written February 28, 2006. It sounded like the federal agent's sexual assault case all over again, except this victim had more trouble remembering what happened. I knew I could use some help on this one, but what?

I overheard another agent make an appointment over the phone to speak with an OSI psychologist in DC regarding a different case. Our psychologists not only worked with agents, they also helped with cases. The shrinks were in such high demand that we couldn't simply call one up or walk into their office—we had to make appointments. This one happened to be a former marine.

I said to the agent, "Hey, when you get done with him, could you see if he'll answer some questions for an interview I'll be conducting?"

The agent did, and the psychologist agreed to talk with me. I told him about the mechanic. "I have a six-photo lineup that I want him to look at to see if he can identify the perpetrator. Because the incident happened some time ago, he was drugged, and he may not *want* to remember what happened, how can I help him?"

"Go back a couple hours into the night and start by asking what he does remember—and make sure it's in detail—colors, smells, cars, and so on. That'll prime his mind to go further."

"Thank you," I said.

I called the mechanic, and he agreed to come in the next morning.

When the mechanic arrived, his physical similarities to the federal agent struck me—he was tall and muscular, with olive-colored skin and short, dark hair. They looked a lot like me too. Devery Lane Taylor favored a type—he could be a serial rapist.

Agent White was with me, and he seemed to notice the resemblance too. "Wow."

We interviewed the mechanic, and I did exactly as the psychologist told me, except I asked him to recall things from more than a couple hours before the incident. Lesson from an old frogman cliché: "If it's worth doin', it's worth over doin'."

"Before I left the house, my wife and I had an argument," the mechanic said. He went through the night in detail.

He put his face in his hands and his elbows on the table. Then he described Taylor.

I slipped my six-photo lineup across the table and under his face.

The mechanic opened his eyes. He jumped from his seat and almost fell. He avoided looking at the pictures.

"What's the matter?" I asked.

His muscles tightened as if he was about to make a run for it. "I just saw him."

"I know you don't want to look again, but you've got to tell me which one it is."

His finger trembled as he pointed to Devery Lane Taylor's picture. The mechanic's whole body shook.

"You all right?" I asked.

"I think I need a cigarette."

"Okay. Come on, and we'll step outside."

We left the building, and with unsteady hands he lit up. Each exhale of smoke calmed him a bit.

I knew where Taylor lived, and I wanted to strengthen my case. "I'm going to take you to get something to eat," I said.

"Thanks," he said.

I drove him and Agent White to a fast-food drive-through, and we ordered cheeseburgers, fries, and sodas.

On the way back, I said, "Look, I'm going to drive over this bridge, and I'd like you to direct me as best you can to where you think you were that night."

The mechanic washed down a bite of cheeseburger with some Coke. "Man," he said.

"Listen, it'll really help the case if you can do this," I said.

He directed us past Taylor's house and said, "Stop. I've seen this apartment complex, but this isn't the place. I have a friend that lives here. Circle around."

I drove us around the block, and he mentioned another house as a possibility. After he took us full circle, the mechanic stopped us again.

We were in front of Taylor's house.

"I don't know," the mechanic said. "I think I'm close, but I don't know for sure. It could be this one, but I don't know."

I was bursting inside, but Agent White and I kept poker faces. "Thank you," I said. Now we knew the mechanic's rape had been committed by the same guy, and it had happened in the same place.

"I'm sorry I wasn't able to help," the mechanic said.

"No, not at all," Agent White said.

"We really appreciate your time." I eased off the brake and accelerated.

The rapes were roughly a month apart, suggesting Taylor had a monthly habit. *How many times has this creep done this and gotten away with it?*

We returned to the base and dropped off the mechanic in the parking lot outside our office building. I walked inside and had barely sat down and started my report when the victim I'd interviewed in the hospital called me.

"How're you doing?" I asked.

"You know, I returned home back west, and I'm getting therapy and all, but I've been having a real tough time, man. I think I might lose my job," he said.

"Oh no," I said.

"Have you found the guy yet?" he asked.

"Yeah, I'm pretty sure."

"Who is he?" the federal agent asked.

As a federal agent, he could hop on a plane at any time and fly anywhere in the US with his badge and his gun. "I can't imagine what you went through, and I can't pretend to. I think I know what you're thinking, and I'd probably want to do the same thing, but listen—don't do it. Let me do my job. You've trusted me this far. Let me take care of this. You have a wife and a daughter, and you've got to think about them."

He went quiet. "You know, man, you're the only one who's ever said that to me. I appreciate that. I'm going to let you do your thing. You don't have to worry about me."

"You sure?" I asked.

"Yeah."

"I'd like to send some agents out there with a photo lineup that I'd like you to take a look at. Could you do that for me?"

"Sure."

Later he selected Taylor's photo out of the six.

Kelly and I hadn't hit it off so well in the beginning, but as we realized each other's strengths and weaknesses, we appreciated one another and worked more and more together. We became partners and combined our cases. She'd turn out to be the best criminal investigator I'd ever worked with. I had decent instincts, but like most frogmen, I hated the paperwork. Kelly was sharp on both fronts, and when you went to court, a solid case report was essential.

We found out who Taylor's friends were and interviewed them. One of them was a jealous ex-boyfriend who was ready to dime him out on all kinds of things, and we recruited him as an informant. He told us about two other people Taylor had raped, and we contacted both. One of them wanted to meet us at an IHOP.

Kelly and I arrived first at the pancake house restaurant and took a table. It was senior citizen happy hour, and a room full of elderly people ate their meals. Two young, flamboyant guys dressed in purple and pink shirts walked through the door. One was a tall, buff Hispanic dude who seemed to fit the profile of Taylor's targets. The other was as skinny as a runway model. We waved to them, and they came over to our table. They introduced themselves. The buff guy was the possible victim. Kelly and I introduced ourselves. The four of us stood out like turds on pancakes. *This is just weird.*

"I'll take notes," I said.

Kelly began the interview. "Can you tell me about the incident?"

The pair seemed to be boyfriends, and Runway Model seemed to take a protective masculine role. "You're investigating the rapist, right?" he asked. "Not something else?"

"Yes," Kelly said. "We need to know about the incident."

Buff patted his friend on the shoulder. Buff was bigger, but he seemed to take a feminine role in their relationship. "It's okay. It was my birthday, so a bunch of friends came over to my house for a party—including Devery Taylor.

"He hung out by the pool with me and asked if I wanted a shot. My friends were talking about going out bar hopping, and I didn't want to get too drunk too early, but I figured one shot wouldn't hurt, so I said, 'Sure.'

"Devery left and came back with two shots, and we drank them. Suddenly I didn't feel well, so I told everyone to go on without me. Then I went to my room, locked the door, and laid on the bed."

"Then what happened?" Kelly asked.

"I dreamed that a guy was having sex with me." He proceeded to go into graphic detail and then started to cry. "I woke up and Devery was on top of me."

I was so embarrassed that I tried to bury my face in my notes. I could feel elderly eyes staring at us.

Kelly seemed to be enjoying the situation, like it was some bad reality TV show. "What'd you do?" she asked.

Buff waved his hands wildly. "I pushed and kicked him off me and shouted, 'Get out!' He got out. All my friends were already gone."

I felt like now everyone in the restaurant could hear us and was saying *what-the-hell?* I second-guessed the idea of meeting with these guys at the IHOP, but it was where they felt safe, and if it gave us what we needed, I was willing to endure it.

"I thought you said you locked the door," Kelly said.

"I did," Buff said. "Later, I saw that the frame was all busted up as if he'd kicked the door in."

Now we had a third victim and a possible fourth. We knew we had a serial rapist.

How long has this guy been doing this? Kelly and I finished the interview and returned to the base. We checked out all the places Devery Taylor had been stationed in the air force. Then we called those bases and asked them to dig up any old cases they had.

More cases popped.

We asked the agents at those bases to do the interviews and send them to us. They did.

Headquarters suggested we put out a message in *Air Force Times* asking anyone with information to call OSI. We did.

A civilian medic from Pensacola called and reported that Taylor had drugged and sexually assaulted him. Another mechanic called in and said Taylor raped him. When the dust settled, we had twenty-three victims.

This was also the time of President Clinton's "Don't ask, don't tell" policy for the military, which protected closeted homosexual or bisexual men and women but prohibited openly homosexual or bisexual men and women from serving.

It also prohibited the military from harassing or discriminating against closeted homosexuals and bisexuals. In our investigation, we had to tread carefully so as not to violate this policy. We consulted with military lawyers, who warned us not to "out" any closeted homosexuals or bisexuals. I told interviewees and victims, "I don't care about your sexual orientation or gender. Everybody has a right to be protected and to receive justice. I simply want to lock away a predator. We can't let him do this to other people."

Kelly was bravura at digging up cases, and I excelled at focusing on the victims who were most likely to show up in the courtroom and testify.

I called the federal agent to ask if he'd come out and testify. His wife answered the phone, and I identified myself. "Can I talk with your husband?" I asked.

She cried. "I so much appreciate what you're doing for him and for talking with him." She sobbed again. "Thank you so much."

The agent got on the phone, and I could hear his wife sniffling in the background.

"I was wondering if you'd be willing to come to the trial and testify," I asked.

"Yes," he said.

After talking to the victims, we narrowed the twenty-three cases down to nine who would testify. We zeroed in on their cases.

In the meantime, we ran surveillance on Taylor—tailing him and so on—and used confidential informants to help us. This generated information about other victims and the circles Taylor ran in. He was well connected in the gay community. One informant tipped us off that Taylor was about to get rid of evidence. We watched him pack up things from his house in garbage bags and go dump them. Then he sterilized his car. We surreptitiously collected the garbage bags that he'd dumped. He withdrew a lot of money and talked about flying off to the Middle East.

Kelly and I had already shown our faces to Taylor, so we couldn't go undercover to observe him—and I was happy with that. Some agents dressed up in tight pants and wife beaters with creative designs on them. Others wore jeans and blazers with no shirt. They went to gay bars that Taylor frequented and observed and reported on him. One of the bars had an underwear dance contest. Men danced in their underclothes for the crowd. An agent from another detachment helped us out and got so into his undercover role that he entered the underwear dance contest—and won!

What the hell!

The winning agent's commander was irate. He couldn't figure out what to do with the two hundred bucks the agent won. He didn't know how to log it, and the agent couldn't keep it. I don't know what they ever did with the two hundred dollars.

✧ ✧ ✧

Putting Devery Taylor in jail and holding him there until his trial was a challenge. Military arrest authority is picky. A suspect has to be a threat to the military community—such as someone who is likely to have committed murder and may murder again—before he is put under pretrial confinement. The base's second-in-command, the executive officer, acts as magistrate and makes the ultimate decision. We held a hearing.

Taylor's lawyers argued, "Devery Taylor has no criminal history, is an outstanding officer, and he is not a threat to the military community. There is no reason to put him in pretrial confinement for a crime that he hasn't committed. He is innocent until proven guilty."

I couldn't believe my ears.

The executive officer turned to me and asked, "What would be your suggestion?"

"Sir, you and the commander are in charge of military men and women who live on and off the base. You know civilians outside of the base. What're you and the commander going to say to them when one of them or their sons becomes the next victim—when you knew there were already several victims in the area—and we did nothing at all to prevent it right here, right now."

The executive officer thought for a moment. "Arrest Devery Taylor and put him in pre-trial confinement."

I wasn't needed during the trial to give testimony, and I wasn't excited about the possibility of my name and picture appearing in the media—especially since this case was garnering national attention. On the other hand, Kelly was at home in the courtroom and the limelight.

The trial began on February 19, 2007. Taylor claimed he was the victim of a gay roundup. When the federal agent showed up for testimony, he leaned over to Kelly and asked, "Are some of those guys gay?"

She nodded.

He sank in his seat.

After two weeks of graphic and sometimes emotional testimony, a jury of nine air force officers found Captain Devery Lane Taylor guilty on all counts of unlawful entry, kidnapping, attempted sodomy, and forcible sodomy. Taylor's civilian defense lawyer claimed that Taylor was not a repeat offender and asked for a sentence of ten years with the possibility of parole. Captain Eveylon

Westbrook, the military prosecutor, explained how Taylor began as an opportunist and ended up a predator. She said, "Each of these victims met the accused only briefly, but they will suffer for the rest of their lives."

Captain Devery Lane Taylor was dismissed from the air force, the equivalent of an enlisted person's dishonorable discharge, and sentenced to fifty years in Fort Leavenworth—until he's eighty-eight years old, if he lives that long. He was led out of the courtroom in leg irons and handcuffs.

Several months after the trial ended, my partner Kelly was transferred to narcotics. Because we worked so well together and had seen so much success, she bugged the leadership to transfer me over there as her partner. Commander Jameson knew I was jonesing to run counterintelligence in a war zone, the primary reason I joined OSI. "You need to learn how to run confidential informants before you can get an assignment in a war zone," Commander Jameson said. "The best place to do that is narcotics."

I grew a beard and let my hair get long. I wore a tank top and a flannel shirt with jeans, boots, a badge, and a gun, and I rode to work on my Harley. I ran sources and surveillance and netted the little fish, which included some guys on base involved in an ecstasy ring. Kelly and I also helped local law enforcement capture the bigger fish. After doing a year in narco, I got my wish—I went to war.

PART II

THE HUNT

When you hunt men, men will hunt you.

CHAPTER 16

IRAQ

I STEPPED OFF THE PLANE at the Balad Air Base in Iraq, and a dry gust of heat blasted me. A gray haze hung over the base, and the air smelled a funky mix of metal, burning tires, and jet fuel. A red-headed guy about my age met me on the runway. "Agent Treadway, I'm Red."

I'd heard that Red was the superintendent at my Expeditionary Detachment (EDet) here in Balad. "You're the supe, right?" Red was the highest-ranking enlisted man in the detachment and the commander's right hand man. Although the operations officer and other officer agents outranked him, he had more experience as an agent and was revered as such—much like a chief in a SEAL platoon.

"Yep."

"Good to meet you," I said.

"Likewise." He shuttled my bags and me in his black SUV across the base to the EDet compound. After I stowed my stuff in my personal room, he took me to another room.

A stuffed toy—a lime green baby frog with skinny legs and arms dangling down—hung from an office sign above the door. "This is your office as our new operations officer," Red said.

I pointed to the frog. "What's that?"

"That's you and your new call sign. Welcome to Iraq, Kermit." He walked away proud of himself, and I understood there was no negotiating.

I walked inside, turned on the light, and sat in my chair. Other than the stuffed Kermit on my door, the office was unremarkable. A knock sounded.

Nate stood in the doorway. "Long time, no see!"

"Nate!" I said, "I didn't know you were here."

Then another familiar face poked in.

"Mac!" I called out. "No way!"

111

"Small world," Mac said. "Great to have you here, buddy."

"This is awesome," I said.

We did some backslapping and catching up on what we'd been doing since FLETC, but I did feel a bit awkward. Back then, we were classmates, but now I was their ops officer, and I'd have to lead them. I'd need to ask them to do things they didn't want to do, and our friendship couldn't get in the way of that.

Both Red and Commander Mitchell gave me something in addition to my new call sign—they put their faith in me to train the agents to be more tactical. On top of that, I divided our responsibilities into geographical areas.

Soon we learned of a high value target in Huey's and my area. The HVT was codenamed Kaiser Soze, who hustled up the money to bankroll insurgents to plant IEDs and mortar us, and he was directly linked to al Qaeda terrorists. He was on our kill or capture list: wanted dead or alive.

Huey was the youngest agent in our expeditionary detachment and one of the strongest. He could be goofy as hell, but he was Johnny-on-the-spot: always on time and ready to go.

Huey briefed me on his informants with files on each one. He proudly showed me a stack of reports. "They've given us lots of intel."

I was less enthused. "Which of those files has decreased the number of mortar attacks, the planting of IEDs, or changed the battle in a significant way?"

"Well…"

Exactly. One file did catch my eye. "Who's this guy?" I asked.

"That's Bones. All he talks about is wanting a contracting job on base or getting his friend out of prison down in Baghdad."

"Where does he live?" I asked.

Huey showed me Bones's village on Google Maps.

I almost shit myself. "He lives in the same village and neighborhood as Kaiser Soze! Dude, why haven't you been using Bones to target him?"

Huey shrugged his shoulders.

"There's no way Bones lives that close and doesn't know who Kaiser Soze is. Let's talk to him."

Huey called Bones and asked him to pay us a visit. Bones agreed.

The next morning, a lieutenant who could be a double for the actor Jimmy Stewart in *It's a Wonderful Life*, called me.

"How's it going?" I asked.

Jimmy Stewart had a slight stutter and spoke slowly. "It'd be better if I had a light-all here at the gate." He wanted a tower of lights mounted on a small trailer that also carried a generator for power. The trailer could be easily hitched to a truck and moved.

"Oh?" I said.

"At night, the light out here is so bad that it's a pain in the ass to check faces and IDs."

"I see."

"Your visitor is at the back gate," he said.

"Okay, escort him to our trailer," I said.

The gate guards would process our visitor as if he was one of the base contract workers.

Huey and I grabbed our terp, Ibrahim, and we took drinks from the refrigerator and drove in my black armored Suburban across base. We parked in a dirt parking lot inside the gate, which insurgents often tried to mortar so they could hit Iraqis coming and going from work on base. Guard towers overlooked the area.

Huey, Ibrahim, and I strolled past Jersey walls that protected a gravel compound with trailers in it. The Jersey walls also limited visibility from the outside. We waited outside of our trailer. Huey and I wore our OSI badges showing that we were law enforcement and, as such, the only ones authorized to carry pistols in the chow hall, hospital, or anywhere else on base. The military restricted weapons-carry on base to official use only—troops preparing to go out on missions or returning from them, law enforcement, or sentries. As agents, we were always armed.

Military police brought Bones to us. True to his codename, he was a skinny man.

Huey and I greeted him, "*Salaam alaikum.*" Peace be unto you.

"*Salaam alaikum,*" Bones said.

We engaged in small talk and entered the trailer. Wooden planks creaked under our feet. We sat on gray vinyl chairs around a rusty table. The décor was lacking, but we had something much more important—air conditioning.

We sat down, and Ibrahim handed out drinks. Huey was always drinking protein shakes, but he didn't drink them during meets. Instead, he had a soda.

"How's your family?" I asked.

Ibrahim translated.

Bones said something in Arabic and Ibrahim translated. "Wife and kids are fine."

I made a mental note that he was married with children. My work in narcotics stateside taught me how to work with informants. I learned how I could help someone out so they could help me out. Here I intended to use those skills again. "Maybe we can help out your family—toothpaste for your wife or toys for your children."

Ibrahim continued to translate.

"All I want is a job on base and to get my friend out of prison," Bones said.

Huey showed him a surveillance photo of Kaiser Soze. "Do you know who he is?"

Bones shifted in his seat as if I was asking for some real dirt and he was a bit anxious about it. "Yes, of course. You know, he looks like you."

Kaiser Soze was the same height and had the same beard, short hair, and tanned skin as me. It felt weird. "I've seen photos of him, but I hadn't really noticed the resemblance until you mentioned it. He's a bad guy."

Bones nodded. "Yeah, he's a bad guy."

I turned to Huey and asked, "How do we get Bones a job on base?"

"He needs to be vetted by the army's Criminal Investigation Division and the Iraqi government too. Plus, his employment has to be in line with the Status of Forces Agreement between our countries."

"Sounds like a lot of hoops to jump through," I said. "Maybe getting his friend out of prison will be easier." I looked at Bones and asked, "What is your friend's name?"

Bones finished taking a sip of his drink. "Sami Al-Zuhairi. He's my best friend. His family is rich, and he has nothing to do with terrorists. He has a wife and a little girl. I worked for him, and after he was taken away to Baghdad, I lost my job."

Sami Al-Zuhairi was as common a name in Iraq as John Smith was in the US. It would be difficult to locate this man, let alone free him. Despite the challenges, I told Bones, "We'll look into it, but first you have to show me that you can help us with Kaiser Soze."

Bones set down his drink. "Okay."

"Do you need money or anything like that?"

He shook his head. "I don't really care about money—only a base job and my friend."

Sirens blared—a mortar round was incoming. Huey looked at me like he'd never heard the sirens before. I didn't know if it was because the location of our trailer was closer to the sound of the sirens or what.

The outside noise of running footsteps on gravel made me nervous. I asked Huey, "Do you know where the bunkers are on this part of the base?"

Huey shook his head. "Oh, hell, what do we do?"

A mortar slammed into the ground nearby—*bam*! It shook the whole trailer, and we vibrated.

I laughed. "Nothing we can do about it now."

Bones seemed like he was about to piss himself.

I stared him in the eye and said, "That's why we need your help."

Bones touched his chest. "*Inshallah*." God willing.

The next couple of meets, we played a game of us testing one another, both of us trying to see if we could trust each other.

Another source told us about an Iraqi who worked on our base. The worker could use some extra money and lived in Kaiser Soze's area. The source arranged for the worker to meet Huey and me on base, and we developed him as a new asset. We tasked him with verifying the information that Bones had given us, but we didn't tell him about Bones or what he was saying. Likewise, we didn't tell Bones about the base worker.

Huey and I used their intel to develop a pattern-of-life on Kaiser Soze. During one of our meets at the trailer, Bones told us, "Kaiser Soze is out of town a lot, but he's always home with his two wives and kids on Thursday nights, and every Friday, he goes to the mosque to pray." We heard the daily calls to prayer at least three times a day, called out from a loudspeaker on a nearby minaret: *Allahu akbar*. God is great. "Kaiser Soze has several bodyguards, and at least one is usually with him."

I showed Bones a map and asked, "Can you show us how he goes to the mosque?"

He pointed to a large village on the map. "This is his house." Then he traced his finger from the house to a bridge that crossed a canal to a mosque in a smaller village on the other side.

"Fantastic," I said.

The army frequently raided Kaiser Soze's neighborhood to find his insurgent buddies, but the army kept coming up goose eggs or finding only warm food and a burning cigarette. Sometimes the army would chase the insurgents out of town, but they would hide in the heavy brush under palm trees next to the Tigris River then disappear into escape tunnels.

Once I developed Soze's pattern-of-life, and when I was close to having a mission plan, I visited the Joint Defense Operations Center (JDOC). They had more large video monitors on the wall than a sports bar. There I talked to an army First Cavalry artillery officer in charge of JDOC, Major Sherwood. He was a cool country dude who sounded like he was from Arkansas.

"I'd like to put together a package to snatch Kaiser Soze," I said.

Major Sherwood pointed up to a monitor. "My men are in his neighborhood right now."

Someone in the bushes next to the river opened fire on his troops. Major Sherwood pounded the desk with his fist and raised his voice over the radio: "Go kinetic on their asses!"

Apache attack helicopters unleashed hell from above. Then it was quiet.

Major Sherwood's troops patrolled into the bushes to investigate. They found an insurgent slumped over a Russian belt-fed PK machine gun mounted on a bipod. The major shook his head before turning to me. "I didn't start it; they did. They asked for it; they got it."

I gave him a moment to unwind.

"What's on your mind?" he asked.

I took a breath. "Can your guys hold off on doing raids in Kaiser Soze's area for a while, so he gets more comfortable? Then we can grab him."

"We've run so many missions trying to get this guy, and he always gets away. Might be good for us to take a break. Yeah, we can do that."

"Who can best action this?" I asked.

"There's a Special Forces unit at another FOB that'd be good," Major Sherwood said.

"That might be what we need," I said. Instead of trying to insert by vehicles into Kaiser Soze's neighborhood, where there was only one avenue of approach and the danger of hitting IEDs, a Special Forces team would be able to insert via helicopter on fast ropes or whatever.

"There's someone else you might like to meet," Major Sherwood said. He led me over to a console where a man typed on a keyboard. "This is our TACP."

I recognized the acronym for the air force's Tactical Air Control Party, but I was curious. "What exactly do you do?"

The TACP looked up from his monitor. "I direct fire from aircraft in support of conventional army operations. Before Predators land on our base, I have control of them for an hour."

I got excited. "Dude, I have a target I want to look at. Can you help me out?"

"Where's it located?"

I showed him on a map. "I need to do recon for a Special Forces team."

"When can you come back?" he asked.

"When can you get another Predator?"

"Tomorrow at around 13:00."

I returned the next day at noon, sat down with the TACP, and we waited for his Predator to show. Somebody in another part of the world had control of the Predator while it was out on its mission. After 13:00 passed, the drone came into our area, and the TACP tapped on his keyboard, patched into it, and took control with his joystick. It looked like a video game, except on a much larger monitor—and this was for real.

Kaiser Soze's house came into view on the screen with a high wall surrounding it. From the ground, one couldn't see into his property, but from the drone, I could see everything. There were no dogs or patrols, but between the front gate of the perimeter wall and the front door of the house was a cage-like corridor. Its length was about seven paces. It would slow down any entry team, especially if they were caught unaware of it. "The SF team will have to get inside the cage to reach the front door."

The TACP tapped his keyboard and took pictures of Kaiser Soze's home. He also made measurements of everything, including the space in front of the property—which happened to be large enough to land a Black Hawk helicopter carrying an SF team.

We would have to catch Kaiser Soze before he squirted into the orchards and disappeared into the insurgent tunnels there. Just in case we weren't fast enough, I figured we could place a blocking team between the orchards and the village to cut off his escape. In the SEAL Teams, it would've taken me three days to do all the recon and surveillance that the TACP collected for me in an hour. I printed everything and put it in my target package. It amazed me how much information could be collected without putting any of our troops in harm's way—and the target on the ground had no idea what was happening.

"You're awesome," I said.

"I know."

CHAPTER 17

KAISER SOZE

ON THURSDAY OF THE SAME week, the other agents and I saddled up and made the twelve-mile ride out to FOB Poliwoda to meet with the Tenth Special Forces Group (SFG)—more commonly known as Green Berets. When I was at SEAL Team Five, we trained in the same mountains of Montana that their unit trained in for cold weather ops. It was ironic that their specialty was winter warfare, but here they were in the heat of the Iraqi summer.

Huey and I walked inside the gates of the FOB with our terp, Ibrahim, while the other agents waited outside with our vehicles. In the compound, Special Forces sergeants trained Iraqi scouts using dry-fire practice. SF soldiers were master trainers, teaching indigenous forces military tactics and techniques. Twelve men, called an A-Team, would go into an area and train a hundred soldiers, creating a foreign internal defense. The Green Berets were a force multiplier.

The A-Team consisted of a commander, who held the rank of captain. His assistant commander was a warrant officer. Next in command was the team sergeant, usually a master sergeant. His assistant, commonly a sergeant first class, helped with operations and ran intelligence. Under them served two of each: weapons sergeant, engineer sergeant, medical sergeant, and communications sergeant—whose ranks ranged from sergeant to sergeant first class. Although each had their specialty, they cross-trained in at least one other teammate's specialty.

The A-Team commander, a tall, athletic captain, escorted the three of us to his office. There, I showed him and his team sergeant my target package.

The captain had a mellow disposition and an effortless smile. "This is good stuff."

The team sergeant held up the pages. "How'd you put this together?"

I told him a little about our human intelligence, the drone, and some other methods.

"Yes, but what kind of background prepared you to put together a package like this?" the captain asked.

I explained my experience in the SEAL Teams as a sniper and in the air force as an OSI agent.

The captain nodded. "That makes sense."

"Do you know Pepper Tagle from SEAL Team Five?" the team sergeant asked.

"Yes," I said. Pepper had a Yosemite Sam moustache, way out of navy regulations. He trained my platoon in the California desert in preparation for a Desert Storm deployment. We respected him, and I had the feeling he liked me. I learned early in the Teams that if a seasoned operator went out of his way to give you a bad time, he thought you were worth the effort.

"He taught me with my former A-Team how to do combat swimmer ops with the Draeger," the team sergeant said, referring to a rebreathing diving apparatus.

"Oh yeah, I remember when he was teaching you guys. I was at the compound then."

"Small world," the team sergeant said. "Too bad he isn't around anymore. Did you hear?"

"Yeah, he was doing contract work, and he died with some other Team guys in a plane crash off the coast of Spain."

The captain, team sergeant, and I chewed the fat for a bit. Then the captain asked, "Hey, you're coming with us tomorrow, right?"

"Hell, yeah," I said. "Can I bring my terp?"

"You bet," the captain said.

The team sergeant nodded. "Great!"

When the other agents and I returned to the base, one of my sources told me that there would be a funeral in Kaiser Soze's area. A mix of about three hundred good Iraqis and bad Iraqis would attend. This would make it nearly impossible to snatch our target without hurting innocents, especially if shooting broke out. Also, the bad guys would outnumber us.

Before I picked up the phone to call the Special Forces captain about my concerns, he called me.

"We're getting intel about a funeral in the area," he said. "We don't do funerals anymore."

"Yeah, I'm receiving that intel too," I said. "We better call this off."

Kaiser Soze lucked out.

I waited a week after the funeral to see if he returned to his routine, and he did.

Bones was tired of waiting. "Hey, are you going to act on this or what?"

The following Friday, Bones kept watch on Kaiser Soze's neighborhood. Once again, the TACP had control of a Predator drone that watched the target area, and the Tenth Special Forces conducted surveillance with their Hunter drone.

We agents drove to the south end of Balad Air Base and linked up with soldiers who belonged to a company from Third Infantry Division. These men were more trained and accustomed to hitting doors, cracking heads, and getting after it than the artillery unit they were attached to.

Our three-Humvee agent convoy slipped into the middle of the larger infantry convoy, and we rumbled through the base. We exited the gates, test fired our machine guns, and headed out. Fresh holes beside the road marked recent IED detonations—one was still smoking.

We rendezvoused with Iraqi soldiers, minus their cell phones so they couldn't give away our actions and could focus on the mission. The Iraqis hopped in their military vehicles and lengthened our convoy.

Next, we halted in front of the SF unit's base. There, Huey, Ibrahim, and I exited our truck and walked through the gates. We made our way to a concrete building and up to its second floor. In plastic chairs around a long, brown table sat the whole Special Forces A-Team: the captain, his executive officer, team sergeant, assistant operations and intelligence sergeant, two weapons sergeants, two engineer sergeants, two medical sergeants, and two communications sergeants.

The three of us sat in the empty seats at the end of the table. I briefed the A-Team: "Our window of opportunity to bag Kaiser Soze is between 10:00 and 13:00. We know he's going to go to the mosque at 12:00. Again, our total window is three hours. We have men from the Third ID who'll insert as a blocking force in APCs and Humvees between the village and the grove next to the Tigris."

Both Huey's and my phones rumbled.

"Excuse me." Huey stepped out. When he returned, his face was filled with concern.

"What is it?" I asked.

"There's a sandstorm, and the Black Hawks are going to be delayed getting off the ground."

Strike one.

"When do they expect the storm to clear?" I asked.

"They aren't sure," Huey said.

I shook my head. "We'll have to wait."

"Our window's closing," an SF sergeant said with disappointment in his voice.

I was disappointed too. "I know."

I called the other agents in the convoy and let them know. My teammates, the infantrymen, Iraqi soldiers, and A-Team waited for the sandstorm to clear.

When noon came around, I lost contact with Bones. My guys back at the base couldn't reach him either.

Strike two.

I sat at the table with the whole A-Team staring at me. Half of them said, "Let's go."

"Hey man," a young guy said, "I'll ride my motorcycle up there and see if Kaiser Soze is home." He was serious.

The SF men on the other side told me, "Naw, man, don't do it. Don't burn your source."

I turned to Huey and asked, "How are we on the helos?"

"Still a no-go," Huey said.

I looked at the captain and asked him, "What do you think?"

"It's your op. I'll let you make the decision."

Oh shit. "Can I use your comms room?" I asked.

The captain got up. "Sure." He escorted me out of our meeting and into a room where communications equipment wrapped around the interior in a horseshoe-shape. Then he showed me how to call Balad Air Base.

No one had heard from Bones since noon.

I radioed the TACP who controlled the Predator drone. "What've you got?"

"Listen," the TACP said, "three cars pulled up to the target house, and a dozen guys poured out with AKs. One man came out of the house."

"Can you tell who came out of the house?" I asked.

"No. All of them got in the cars, and they took off."

Strike three.

Signals Intelligence (SIGINT) were the ones who intercepted communications, whether it be face-to-face or via electronic devices. They radioed me. "Kaiser Soze's cell phone is in the house."

I called back to the TACP. "Can you follow those cars?"

"Yeah, I've got eyes on them right now," he said.

I thought we might assault the three cars, but that would be a totally different plan from what we'd prepared for, and I wasn't exactly sure where the vehicles would be when we caught up to them or what would be waiting for us.

I looked at the captain standing next to a stack of radio electronics.

"It's your op," he repeated. "I'll be in the meeting room." Then he left me alone in the radio room.

I meditated on it for a minute. Kaiser Soze was responsible for a lot of people being killed—Iraqis and Americans. Some of his family members were part of the insurgency. But I couldn't put agents, infantrymen, Iraqi soldiers, and the A-Team in harm's way for something I was unsure about.

I returned to the meeting room. When you abort a parachute jump, you put your arms across your chest and shake your head. I felt like doing that. Instead, I ran my hand across my throat and said, "We got to cank it, fellas."

Half the A-Team complained. "Ah man. What the hell?"

The other half said, "Good call."

The captain's face and shoulders relaxed. He seemed pleased with my call.

"I'm going to go tell my guys," I said.

"Next time we'll get him," the captain said.

I forced a grin. "Next time."

I went outside and gave my team the news. The agents were angry. Croft was close with a SIGINT guy, and he must've given her some information because she argued with me: "Kaiser Soze's phone is in his house."

I stood my ground. "I'm not going to put guys in harm's way to capture a phone."

Croft's gaze became icy.

"I got to have more validation," I added.

The trip back to the air base was quiet. I felt as if I wanted to get Kaiser Soze more than anyone. I wanted to retrieve my MK-24 .308 sniper rifle from the Teams and Wookie and go out at night and patrol on foot to the vegetation next to the Tigris River, stalk through the water canal, and wait for Kaiser Soze to cross that bridge. Then I could squeeze the trigger—finish it.

But that's not how it was done here. We had to try to capture him alive. If he gave up one or more insurgents higher up in the food chain, taking him alive would be worth far more than taking him dead.

The next day, Jimmy Stewart called me. "Do you know anyone who has a spare light-all somewhere?"

"Sorry, I don't," I said.

"Bones is here."

"Thanks."

Huey and I met with Bones in the trailer.

"What the hell happened, man?" I asked.

Bones moved his hands excitedly. "Kermit, at noon, Kaiser Soze didn't go to the church. Three cars pulled up, and he got in with some men and left. So I left."

We finished debriefing Bones and sent him on his way.

During the drive back to the compound, Huey asked me, "Who do you think tipped Kaiser Soze off?"

"Maybe someone in the Iraqi team had a hidden phone. Maybe a villager friendly to Kaiser Soze spotted the movement of our caravan and contacted him. Could've been an Iraqi spy working on our base. I don't know."

We parked at the EDet compound, and I dragged my ass back to my office. Huey returned to the bullpen. I overheard him tell the other agents about our meeting with Bones: "Kaiser Soze's phone was at his house, but he wasn't. Kermit made the right call."

I wanted to smile, but I was still too pissed that we'd missed our target.

CHAPTER 18

IED PLANTERS

ON THE EVENING OF SEPTEMBER 5, 2007, First Cavalry soldiers drove out on patrol several miles from base. One of their Humvees hit an IED that blew up and flipped the vehicle. One soldier was wounded. Dane Balcon, nineteen years old, and William Warford, twenty-four, were killed. We agents attended the fallen soldiers' memorial ceremony, where a Battlefield Cross was erected—the muzzles of the fallen soldiers' rifles were stuck in their boots with their helmets on top.

The First Cav was furious. They wanted the insurgents who did it, and shortly after the funeral, they went out after them—that was their way of mourning. The soldiers of the First Cav inspired me. They were artillery troops doing the job of infantrymen. When two of their men were killed, they didn't get bogged down in sorrow; they got up to fight back.

Around this same time period, Red, Gator, and Hank shipped back to the States, replaced by three new agents: Tom, Dave, and Jeff. Tom became our new supe—Commander Mitchell's new right-hand man. Almost six-feet tall and fit, he had closely cropped blond hair and a cropped beard. He'd served in Operation Restore Hope II in Somalia and the Gulf War in Iraq. He was the perfect fit.

Gator's substitute was Dave, who had a smile and a laugh that infected people around him, even if they didn't know what the joke was. Before arriving, he'd used surveillance countermeasures to protect some of our nation's most sensitive programs from enemies. He was passionate about his work. It was just after chow when he stepped off the plane, and Mac, Orion, and I went out to pick him up. We exchanged handshakes. He shook his head, gave us an odd look, and said, "Is that a check-off item when you get here? You've got to start lifting a lot?" All of us had been pumping stacks of iron.

Jeff looked like Burl Ives, the Snowman narrator in the classic TV stop-motion animation, *Rudolph the Red-Nosed Reindeer*. Although he had more time as an investigator under his belt than the rest of us, his contributions to our EDet were yet to be seen.

Not long after their arrival, the army put on a 5K run, and some of us agents entered, including Commander Mitchell, Dave, and me. We ran the route through the base. Commander Mitchell was in tip-top shape, but I passed him. Dave was an avid soccer player, and he ran like one too. He blew my doors off. At the turnaround point, spectating agents from my unit watched Dave kick my ass and shoot out way in front of me. I felt belittled. I gave it everything I had and more to catch up to him. At the 4K point, he slowed enough for me to pass him. I eyed some army runners ahead of me and pushed to pass them too.

After the race, I met up with Dave while I walked it off and caught my breath.

His face was discolored. "Man, I'm having a heck of a time breathing."

"That's the burn pits," I said. The smoke was always thick over Balad.

He grabbed his waist as he walked it off. "My lungs couldn't suck in enough air."

"You'll get used to it," I said. "Great run."

"You too."

When we returned to the compound, everyone buzzed about how Dave beat my ass in the first three kilometers—didn't matter that I crossed the finish line before him.

I smiled. *Good on Dave.*

Croft and Orion gathered intel from an asset who could positively identify the two men who'd planted the IED that wounded the First Cav soldier and killed two others. At 21:00, six of us went over to the First Cav's compound and met outside with a lieutenant I'd worked with before. He was a tall, thin officer who looked to be in his twenties but who acted more mature—an old soul. *I guess this place will do that to you.* With him was his platoon sergeant and a squad leader. I shared our intel with them.

First Cav had their human intelligence collectors too. Although they were young and didn't have as much training or experience as we did, they'd gathered information that matched ours on the same two men. The First Cav regularly patrolled the village where the two IED planters lived, so they knew the area well. It was a town I'd never been to.

Lieutenant Old Soul and his sergeants were fired up. They planned out the mission on an outdoor sand table—showing where our units would enter the village, where the target houses were, and how we'd take them down. Before the witching hour, we grabbed our people, tested our comms, put on our game faces, and mounted up.

Multiple trucks full of First Cav soldiers rolled out first. Lieutenant Old Soul served as the patrol commander, and I rode in the Humvee immediately behind him. Burl drove.

Behind me, Nate drove while Croft navigated, and Dave took the machine gun in the turret. Croft's terp, Shaky, sat in the back seat with the informant. Three more First Cav trucks fell in behind us. One of them was an Armored Personnel Carrier (APC).

We trotted out of the gate, and when we hit the asphalt, we reached a full gallop. Our posse left the blacktop and headed northeast, kicking up dust. Air weapons teams flew above as we tore through back country roads.

We slowed to a stop on the edge of the target village, forming a crescent-shaped perimeter. Booger-eaters squirted towards the palm trees. Two Humvees and the APC broke off the back of our patrol and bolted down the backside of the village. The Humvees in front of the lieutenant's vehicle raced to the other side of the village. Trucks halted, soldiers dismounted, and soldiers chased squirters into an orchard.

Lieutenant Old Soul dismounted and spread a map across the hood of his Humvee. We agents and a handful of his men guarded the perimeter. Huey called down from his gun turret, "I got military-age males on the rooftop next to us. I'm holding on them."

I followed the aim of his machine gun to a building where silhouettes of heads looked over the top. At the base of the building, four soldiers searched for a way in.

I turned to Orion and said, "Let's help these guys out."

"And tell the soldiers about the threats on the roof," Orion said.

Orion and I dashed to the building. The four soldiers continued to seek an open door. Orion and I slipped around to the left.

Huey radioed. "Military age males on the roof have AKs." The AK was a popular assault rifle for our enemies.

We had to move quickly before the men on the roof attacked the soldiers or us. Orion located a side door and opened it. He looked at me and asked, "You want to go?"

"Hell no. Let's get those four soldiers, and we'll all go up."

Orion aimed his rifle at the door, and I went back around the house and found the army guys. "Hey, we got an in over here," I said.

I hauled ass with them back to Orion, and we formed a train next to the door. I briefed them on the men on the roof. "They know we're here."

The soldiers didn't seem concerned. They were jacked up, ready to go.

Orion and I took two men to the top and left their two buddies to clear the bottom floor. There must've been nothing on the first floor because the two quickly joined us upstairs. Tactically we moved onto the roof in the dim moonlight. All we could see were blankets, but we knew what was underneath. It felt weird watching their sleeping act while we knew what was going on. *How can they not know that we know they're there?*

We aimed at a blanket, and one soldier pulled it off. An Iraqi lay there with his AK. We grabbed his weapon and flex-cuffed him. Then we wrapped up the others too.

One of the Iraqis had a peculiar rifle. Having been a sniper, I immediately recognized it as an Iraqi copy of the Russian Dragunov. I took it, and Orion flex-cuffed the owner. Getting my hands on an enemy sniper rifle felt good. The sniper frowned.

We hauled our prisoners downstairs and out to the Humvees. There, we lined the military age males against a wall, facing it. That was our marshalling point. I don't know why, but for some reason, troops stacked the AKs they found on the hood of my Humvee. I put the Dragunov inside my truck on the passenger side. As more soldiers captured more men from different parts of the village, nearly a dozen AKs accumulated on my vehicle.

Croft and Nate came over, and Croft pointed at a house. "That one hasn't been cleared yet."

A ma and pa couple came out of the front door of the uncleared house and stood watching us as if to say, "What the hell's going on?"

We walked over with our terp, Shaky, and asked, "Is anyone else in your house?"

Ma and Pa didn't say anything.

"You better tell us or something's going to happen when we go in," Croft said.

"Are there any weapons in your house?" I asked.

"Yes," Pa said.

We stacked up next to the house. Orion entered first with Croft.

"Clear," Orion and Croft said.

I ventured in with Burl behind me. I held my sights on a hallway when a young man moved across it. "I got one moving into the next room," I called out.

I advanced. The door to the room was already open to the right, so I stepped inside and peeled in that direction. A bed sat in the middle, low to the floor. My corner was clear, but I saw the young man to my left in an open closet, and I aimed at him. The dude froze. Standing on the floor next to him was a loaded AK, and Young Man looked like he was going to reach for it. I shook my head and said, "Uh, uh, uh."

Orion chuckled from the hall as if I'd just quoted some cheesy line from an action movie. "I want to put my fingers in my ears," he said.

Young Guy looked at me. Then he looked at the gun.

I continued to aim. "Burl, you see what I'm seeing?"

"Yeah, I got him."

Several years earlier, I was sent to the Defense Language Institute to learn Spanish. When I returned to the Teams, one of the older bullfrogs said, "That twenty-six weeks of Spanish is some slick shit, but all I need you to tell me is how to say, 'Hands up.'"

I laughed at the SEAL, but he was right, that's all I needed.

I'd picked up a few key phrases in Arabic on deployment to Saudi Arabia. I said the words in Arabic, "*Iirfae yudik.*"

Young Man looked stunned, but his hands popped up.

I told him in Arabic, "*Imshi.*" Come here.

He did.

I grabbed Young Man and said, "I got him. You got the weapon?"

"Got it," Burl said.

I spread Young Man against the wall and cuffed him while Burl picked up his weapon. Then we took him out of the house.

Young Man was lucky Burl and I were of a law enforcement mindset instead of a soldier mindset, or things may have ended differently.

We shuttled our prisoner to the marshalling area and put him in the lineup with the other prisoners. Nate and a soldier kept their weapons trained on them. Nate wasn't a smoker, but he had a lit cigarette in his mouth. I had no idea where he got it from. With his goatee and windswept black hair down to his shoulders, he looked like a hipster commando.

Orion and Croft took Young Man and escorted him into the headlights of Croft's Humvee. Our asset remained tucked away in the Humvee as he identified him. "No, not him."

Orion and Croft grabbed the next guy off the wall and put him in the headlights. Again, their asset identified him. "No."

I walked over to see Lieutenant Old Soul, who continued to study the map on the hood of his Humvee. The handful of soldiers around him, save one, had gone to help the others. Now it was up to us to hold the perimeter, clear buildings, guard prisoners, and ID them. Doing all that in full body armor and carrying gear sapped the energy out of me, so I was happy that I'd cleared the last house.

Lieutenant Old Soul stabbed the map with his finger and said, "We've got to clear this target house over here."

"Are you asking me to do it?" I asked.

"Could you?" he asked.

Out of the dark and into the light of the Humvee stepped a lieutenant colonel, the battalion commander. He was in charge of the army section of our base, called the Anaconda Logistical Support Area, and the FOBs—the head honcho. I'd never met him before and didn't even know he was in our convoy.

"Evening, sir. How you doing?"

"Good," the battalion commander said.

I returned my attention to the map and put my finger on a large property. "This one right next to us?"

"Yes, this one," Lieutenant Old Soul said.

"Yeah, we better. It's right on top of us. Can you give me any guys?"

At that moment, three soldiers turned a corner and came toward us, huffing and puffing.

Lieutenant Old Soul grabbed one of them by the shoulder and pointed to a large, gated courtyard beside us and said, "I need you men to clear this building."

"Okay," one said.

The cement walls around the target house were seven feet high, and a metal gate with bars was closed. We moved closer. I tried to open the gate, but it was locked.

One of the soldiers was a tall black guy, bigger than me.

"Hey man, you want to try and kick this in?" I asked him.

He kicked. It rattled loudly but didn't budge.

Holy shit. We just let everyone inside know that we're coming to visit them.

"What do we do now?" a soldier asked.

In the turret of one of the Humvees was a machine gunner with his weapon pointed down into the courtyard of the target house.

"Follow me," I said.

I ran beside the wall, hopped up on the gunner's Humvee, climbed on top of the wall, and jumped down into the courtyard. I forgot how bad my knees were until I landed. "Ungh."

The courtyard was deadly quiet—I was all alone. *Where are the other guys?* They seemed to take forever. *Are they coming?*

The house was expansive. I aimed at the front door and a window next to it. I couldn't assault the house by myself. *Where are my three guys?*

Then I heard three crashes followed by grunts.

I turned and spotted three bright, toothy grins in the darkness. The soldiers seemed to be digging this. They each took a knee.

I rose to a crouch, and they shadowed me. I led them to the front door. It was locked.

Two more soldiers jumped down into the courtyard and joined us. We turned around and the last guy became point man and led us to the back of the house. The door was open there, so we went in.

At the foot of a flight of stairs, an Iraqi threw something down behind a huge clay pot.

We pointed our weapons at him, and he fled up the stairs. Behind the pot was an AK rifle he'd discarded. I ran upstairs. I heard the bootsteps of more soldiers flow in behind me and follow me up.

I hit the second floor. Off to my left was a room. A soldier and I slipped inside. It was mostly empty except for a bed. All around us came the sounds of more combat boots rushing into the house and Americans calling out, "Clear! Clear!" The situation seemed secure enough for me to take a moment to search for intel, so I did.

A senior noncommissioned officer came into the room with his weapon at his side. He took one look at my unconventional appearance and seemed to wonder how I got mixed in with his conventional troops: "Who the hell is this guy?"

I didn't know who the hell he was either. He wasn't in the brief back at the base, and I hadn't seen him jock up with us. "There's nothing in here," I said.

He left the room.

I did too.

Other soldiers found the man who'd thrown his AK behind the clay pot and fled upstairs.

I was finished, so I walked downstairs and stepped out of the house. Soldiers who'd chased booger-eaters into the palm trees had returned, and this was one of the first houses they came to. Some were in the courtyard. I climbed the wall and returned to where Nate and another soldier were guarding prisoners. Nate had missed out on most of the action, and he looked bored.

Troops came from the building I'd just left. "Let's clear another building," one said, "You coming?"

My knees hurt, I was dripping with sweat, and I was smoked. I turned to Nate and asked, "You want to go?"

Nate dropped his cigarette and put it out with his boot. "Can I?"

There were so many soldiers that I wasn't too concerned. "Yeah."

He ran off with the army guys.

I stood there and caught my breath. The AKs were gone from the hood of my Humvee—somebody must've secured them somewhere in our convoy. I watched the prisoners go through the identification process. The man who'd thrown his AK down behind the clay pot and run up the stairs took his turn to stand in front of the Humvee lights.

"Yes, that's him," our asset said. "He's one of the two who planted the IED."

"We got him," Croft said.

"Hell yeah!" a soldier cheered.

The second IED planter was also identified in the lineup. The First Cav happily stuffed them in the back of an APC. We released the other prisoners, and I hopped in the Humvee with my newly acquired Dragunov sniper rifle. I planned to mount it on the wall in our compound as a memento. Our posse rolled out of the village. *Justice.*

CHAPTER 19

OLD MAN HAJIB

ONE AFTERNOON, I GOT A phone call. The caller ID displayed Jimmy Stewart's number. I expected him to bitch to me about wanting a light-all again. "What's up?" I asked.

"Here at the gate, I've got a little old man who looks like a dirt farmer, wearing a red and white keffiyeh, white dishdasha, and flip flops. He brought another man here at gunpoint," Jimmy Stewart said. There was yelling and chaos in the background.

The little old man sounded like one of my assets, but I couldn't quite process what I was hearing. "*What?*"

"The little old man says his name is Hajib, and he knows you. He says he caught an insurgent."

"Yes, Hajib is helping me. Who's the insurgent?"

"Wait one," Jimmy Stewart said. There was more shouting and confusion. "Khalid Zogby."

I didn't recognize the name. "Cuff Khalid and hold him until I can check this out. I'll call you back." I went to our intel analyst and gave him the name.

Soon the intel analyst replied, "He's green." He was an insurgent.

I called Jimmy Stewart back. "Khalid is a bad guy. Bring him in."

"Will do," Jimmy Stewart said. "This Hajib is a stud."

I smiled.

✧ ✧ ✧

At the end of the day, the EDet continued to buzz. There always seemed to be something going on 24/7. Nate's work spilled into the evening, and he met with our intel analyst in the bullpen and discussed collecting information and targeting an insurgent. Tom kicked back on the patio and smoked a cigar. Mac,

Dave, Croft, Orion, and Burl reclined in the family room and began to watch another season of *The Wire*.

I left the buzz and climbed the stairs two stories to the rooftop. Sandbags covered the deck to dampen direct hits from mortars, and a five-foot wall surrounded it. Antennas sprouted up as if from a porcupine. It was a good place to get reception for the Iridium satellite phone that we used to make calls to the States. Although the reception was clear, we were next to the airfield, and F-16 fighter jets, supporting missions all over Iraq, screamed in and out of our conversations. C-130 cargo planes landed and took off too. At the far end of the runway, helicopters came and went.

The rest of the base spread out on the opposite side of our building. In the shadows beyond some streetlights were barracks and the wooden shacks that housed Burger King, Pizza Hut, and Baskin Robbins. Nearby was a base exchange where one could buy retail items, from uniforms and toothpaste to civilian clothes and electronic devices. The hospital was constantly busy with people going in and out 24/7, including friendly Iraqis.

The night air was twenty degrees cooler than the daytime, and up on the roof it usually felt a degree or two cooler. The air smelled of jet fuel and the stink of metal and tires from the base's burn pit. A gray haze perpetually covered the base.

A picnic table occupied a spot near the center of the roof. It was too large to fit up the stairwell, and sometimes I wondered how it got up here. I sat down on it.

Nate appeared on the rooftop. Each week, like the rest of us, he used the satellite phone to call his family. His sister was a schoolteacher, and her students made paper cutouts of a character named Flat Stanley and sent them to him to give to Iraqi children. Then Nate took pictures of the Iraqi kids with their Flat Stanleys and sent them back to the boys and girls in his sister's class.

He sat down and joined me, wearing one of his Columbia outdoors shirts that buttoned down the front and had long sleeves that he rolled up. Sometimes he wore the shirts on missions. They were usually tactical colors, sand-colored or brown, but he had a light blue one too—that's how he rolled. Sometimes he liked to talk about his favorite place to sail—the Gulf of Mexico.

"We're operating at a high-ops tempo," Nate said. As an EDet, we'd been running meets outside of the wire with informants three to five times a week. Once or twice a week an asset would come on base to meet. We actioned targets about once every week or every other week. Nate added, "I miss Hank."

"Me too," I said.

"Burl isn't much help in developing informants, conducting meets, or putting together packages for action. He has his moments, but Professor and I do most of the work."

I'd noticed that while Nate went outside the wire as much as possible, Burl went out as little as possible. "Burl writes nice reports," I said.

"Yeah, he can do that. But I'm looking for targets."

I tried to change the subject a bit. "Looks like you're helping Mac and Dave verify a lot of information," I said. Nate's area was adjacent to theirs.

"They're helping me."

"Croft and Orion have had some outstanding successes too," I said.

Professor showed up with some Arabic *chai*, a spiced tea. "Freshly brewed." We respected Muslim customs, and alcohol was prohibited on the air base.

Nate and I thanked him.

Professor went back downstairs and left us alone.

Nate took a sip of his tea. "We've gone from forty-four mortar or rocket attacks a week to about eleven. There are so few now that when a mortar comes out of our AO, we take it personal."

I took a drink. "Yup! That's what happens when you take bad guys out of the battlespace."

"We're shutting them down," Nate said proudly.

He was fearless, but that was a two-edged sword, and I wanted to talk to him about it—not so much as a leader but more as a big brother or friend. I took another swig of tea. "I was like you when I was your age in the Teams—aggressive and ready to fight."

Nate grinned.

"You got to be careful out there."

"What do you mean?" he asked.

"When you get in over your head out there, who do you think is going to come and get you?"

Nate smiled. "You."

"I'm not Superman. We all got to get whoever's in over his head, but we're not a direct-action team. Yeah, we're getting better in the training and shooting, but that's only to give us a chance to break contact, or at worst, hold our own until a QRF or Air Weapons team saves our asses."

Nate's grin shifted to a look of disappointment.

"You're our most effective agent," I said. "It's good to have that aggressive mindset, but don't unleash it unless you have to. Just like Commander Mitchell and Tom, I want to keep you, me, and the rest of our team on this side of the dirt."

Nate seemed to soak it in. He drank the last of his tea and put his cup down. Then he looked me in the eye and said, "I'll be careful."

Incoming mortar sirens sounded. Two Katyusha rockets swooshed over our heads and hit the gravel two hundred yards from us near the airfield: *boom, boom!*

Nate and I scrambled downstairs like rats.

Jack's first SDV Platoon at Little Creek

SEAL Team 5, Delta Platoon 1990.

SEAL Team 5, Jack with M-60 double loadout, 1,000 rounds, for desert warfare.

Special Agent David Wieger. (Courtesy USAF)

Special Agent Nathan Schuldheiss.
Courtesy USAF)

Special Agent Thomas Crowell. (Courtesy
USAF)

Iraq, early EDet Group photo. Nate is on the left.

Iraq, Jack visiting the sheik.

Weekly range work at Balad Air Base.

Running agents thru course at range Balad AB.

Mac, Jack, and EDet Commander Mitchell.

Dave in a Humvee. (Courtesy USAF)

Nate in a Humvee. (Courtesy USAF)

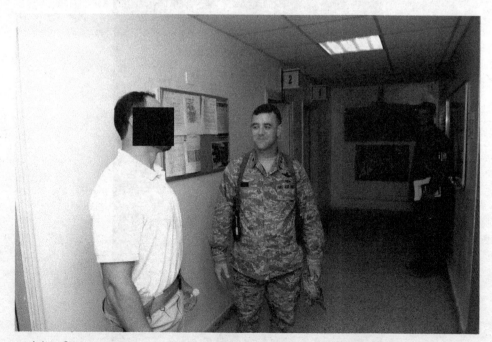

Jack briefing Brig. Gen. Burt Field, Balad Air Base Wing Commander, confiscated weapons in the background.

Tom. (Courtesy USAF)

Tom at work. (Courtesy USAF)

Dave up to his antics in the Bullpen.

Dave and Iraqi kids outside Balad. (Courtesy USAF)

Nate giving Flat Stanleys made by US kids to Iraqi kids.

Nate and Mac with Citadel flag, 3rd Infantry Division in background, before mission to capture a high value target.

Kids gather around Santa Nate bringing toys and candy.

Christmas in Iraq. Commander Mitchell, Interpreter, and Jack.

Jack with Iraqi kids after op in Kaiser Soze's village, kids flexing like the Hulk.

Jack and Orion during mission, five captured bad guys in vehicle in background. Three were released then struck by hellfire rocket, three days later while mortaring our base.

Jack and Dave two days before Dave's last mission. This photo is at the Knox Building in the Hall of Heroes.

Balad Air Base, more than 300 Airmen and Soldiers bow their head in prayer at Memorial for Dave, Nate, and Tom. (Courtesy USAF)

Balad Air Base, SMSgt Anthony Turner consoles MSgt April Spiczka at memorial service for Dave, Nate, and Tom. (Courtesy USAF)

Brig. Gen. Burt Field pays his final respects to Dave, Nate, and Tom. (Courtesy USAF)

Honor Guard unveils portraits of Dave, Nate, and Tom. (Courtesy USAF)

Special Agent David Wieger. (Courtesy USAF)

Special Agent Nathan Schuldheiss. (Courtesy USAF)

Special Agent Thomas Crowell. (Courtesy USAF)

CHAPTER 20

INEFFECTIVE FIRE

FROM THE VICINITY OF A nearby village, insurgents continued to fire mortars and take potshots at soldiers. The First Cav wanted to suppress it, so they called me up, and I went to talk with them. I understood where they were coming from. My fellow agents had gone out with First Cav, collected intel from villagers, and spotted new routes we could use for our meets with informants, and my plan was to do the same.

Several First Cav Humvees lined up in the pale moonlight, and I loaded up in the second Humvee with Lieutenant Old Soul. Huey and Ibrahim sat behind us. We rolled out a few miles to a town that I wasn't too familiar with. The population was around a couple thousand people. We stopped and broke out of the vehicles.

"I'm going with the First Cav interpreter," Huey said. "We can cover more ground if we split up."

I figured he was safe with all the soldiers and their firepower, so I said, "Go for it."

Ibrahim stayed with me, and we followed the troops, who poured into town. The soldiers moved aggressively, kicking in doors and shouting questions.

I turned a corner into a narrow alley, and a strapping soldier held an Iraqi by the neck with his face shoved into the Kevlar plate on the Big Soldier's chest. He yelled at the Iraqi, but without an interpreter, their communication was limited. A couple of Big Soldier's squad mates huddled around him. They were likely at the funeral of the two fallen soldiers, and now their lives were in danger from whoever in this village was mortaring and taking potshots at them and their buddies. They were frustrated and cleaning up the mess as best as they could. Being aggressive made a booger-eater think twice about making a move. Now I understood why adults cleared the streets and mothers pulled their children inside when we showed up. Under these circumstances, there was no way I was going to be able to get any Iraqis to work for me.

I told Big Soldier, "Hey, he ain't going to tell you anything like that. Let me have him."

Big Soldier turned the Iraqi over to me.

"I'm here to help," I said. "I just got you out of trouble here."

Ibrahim interpreted.

The Iraqi didn't say anything.

"You want to talk to me a little about what you know?" I asked.

"I can't tell you anything," the Iraqi said.

A man from the village squirted off, and Big Soldier and his buddies hauled ass after him. A pair of soldiers jumped a wall and followed. I chased the squirter with Ibrahim at my side. The soldiers split off and spread out into various directions. With them thinned out like that and not knowing what they were heading into gave me a bad feeling.

I stopped running. I didn't want to go any further. I turned back and the Iraqi was still there in the alley. *I'll stay with him and see if I can work him a little bit.* I walked back to him. When I reached the man, I asked, "Who is the guy that took off running?"

The Iraqi shook his head.

"What did he do?" I asked.

"I don't have any part of it," he said.

"Do you need help—like money or something?"

"If I tell you anything, the insurgents will kill me."

"I can protect you," I said.

"I'm afraid."

I kept trying. "I can protect you from the insurgents."

"I'm afraid of you too," the Iraqi said.

"You don't have to be afraid of me. I'm here to help you."

"Please, let me go," the Iraqi said. "If they see me with you, they'll kill me. I don't want any part of this."

The situation was hopeless. I looked around. There were no soldiers in sight. Ibrahim and I were all alone. Danger loomed, and my gut became more uneasy. I turned to Ibrahim and said, "Let's head towards the convoy."

We made our way through the village. Our terps were unarmed, and Ibrahim was no different. Even so, I'd taken them out to the range and showed them how to shoot the rifles and pistols.

"You know where my pistol is at," I said.

"I know," he said.

If things got bad, he would take it. Or, if I became incapacitated, he could use my rifle. I pressed forward in the direction of the trucks, but I couldn't see them yet. I aimed my muzzle at windows where snipers might be. I scanned ahead for any surprises. I checked the alleys on both sides in case the squirter circled back around and ambushed me. I aimed up, down, and sideways. Friendly soldiers could pop out on me, and I had to be careful not to shoot one. I hadn't realized we were so far separated from the trucks, and my stomach twisted and turned with each step.

I aimed up at a window. Suddenly a figure dashed out at me from below. I jerked my weapon down in the direction of the threat and clicked off my safety. I held my finger straight but didn't put it on the trigger yet. From the shadows of the alley came a First Cav soldier. I aimed away from him and flicked the selection switch back to *Safe*.

I exhaled. "Did you see which way the others went?"

"No," he said. "They all split up."

I pointed my muzzle ahead. "Well, we're heading back to the convoy."

He joined Ibrahim and me on our way back. It felt better to have the soldier's gun at my side. Then another linked up with us—the more the merrier. We covered each other as we moved tactically towards the convoy.

Half a dozen soldiers had already rallied up at the convoy when we arrived. The others returned too. "We got nothing," one told the lieutenant.

Finally, we mounted the trucks and rolled out of there. *This isn't going to be an effective way for us to develop informants.*

CHAPTER 21

THE IRAQI CAPTAIN

NATE'S BEST SOURCE, CODENAMED BAGHDAD Bob, infiltrated a group of insurgents connected to al Qaeda, and he became their newest member. Baghdad Bob observed their activities and reported back to Nate. When the local Iraqi military rounded up some of the insurgents, Baghdad Bob was swept up too. Nate wanted to secure his release. It wasn't safe to travel outside of the wire in anything less than a three-vehicle convoy, so the other agents and I escorted Nate, his partner Burl, and their terp, Professor.

We drove out to FOB Orion, where Baghdad Bob was imprisoned. Both US and Iraqi forces shared the base. Then we pulled into the parking lot and stopped. The temperature was a hundred and fifteen degrees, and there was no shade. It was even hotter in the Humvees, so we stepped out and lined up against a cement wall. There we soaked in sweat, waiting for the commander of the local Iraqi military unit—a colonel—to come out and talk with us.

Instead of the colonel, a six-foot-tall, unshaven Iraqi wearing a captain's uniform swaggered into the parking lot.

Our posse didn't look like the other soldiers in the area, and he gave us an odd stare.

Nate explained why he was there, and Professor translated. Burl took notes.

The captain stood with his feet far apart, held his elbows wide from his body and stuck out his chest. "I don't take orders from anyone—not even my boss, the colonel."

"Baghdad Bob is one of our guys," Nate said, "and we need him released."

The captain bared his teeth and flared his nostrils. "I can't believe you have the audacity to come here and demand something from me!"

"Baghdad Bob is on our side," Nate said. "We need him."

The captain stepped into Nate's personal space. "He's not on our side. He runs with insurgent groups tied to al Qaeda. He can rot in jail."

Nate and Professor stepped forward, too, and their faces were in the captain's. "No, he's reporting on the insurgents for me," Nate said. "I want him out."

The captain pointed at FOB Orion. "The Iraqi military here is mine. This prison is mine." Then he swept his hand out towards the city of Dujail. "I own that too."

"Who are you?" Nate asked.

"Captain al-Hakim. Don't forget it."

"I won't," Nate said in a controlled tone. He turned and calmly walked to the Humvee. All of us mounted the vehicles.

Nate slammed his door. Then he fired up the Humvee and peeled out.

Captain al-Hakim glared at us before we left him in a cloud of dust.

I didn't like or trust Baghdad Bob, and Captain al-Hakim was one of our allies, so I sympathized with him. I understood what it was like to capture a bad guy only to have someone else release him from jail.

Later Nate phoned and emailed the multinational forces in Baghdad. Shit rolled downhill and landed on Captain al-Hakim's head. Baghdad Bob was freed from jail.

However, this was far from over.

CHAPTER 22

MOPED

A SHIA VILLAGER WAS WILLING to give Mac and Dave information about Sunni insurgents. Mac and Dave tried to encourage him to meet them at FOB Orion, but he wouldn't do it. He wanted us to go far from the base, closer to his village, to meet with him, but we wouldn't go. We understood how dangerous it was for Shia informants to travel through Sunni-controlled territory on a regular basis, so we found neutral ground that seemed safe. After the sun dropped out of the sky, once again, our whole EDet exited the gate in our three-Humvee convoy.

Our rendezvous spot wasn't too far from FOB Orion, so if we needed help, we could get a lot of it quickly. Nearby was the city of Dujail, populated by almost one hundred thousand people, most of whom were Shia. We approached an area that looked like the entrance to an outpost that someone was beginning to set up. The road was still paved, and there was a turnoff that was easy to miss, which is why Nate led us there—he never missed. He turned onto a dirt road, and we followed. After a couple hundred yards, we passed six-foot-high staggered barriers with small berms on our left. We passed an old cement pump house surrounded by a lot of bushes and trees—natural cover and concealment that was spy-worthy for a secret rendezvous. We settled into a perimeter in the vegetation and waited.

The sound of a small motor hummed in the distance. Gradually it became louder. Then a small light flickered between the barriers. A moped pulled up and stopped at the designated point.

Two agents intercepted the person. It was the informant. The agents searched him before escorting him inside our perimeter. There, he talked with Mac and Dave.

Pop, pop. Gunfire sounded from our rear. I turned and strained to see where the shots had come from, but I couldn't pinpoint them. I keyed my inner squad radio and called Commander Mitchell, who was also guarding the perimeter, but for some reason, he didn't respond.

Pop, pop.

I couldn't see anything of significance; I could only hear the gunshots. A silhouette appeared, and I aimed at it. Then I recognized who it was—Commander Mitchell. I lowered my weapon.

He approached me and whispered, "Hey, Kermit."

"What's up, sir?"

"There's shooting going on over there," he said.

"Did you go check that out by yourself?"

"Yeah."

"Hey, sir, don't do that. Always grab one of us to go with you."

"All right, will you come with me?"

"Yes, let's go." Like I taught the agents, I let them know where we were going, so they wouldn't mistake us for bad guys when we returned to the perimeter.

Commander Mitchell and I went as far out to the edge of our perimeter as we could. *Pop, pop, pop, pop.* I could barely see muzzle flash, but I couldn't see where the rounds landed or figure out what they were shooting at. I thought I heard a vehicle or two near the muzzle flashes. Then I thought I saw a truck.

I radioed my turret gunner. "Call the FOB and ask them if any of their guys are in contact out here."

Several minutes later the gunner replied: "Negative. None of them are in contact anywhere."

"How about their Iraqi soldiers?" I asked.

After a short delay he said, "Negative."

"I don't know what to make of the gunshots," I said.

"I don't like it," Commander Mitchell said.

"Me neither."

There were no houses or farms or any reason for anyone to be in that area. All the same, it was far enough away to be ineffective, and we continued with the meet.

I kept an eye out to see if the gunshots or vehicles came closer.

We finished and watched the Shia walk to his moped and drive away. Then we jumped in our trucks and motored back to base.

The informant had told Mac and Dave about a Sunni insurgent who had weapons and explosives and was making the initiators for IEDs. He didn't know what the firing to our rear was all about.

We gathered in the classroom, where Commander Mitchell voiced his concern, "Someone was out there taking potshots. It's strange that the military in that AO gave no reports of gunfights going on or anything like that. You all know what it looks like. We were in the middle of nowhere. There's no reason for anyone to be out there at that time. It's like someone knew we were there."

"We can't ignore what happened," I added. "We were miles from anything inhabitable. We have to assume someone was out there conducting recon by fire so they could get a reaction out of us, confirm our presence, and figure out our location, either so they could disrupt us or attack us."

The new guys—Tom, Dave, and Burl—nodded and leaned forward in their seats. They seemed to support what Commander Mitchell and I had said. The veterans—Huey, Mac, Nate, and Croft—crossed their arms, rolled their eyes, and looked at their watches. Orion had enough tactical sense to understand the situation, and he'd lost a good buddy in Kirkuk, but he was one of the old guard in our EDet, and he seemed conflicted. None of the agents said a word, but I could see the bullpen was split.

We finished jocking down, and the agents put their radios away in the comm room. When I went to put my comms away, I overheard Croft say, "He's overreacting. He's acting like there's something to worry about, and there's not."

Someone agreed.

I couldn't believe these agents' complacency. I was furious. I hadn't raised my voice in a professional setting in ten years, not since I was a BUD/S instructor. I burst into the comms room. "Listen, this isn't a game! You're patrolling with Kevlar, armored Humvees, and guns for a reason! These insurgents know by now that after we go into a village, their buddies end up in some shithole prison in Baghdad or die. They're going to start connecting the dots. After we visit, people vanish. You can't be complacent. If you hunt men long enough, they'll hunt you back."

The comms room went deadly silent.

The next day, we put together a mission and briefed the First Cav. With them were paratroopers from the 101st Airborne Division, who were preparing to relieve them. Because we now had ample military support, we only needed one truck full of agents for this mission. The target was in Mac and Dave's area, so they went. Nate joined them—it was hard to keep him out of any mission. He always wanted to be part of whatever was going out. I stayed behind at the JDOC and monitored their mission.

Major Sherwood directed his soldiers and air assets from the JDOC via radio as if he were an orchestra conductor. If he'd had a drone or other air asset, he could've used some of the big screens to feed him live video. He shared the room with air force security, who sat in the room 24/7 watching jumbo video monitors that devoured video feeds from all over the base, especially the airfields.

Mac, Dave, and Nate captured the insurgent and his cache, and they collected intel on another insurgent.

The First Cav radioed back to the JDOC: "We're still working this target. Can we get some more men to take down this other insurgent the agents IDed?"

Major Sherwood gathered some more troops from First Cav and the 101st to go out. Then he turned to me and asked, "Can we get an agent to go with us?"

"Yes, sir," I said. I called Commander Mitchell and gave him the details.

"Ibrahim can translate for you," he said.

"Thank you, sir." I hung up. Then I called Ibrahim and said, "Hey, buddy, we need to action a target—jock up."

"When?" Ibrahim asked.

"Right now. I'll be there in a minute."

"Will do," he said.

I rushed out of the command center. The sky was cloudy, and it was raining. I hopped in my operations officer vehicle—the blacked-out, armored Suburban—and drove across base to the EDet compound where I put on my body armor, comms, and other gear. Ibrahim was already jocked up.

I drove him out to the gate, where a convoy of soldiers were arriving. The First Cav guys recognized us, and we loaded into their vehicles with the 101st Airborne and rolled out of the gate.

It continued to rain as we rode through farmland. We came to a turn, and somehow, we got split up and my vehicle took the lead. The paratrooper in the gun turret of my Humvee looked like he wasn't much older than nineteen, and he started fidgeting a lot. His position up in the gun turret gave him a better view of the road than the rest of us had.

"This is my first op," the young paratrooper said. "What the hell am I supposed to be looking for?!"

"IED's," an older paratrooper called out.

"What the hell does an IED look like?" the young paratrooper asked.

"Look for any dirt that's been freshly overturned," I said.

The young paratrooper was impatient. "That all?"

Sometimes an IED would go off, and the insurgents would put an IED in the same spot. "Indentations on the road with something in them," I said.

"Okay," he said.

I didn't really know either. It wasn't easy. An IED could be detonated by the pressure of a vehicle rolling over it. Or it could be connected to a wire that an insurgent fired with the flick of a switch. Insurgents sometimes used cell phones to trigger IEDs too. Then they started using infrared, like that commonly found on a garage door in the States—except, instead of protecting the car from the garage door closing on it, an explosively formed penetrator pops up from the ground, pierces the vehicle's armor, and explodes inside. They kept changing their tactics, and we kept changing ours to protect our patrols.

"Anything that looks out of the ordinary," I said. "You call it out, and we'll stop and take a look."

"Okay." He seemed calmer.

I sure as hell wasn't calm.

My driver set a pace slow enough that we could spot something suspicious in the road but fast enough to avoid being an easy target. He steered onto a muddy road. I hadn't seen a Humvee get stuck in the mud while I was in Iraq, and I didn't want to change that trend.

The rain stopped as we halted at the target house. We unassed the vehicles. Helicopters flew between us and the dark clouds.

Mac and Dave spoke with a prisoner, a young man in his early twenties. His upper body drooped as if he carried the weight of a really bad day. Soldiers held the perimeter while Nate and others brought things out of the young man's house and laid them in a dirt driveway: tools for making IEDs, electric initiators, demolitions, RPGs, and a Dragunov. It looked like an insurgent's yard sale.

There was too much stuff in the driveway to belong to one guy. He had to have been holding some of it for others and working with them.

"Got the location for the next target," my driver said.

I loaded up with Ibrahim and the army guys in our convoy, and we pulled out. Mac, Dave, and Nate stayed behind to wrap up the young guy and finish collecting intel.

My convoy rolled out of Mac and Dave's area of operations and entered Nate and Burl's stomping grounds. We turned off the road and parked on the corner of a dirt road where a single-story, L-shaped house sat by itself. There were no walls around it, and in the back was a garden.

"This is it," the driver said.

Across the dirt road to our left was another house. A man wearing a *keffiyeh*—a checkered Arab headdress—and two adolescents stopped working in their yard to gawk at us.

None of the troops in my convoy moved, so I jumped out, dashed to the target house, and took a knee outside of it. I aimed my M4 at the front window and then the door. Seven young paratroopers poured out of their trucks and took a knee in a line behind me as if I was the head of the choo choo train.

"Are you one-man, sir?" a paratrooper asked, referring to the first man in a shooting train.

I was older than them, had a beard, and had taken the lead, so they assumed I was in charge. "No, man," I said. "You guys got this. Just be careful breaching that door because this guy is supposed to be an IED maker."

"Roger." The paratroopers hauled ass to the door and entered without hesitation.

Their teammates had already broken out and protected our perimeter while the gunners up in the turrets on the Humvees scanned our surroundings.

Soon the paratroopers came out of the house carrying a box of crudely made IED initiators with wires coming out from toggle devices wrapped in black electrical tape. The intel was good, but nobody was home. Word must've traveled to this IED maker before we arrived.

I glanced over at the gawkers by the house across the dirt road. Then, I recognized the man wearing the keffiyeh. He had *wasta*, or clout, in his village, and he'd volunteered to be an informant. The young men with him were his sons, whom he'd also volunteered to give intel. Wasta never came in by himself to talk—only with one or both of his sons. He never gave us intel of significant value. And he sure as hell never told us about this IED-maker living across the road from him. *How could he not know? Son of a bitch.* He and his sons recognized me and went back in the house as if they didn't know me or have any part of what was going on.

Later, I told Nate, and he became heated.

The next day, he called Wasta and asked, "Hey, we're going to want to talk with you later. How could you not tell us about this IED maker living across the street from you?"

Wasta wouldn't answer, and he ceased communicating altogether. He was full of shit. He sent one of his sons in for a final meet with Nate and Burl.

Nate figured that Wasta was trying to be more dominant in his area, and he was hoping to use us and the soldiers to go after his rivals. Wasta wanted to be the head honcho. Now he was a throwaway, and Nate and Burl stopped using him.

CHAPTER 23

HOLLYWOOD

HUEY INVESTIGATED THE FALSE IMPRISONMENT of Bones's friend. He obtained photos of him and the real insurgent—their faces didn't match, and Bones's friend was noticeably younger. The US snatched him and imprisoned him in error. The only significant thing that Bones's buddy had in common with the insurgent was the same name—Sami Al-Zuhairi—as common as meat on a kebab.

I called the intelligence division under the Multi-National Force–Iraq (MNF-I), which was composed of US, UK, Australian, Spanish, and Polish militaries. They operated out of Baghdad in Saddam Hussein's Water Palace—a sixty-two room resort complex with multiple villas and mini palaces on a man-made lake stocked with large bass. I liaised with an OSI captain and lieutenant colonel there. They helped Huey and me deal with Task Force 134, which was in charge of detainee operations throughout Iraq.

Huey put together the paperwork. Most agents need to have their reports and other paperwork edited, but Huey seemed to get everything right the first time—considerably more challenging in this instance.

Since Bones had put forth a lot of effort and risked his life to give us information about Kaiser Soze, it was our turn to hold up our end of the bargain and get Bones's buddy out of prison.

There was another reason I wanted his friend released. His home was in the same area as another target I wanted to wrap up—an insurgent leader named Rafiyat. He wasn't as powerful as Kaiser Soze, but he was an on-the-ground lieutenant, directly responsible for hit-and-runs that had killed at least half a dozen Iraqis who were US allies. Rafiyat also attempted to kill American soldiers with IEDs and ambushes. He was ruthless, and the US Army wanted him badly.

I received a phone call. It was Jimmy Stewart. "I have my light-all! I have my light-all!" he said.

After all your pissing and moaning… "Congratulations!" I said.

"I can't believe they finally gave me one. Now we can see faces and IDs better at night. Oh yeah, your man Bones is here."

"Thanks."

Huey, Ibrahim, and I met with Bones at the trailer, and I told him, "You did what we asked, and if you keep helping us, we're going to go get your friend."

Bones looked tired. "I'll keep doing this."

Several mornings later, Huey, Ibrahim, and I lifted off from our base on a Black Hawk helicopter. Gunners tested their 240 Bravo machine guns over the sides of the helo and into the Tigris River before we turned and flew southeast. We soared over Fallujah and the Euphrates River. Soon we landed in Baghdad.

A blacked-out Suburban drove up to the helo pad. Out stepped my friend Baker from OSI training in Glynco, Georgia. He was the one who threw the great parties and whose bike had been ridden down the stairs by the army Ranger. I trusted him more than a lot of guys I worked with.

Baker shuttled us to a room for the evening, and after we dropped off our luggage, we went out to dinner. A couple of his friends from the State Department joined us. Baker caught me up on what he was doing in Baghdad, and I told him what we were doing in Balad.

"Can I visit sometime?" Baker asked.

"Sure," I said.

"You know other agencies are watching you on this—getting this guy out of prison."

"I won't screw it up," I said.

"That's not what I mean. This hasn't really been tried before. They want to see if it works."

"I didn't know there were that many eyes," I said.

Baker's State Department friends grinned.

The next day, Baker drove Huey, Ibrahim, and me to Camp Cropper on the outskirts of Baghdad, near the International Airport. Originally, it was used as a detention site for high-value detainees. Saddam Hussein was imprisoned there until his execution. Later, it was used to hold detainees from all over the country. Its living conditions were bad, the guards were severe, and medical care was inadequate. Bones's friend had no idea we were coming to spring him from this shithole.

Inside Camp Cropper, Huey handed an officer the paperwork. He looked it over.

My heart rate elevated, but I breathed long and deep. I was nervous, but I didn't show it.

The officer set the paperwork down and disappeared into a secure room.

"Is something wrong?" Huey asked.

"I don't know," I said.

The officer returned and handed me a plastic bag with something inside. "These are his belongings."

I took the bag and looked at what was inside—a pair of mirrored sunglasses. That was all Bones's friend had when they arrested him.

Military police escorted Bones's friend to us in handcuffs with a black bag over his head. He'd obviously changed out of his prison uniform because he came out wearing tennis shoes, jeans, and a long-sleeved hoodie. He appeared to be in good physical shape.

Huey and I escorted him to the gate. I worried that someone would tell us that there was a problem and stop us. The gate guards and the soldier in the tower eyed us carefully. At any moment, they could put Bones's friend back in jail and ruin everything. Our plans to catch Rafiyat and Kaiser Soze could unravel. I wanted to run, but I walked.

We cleared the gate and walked several hundred yards to our Suburban, which was parked next to a vacant helo pad. We were on the sprawling Victory Base Complex. The Water Palace was part of the same complex. Baker sat behind the wheel, and I took the seat next to him. In the second row, Bones's friend sat between Huey and Ibrahim.

"How long did you think you were going to be in there?" I asked.

Bones's friend spoke Arabic, and Ibrahim translated. "I have no idea."

"You know what? Neither did anyone else. Nobody who was in charge of that place knew. For all we know, you could've been in there forever."

Before Ibrahim could translate, Bones's friend said, "Thank you. You new best friend."

"You're right," I said. "How would you like to be back home with your wife and daughter before the end of the week?"

"I do anything you want," he said.

That was exactly what we were looking for. I looked at Huey and said, "Go ahead and take off his hood and handcuffs."

Bones's friend had long hair. "Thank you."

I showed him the plastic bag. "This is all you had when you came in, huh?"

His smile widened. I gave him the bag, and he opened it and put on his cop shades. He couldn't stop grinning. He looked like someone from LA.

"Your new name is going to be Hollywood," I said.

Hollywood didn't stop grinning.

The helo that was supposed to pick us up got cancelled. Now I was nervous that we might get stuck overnight, and someone might swoop in, scoop up

Hollywood, and take him back to prison again. I didn't trust anybody. While we tried to find another way out of Baghdad, we picked up some Whoppers, fries, and sodas from a Burger King on the Victory Base Complex. Then we found a picnic bench and sat outside and ate.

Hollywood chowed down and smiled.

I chewed a bite of my Whopper and swallowed it. "Hollywood, were there insurgents in prison who tried to recruit you?"

He sipped some soda. Then he spoke broken English: "Yes. Bad men. I no talk bad men. I no go."

"Are you Muslim?" I asked.

"Yes. But I no crazy. I love family. No love crazy."

I smiled.

Huey asked, "What do you think about the insurgency going on?"

"I no like," Hollywood said. "Bad business. America good—more business. Insurgency bad—no business."

After our meal, we finagled our way onto the manifest with some cargo on a C-130. Huey and Ibrahim sat in jump seats on either side of Hollywood, and I sat across from him. We trusted the guy but not 100 percent yet. We weren't going to take our eyes off of him.

We landed at Balad Air Base and shuttled Hollywood to our EDet compound where we had our own trailer. We got him settled in and posted a watch of agents to guard him in shifts 24/7. I brought him a toothbrush and toothpaste and said, "Hollywood, you need to stay in the trailer tonight, and we'll come visit you in the morning. Hopefully, if we get everything done in time, we're going to link you up with your wife and daughter."

He touched his chest. "*Inshallah.*" God willing.

"They have no idea you're coming home, so you're going to surprise them."

He nodded.

In the morning, Huey, Ibrahim, and I fetched breakfast from the chow hall—bacon, eggs, fruit, juice, and milk—and we ate with Hollywood.

Huey showed him some satellite photos.

I pointed to a place on one. "This is your home." Then I pointed to a spot nearby. "And this is where the other person lives who we want to know about."

"Who?" Hollywood asked.

"Rafiyat."

"I know," Hollywood said. "I think we go same mosque."

I almost choked on my eggs. I thought Hollywood was going to have to at least hunt for Rafiyat. "How well do you know him?"

"He bad man. He trouble. My neighbors no like trouble."

"Yes. We're going to let you go home to your wife and kids. While you're home, visit your mosque and see if Rafiyat shows up. After two days, we need you to come back here at 10:00 a.m. to report to Huey and me. Your meetings with us will continue regularly."

He didn't seem to understand, so Ibrahim translated.

Hollywood nodded. "I need build business. I come back again and again."

He was too perfect. I handed him a sack with some goodies: soap, shampoo, toothpaste, and toys. Sometimes care packages to the military overflowed on our base, so occasionally we tapped into them to give to informants. Then Huey, Ibrahim, and I walked Hollywood to the gate and waved goodbye. He joined the flow of Iraqis leaving the base and passed Jimmy Stewart's light-all. Several taxis sat idling nearby. Then he was gone.

⊕　⊕　⊕

Two days later, Jimmy Stewart called me at the EDet compound. "I've got a new guy here to see you."

"Does he have his slick sunglasses on?" I asked.

"Yeah, he's got cop shades on."

"That's Hollywood," I said.

"Okay, I won't forget him."

Huey, Ibrahim, and I went to meet with Hollywood. While MPs processed him in a plywood shack, I parked my Suburban in the dirt parking lot and we stepped out.

Outside of the gate, Jimmy Stewart jumped up and down cussing. "They mortared my light-all! Those sons of bitches mortared my light-all!" There was a huge, dirty dent in the earth, and it was all black around his feet. His light-all had taken a direct hit, and there was nothing left of it.

"Poor bastard," I mumbled.

Huey and I passed the Jersey walls and strolled onto the gravel compound, where we stopped in front of our trailer and waited.

Soon the MPs brought Hollywood, who looked like he was walking on cloud nine. Inside our trailer, we sat down with him.

I offered him a selection of drinks. Hollywood chose a Coke, and since I usually drank what the asset drank, I had one too. Huey chose the same, and Ibrahim had a water.

"How are your wife and kid?" I asked.

Hollywood continued to grin. "Good. They so happy."

Huey took most of the notes during our interviews, and if I left something out, he jumped in. "Have you seen Bones yet?" Huey asked.

Hollywood took a gulp of his Coke. "No. But I Rafiyat same mosque me. Saturday."

"That's good news," I said.

"He no live house. He and gang live fields or trees Tigris River—always change."

This was the first time I'd heard that. "Why does he live outdoors and not in his house?"

"He know America want him and Rafiyat gang."

Recently, at a JDOC intel briefing, I was informed of a mission involving the 101st Airborne. They'd started running Small Kill Teams (SKTs), each made up of five men. An SKT stayed out overnight near the Tigris River to ambush insurgents who were smuggling in weapons from al Qaeda terrorists. This report said the SKT spotted some men near the water and chased them. Two of the bad guys stopped—one of them took a knee near a tree and pointed his weapon towards the SKT that was moving toward him in a wedge formation. On the left flank was the youngest paratrooper on the team, only about nineteen years old. He saw the weapon in the suspect's hands aimed at his teammates in the center of the wedge, so he opened fire and killed him. The other man surrendered, and the SKT captured him. That happened in Rafiyat's area.

With the new information Hollywood provided, I suspected that Rafiyat and his gang might be the ones who were smuggling weapons in from al Qaeda. "Do you know if he's married?" I asked.

"He married," Hollywood said.

"Does he come home to visit his wife?" I asked.

Hollywood shrugged his shoulders.

"I need you to try and find out if he visits his wife," I said.

"Okay. And I go mosque Saturday—maybe see Rafiyat."

Normally we had to tell people what to do and talk them into doing it, but Hollywood offered before we asked. He was a joy to work with. I couldn't help but smile. "Yes."

Over the next several days, Hollywood reunited with Bones, and they were thrilled to see each other. Hollywood's return invigorated Bones to gather more intel about Kaiser Soze.

When Hollywood returned for our next meet, he told us that Saturday, Rafiyat and four men came to the mosque. They were filthy, so they cleaned off with the mosque's outdoor shower. When they entered the mosque, Hollywood sat near them. We sent Hollywood back out to see if Rafiyat and the others visited the mosque again on the following Saturday. They did.

CHAPTER 24

BEST BUDDIES

NOW WE HAD ENOUGH INTEL on Rafiyat to put together a target package. I visited my pal, Major Sherwood at JDOC. He'd been working on handing the reins over to the 101st Division, but he continued to be the ops boss until the transition was complete.

"I want to hit Rafiyat while he's at the mosque," I said.

Major Sherwood leaned back. "Whoa—we'll have to get approval from the battalion commander for that. Or maybe even the general at MNF-I."

"Sure," I said.

"Let's bring it up at the operations brief."

Because of my EDet's effectiveness in helping take many targets off the battlespace, I'd been invited to attend the army's weekly ops brief, and I tried to bring another agent with me each week to watch and listen.

At the next ops brief, I told the soldiers about my mosque idea. The First Cav soldiers and 101st paratroopers were enthusiastic about it.

"All right, let's get it approved," Major Sherwood said.

The approval process dragged on. At the next ops brief, the First Cav's intel collectors, the young ones without much training or experience, announced that they'd discovered a low-level bad guy, a teenager who'd attempted to plant an IED. "We arrested him at his mosque."

I was disappointed. I was happy they got a win, but I was unhappy because I knew that this would scare higher level booger-eaters from showing up at mosques in the area.

Rafiyat proved me right. He stopped attending his mosque.

Meanwhile, Mac and Dave, whose area was adjacent to mine, gathered intel that Rafiyat had a mistress. The next time I met with Hollywood, he confirmed it. Mac and Dave went to work developing a pattern-of-life on the mistress. Soon they put together a target package.

A few days later, at zero dark thirty, Mac and Dave went out with the First Cav and the 101st Airborne in a convoy. Because the soldiers went with them, they didn't need other agents. Nate joined them for the thrill of it. I stayed behind at the EDet and worked on upcoming missions in my ops office. My door was open, and the sound of the op bled out of the comm room and into my hall.

As soon as the convoy rolled up to the target area, Rafiyat opened fire on them. Then he squirted out the back of his mistress's house. After that, it wasn't clear what happened. I strained to listen. Then someone said, "Target is dead."

At 03:00, the agents returned, but they weren't so fired up. They seemed stunned. "AC-130 got him," Mac said.

"Beautiful," I said.

The AC-130 flew over a kilometer high in the air, and I don't think they realized that the monster gunship was on station. It was a good mission.

The next morning, after I came back from an informant meet, one of the crewmembers of the AC-130 showed up with an empty shell from the 20mm round that killed Rafiyat: "I tell you what, that guy could've been on the Iraqi Olympic track team, he was running so fast." He gave the shell to me. "But he didn't outrun this."

I was by myself a lot. In sniper school I learned to work alone, and my comfort level with solitude increased. I loved working together with a team, but as I got older, I enjoyed my own space more. Here, I didn't go to the chow hall and eat with Commander Mitchell like Tom did frequently. Because Tom was the commander's right-hand man, it made sense. In my case, it didn't feel right. In the Teams, a guy didn't hang out with his boss because he didn't want to be a kiss-ass. For me, that continued in the air force. I wanted Commander Mitchell to be able to tell me things I might not want to hear without holding back. Likewise, I was reluctant to get too friendly with my subordinates because *I* wanted to make tough decisions when the time came. If something didn't look right, I'd tell them. I tried to be friendly with my boss and subordinates, but I wasn't their best friend.

In the evening, agents from the bullpen would gather outside of our building in a gravel pit surrounded by concrete walls, and they'd light a bonfire. Alcohol wasn't allowed on the base, and I don't know if they ever snuck some in. I would've if I was their age. If they did, they were damn sure mature about it, and I appreciated that I never heard about it. They probably talked smack about us older guys—I did about senior frogs when I was young. If that's how they bonded and unwound, good for them.

It wasn't unusual for me to burn the midnight oil working in the solitude of my office. The work is what drove me. It gratified me to get justice for someone who'd been wronged, to take out someone bad like Rafiyat and affect the battlespace. Equally, I was pleased to get someone off the hook for a crime they hadn't committed and clear their name and reputation—like Hollywood.

I heard footsteps in the hall outside my office. Tom poked his head in and said, "All work and no play makes Kermit a dull frog."

I knew he wouldn't take no for an answer. I followed him outside of my office and onto the patio where our analyst, Doug, had already kicked back in a lawn chair. Doug wasn't a Green Beret, but he'd worked intel for the Seventh Special Forces Group before he came to work for us. Tom and I sat in lawn chairs next to him. The two of them were close to forty-years old, about my age, closer than anyone else. We'd all entered the military at around the same time too. Tom or Doug would often grab me out of my office at midnight to go chill out on the porch—by force, if necessary.

In front of us, the Humvees were parked in their usual spots. Doug switched on some AC/DC, "Shoot to Thrill," as background music and handed out cigars that we lit up. Then Professor showed up with tea and handed me a cup. "This is a new one."

I took the cup. "It's always a new one."

Tom, Doug, and Professor watched me with shit-eating grins.

"Bastards." I took a sip. I wasn't used to the tea, and they knew I'd be wired and up until two in the morning. Professor loved to experiment on me with different teas.

They laughed.

Professor came and went, and Doug and I did most of the chatting. Sometimes Tom would talk about his two sons, who were the same age as my children. His family lived on Scott Air Force Base in Illinois, and mine lived on the base in Florida. Sometimes he'd make an observation that cracked us up: "That beanie Huey wears to the gym is as useless as a glass hammer." Tom had picked up where Red had left off, jumping on Huey's ass. Huey was both an irritation and a rich source of humor for us, but he was a top tier agent, and he wasn't scared.

Tom told us about some of his struggles with civilian agents. "When they have something that's mission-oriented and it favors a military agent to do it, they want to be a part of the military. When it's something shitty required of a military guy, they play the civilian card."

I smiled.

In the dim light on the porch, Doug would get me laughing and thinking about funny stuff too. He'd talk about his time in the army. Tom would share old cases he worked in OSI, and I tossed out a frogman story or two.

Tom was always looking after people, even officers and civilians, but especially the enlisted guys, suggesting good career moves to them. Although I was an officer, I started out as an enlisted man. "Kermit, you should think about applying for the Air Force Institute of Technology master's degree—the air force will pay for it."

I took a puff of my cigar. "You keep telling me that."

"Man, you're a good candidate, you got to do it. It's for captains like you. You pick up a language and a specialization in some part of the world. You'd get to live in Monterey, California, for a couple years."

"I already did that Monterey thing for Spanish."

"Yeah, but your family would love it," he said.

I shook my head. "Nah, I don't want to go to school anymore."

"You should do it."

I smiled at his persistence. "I'll think about it."

Kicking back with Tom, Doug, and Professor was one of the rare times I'd slow down and stop thinking about gathering intel and actioning it. They were among my best buddies.

CHAPTER 25

PHOTOGRAPH

SEVERAL DAYS LATER, BACK AT JDOC, I sat down with Major Sherwood at a table with maps on it. He said, "I know you wanted us to hold off on missions in Kaiser Soze's area so he'd relax and you all could capture him, but too much time has passed, and too many problems are coming out of there—IEDs, mortars, and attacks on Iraqi allies. And he's still working for al Qaeda."

"I understand," I said, "I appreciate you guys laying off as long as you did."

"Tomorrow morning, I want to raid his house, whether he's there or not. Send him a message. You want to get in on this package?"

Stirring up that village would probably stir up several insurgents, and I wanted to positively identify them and wrap them up. "Can I bring one of my assets with us to P-ID insurgents?"

Major Sherwood nodded. "Of course." He pointed at a satellite imagery map on the table. "While we're there, I want to tear down this bridge on the canal. This'll leave them with only one bridge to enter and exit the village—limit their movement."

I studied the map to see if it was the same bridge that Kaiser Soze walked on his way to the mosque. It wasn't. "Sounds good to me." Then I tapped the map on trees behind the village that Kaiser Soze and his insurgents always squirted into. "Can we take a team up the back side and insert in this orchard before the convoy gets to the village—cut off anyone who retreats?"

"Definitely," he said. "This'll be a good op to introduce the 101st Airborne to that neighborhood." Major Sherwood paused. "You know the Fifth Special Forces Group will be replacing the Tenth SFG." The Fifth SFG's area of operations was the Middle East, and they hunted terrorists in Afghanistan on horseback. They had a reputation as being regimented and strict—with a long history of successes to show for it.

"I heard," I said.

"Both the 101st Airborne and the Fifth SFG are out of Fort Campbell, and they've trained together. You're going to like working with the 101st more frequently. This is what they do."

I became excited. "All right, maybe we can get after some targets I've been wanting to get at."

Major Sherwood smiled. "This isn't what we do—we're artillery."

I realized he took it as if I couldn't go after targets I wanted to because of his group of arties. The arties were incredibly brave and inspired me. "Ah, hey, Major—I didn't mean it that way."

"I understand," he said. "I appreciate you all working with us."

"You guys did a lot of damage on the battlespace," I said.

Major Sherwood smiled again. "No, no, no—I get it. These paratroopers, that's what they do."

I smiled back at him. "You did it too."

He smiled. "I guess we did, didn't we." He held out his hand.

I shook it. What the arties did, working out of their skill set, was above and beyond the call of duty. They got after it. When they lost guys, they came back stronger. "I'll go get my men," I said.

I went back to the EDet compound and told Mac, Dave, and Ibrahim.

Mac and Ibrahim acted as if it was another day at the office, but Dave acted differently. He wasn't his usual smiling self.

"Me?" Dave asked. He seemed like he didn't want to go.

"Yes you," I said.

⟡　⟡　⟡

Early the next morning, we put on our gear and mounted a Humvee. Dave took the wheel; I sat in the navigator seat beside him; Ibrahim sat behind us and interpreted for my asset, Base Worker, who sat next to him; and Mac manned the machine gun up top. Base Worker wore a balaclava and a Kevlar helmet, and we pulled curtains across the back window to help conceal his identity.

Dave drove to the gate, and we slipped into the middle of the army's convoy—two APCs and four Humvees carrying First Cav soldiers and 101st paratroopers. Leading us was a Buffalo, a mine-resistant, ambush-protected armored vehicle. At thirteen feet tall and twenty-seven feet long, it had a V-shaped chassis that would split a blast away from the truck. Its six wheels were run-flat—in other words, they could function after being punctured. Inside the vehicle, explosive ordnance disposal specialists operated infrared technology to detect

IEDs or other explosives. The EOD specialists could also control the truck's robotic arm to dispose of bombs. Troops had hit IEDs on their way to Kaiser Soze's village before, and we were highly likely to hit IEDs again.

We crossed a canal before following the road to the right of it for two miles. Our convoy halted a quarter mile from Kaiser Soze's end of his village. I turned to my crew and said, "Stay with the convoy and help with the perimeter and P-IDing insurgents. You guys good to go?"

"I'm good," Mac said.

I opened the door. "A handful of paratroopers and I will block Kaiser Soze and his buddies' retreat."

Dave grabbed me and prevented me from leaving the Humvee.

I looked at him. "What's up, man?"

"I don't feel right," he said. "I'm kind of sketched out about this one."

Five paratroopers carrying M4 assault rifles—my blocking team—ran up to my vehicle and stopped, waiting for me to go with them.

I asked Dave, "Is the hair standing up on the back of your neck?"

"Yeah."

"That's a good thing, man. You're not complacent. You need to be that way."

The five paratroopers pushed dirt with their boots, looked around, and rocked in place. They were itching to get it on.

"So it's good that I feel like this?" Dave asked.

"Absolutely," I said.

He smiled.

"You good to go?" I asked.

He let go of my shirt. "Yeah, I'm good."

I looked at Mac again, and he gave me a thumbs up.

I hopped out of the Humvee and dashed off with the paratroopers. I ran in the middle of the pack with them. We beat feet between a ditch and the side of the road. The sides and bottom of the ditch were covered in green grass. When water flowed again, it would be a canal.

Soon, we reached a wall that surrounded the dozen houses that made up Kaiser Soze's neighborhood. We followed the wall almost a hundred yards, past the backs of the houses. On the other side of us was a seven-foot-deep ravine. It was packed with trees—the orchard where Kaiser Soze and the insurgents would boogie to. I took the lead, and the paratroopers followed me to an open gate. Then I gestured that this was our spot to set up on. We took a knee and waited to shoot any bad guys who attempted to leave the neighborhood.

While we stayed at the back gate to catch squirters, I could hear radio chatter that the convoy had rolled up to Kaiser Soze's part of the village. They stopped and set up a perimeter, and troops poured out of the vehicles. Then they cleared house-to-house and rounded up every military-aged male. Soldiers lined the suspects up against a wall.

"Kaiser Soze's house is clear," a soldier said over the radio.

No one had tried to squirt out the back gate, and I needed to go interview whoever the troops had found in Kaiser Soze's house. The five paratroopers and I rose and patrolled through the gate and into the village. We moved tactically through a dirt alley with walls on both sides and two-story houses beyond them until we reached the backyard of Kaiser Soze's home, which was one-story.

I stepped inside his home, where two women and several children, including a teenage boy, were sitting down in front of a handful of soldiers. A tall, thin soldier seemed to be in charge. I recognized him as Lieutenant Old Soul.

"You guys clear?" I asked.

"Clear," Lieutenant Old Soul said. "Kaiser Soze's not here, but we have some of his family members if you want to talk with them."

"Yeah." I called up Ibrahim, and he joined me. We escorted one of the women to another room.

I started with an easy question: "Who lives here?"

She gave me Kaiser Soze's name, which I already knew.

"Who are you?" I asked.

"I'm his wife."

"Do you know what he does for a living?"

"He's a businessman."

"Is he gone a lot?" I asked.

"Yes, he's a businessman. He's always out on business."

"Okay, well, where's he at right now?"

"He's on business in Tikrit," she said, naming the city Saddam Hussein was from.

"When's he coming back?"

"I don't know," she said, "but he's not coming back today."

"Do visitors come here often?" I asked.

"No," she said. She was full of crap. Al Qaeda operatives and insurgents were often their guests.

I took her back to sit with the others and pulled the other woman into a side room. She told me she was Kaiser Soze's other wife and gave me the same story—that he was on business in Tikrit. It was like he told them both what to say.

I took her back and sat her down. The teenage boy looked at me.

I separated him from the others and asked the same questions, except he told me, "Dad is in Tikrit at business school." The kid got the story mostly right.

I took him back in and sat him down. "Thanks guys," I told the soldiers. "I'm done here." I took one long last look at the inside of Kaiser Soze's house. The interior was smaller than I anticipated. Maybe there was another clue to his pattern-of-life.

I went out to the convoy and was shocked to see only four military-aged males lined up against the wall. With a dozen houses in the village, there should've been a lot more grown men. It felt weird. *Where'd they all go?*

I hopped inside the Humvee with Ibrahim.

"Hey," Mac said, "Base Worker is telling us that two of the guys on that wall are hot."

"Which two?" I asked.

"I don't know," Mac said. "He doesn't know enough English, and I don't know enough Arabic. We need Ibrahim."

"I'm here now," Ibrahim said.

I called to a soldier and said, "Bring the first one off the wall and up to the truck so we can P-ID him."

The soldier did.

Base Worker spoke in Arabic.

"No," Ibrahim said.

The soldier brought up the second suspect.

Base Worker spoke again.

"That's one of them," Ibrahim said.

Then the soldier escorted the third one.

"Yes. And he's Kaiser Soze's cousin."

Jackpot.

Base Worker viewed the fourth one. "No."

I called back to our analyst and passed on the information about Kaiser Soze's cousin and the other man our asset had pointed out. "Are these two green?" I asked.

"Yes, they are," the analyst said.

The army guys loaded the two insurgents in APCs—but they weren't quite done yet. We penetrated deeper into the village. A whole lot of little children swarmed around us, and one old man checked us out.

"We got the two insurgents," Dave said. "Let's get out of here."

"Why?" I asked. "The army has this village locked down. Mac's got a hold on it. We're good."

"Can't we just go?" Dave asked.

Ibrahim fidgeted. Dave's reluctance seemed to make him nervous too.

"We can't just head back alone," I said. "We have to wait 'til the army's done to go back."

The army must've brought in another convoy because now there were more soldiers, and they had two High Mobility Engineer Excavators (HMEEs), armored backhoe loaders that could drive fast enough to keep up with Humvees and APCs. Its operators went to work destroying the bridge Major Sherwood wanted taken out. The army went into full-on deconstruction mode.

We dominated the area, but none of us could go anywhere until the job was finished. Now Dave seemed more relaxed.

Yesterday was gone, and tomorrow couldn't be trusted, so I grabbed the here-and-now and took a timeout from the war. My Kevlar vest and helmet felt like a sauna. I breathed in the dry heat, and sweat soaked my skin. Children assembled around Dave and me and chattered in Arabic.

One of them had a soccer ball, and Dave kicked it around with them. They cheered.

I wanted to give them something, but I had no gifts. Then I remembered my digital camera and pulled it out.

"Picture, picture!" the kids cried out in English.

"You kids know who the Hulk is?" I asked.

"Yes, yes, Hulk, Hulk!" They needed no interpreter.

I gestured. "Okay, you guys got to flex like the Hulk."

They made Hulk poses. Then I showed them the digital image on my camera. They pointed, giggled, and laughed.

Dave sat by the canal, and boys and girls gravitated to him. I took their pictures. The kids squealed and went crazy, as if they'd taken a picture with a soccer superstar.

Dave clicked a photo of me sitting with them by the canal—they loved it.

"Picture, picture!" more shouted.

"Okay, okay," I said. I went over to our Humvee and handed the camera up to Mac in the turret. Then I returned to the kids and Dave. With the canal to our backs, Mac snapped our photo.

I retrieved the camera. The children crowded around Dave and me, and we looked at it. Our smiles shone brighter than the Iraqi sun. I'm told that that photo was later displayed in Quantico, Virginia, at the new Russell-Knox building where OSI's headquarters is. That picture is worth more than a thousand words.

CHAPTER 26

HAMMER ONE DOWN

THURSDAY, NOVEMBER 1, 2007, BEGAN much like any other day. Tom and I met with Commander Mitchell in his office. They looked at me as if they expected me to say something first, so I did: "With IEDs, mortars, and rocket attacks decreased around the base, the guys want to push out further and find out who else is attacking us."

Tom shook his head. "Mac and Dave are still hounding you about meeting with Moped, aren't they?" Moped was the Shia informant who'd met with us the night pot shots were taken.

"Moped wanted to meet with Mac and Dave on a Friday," I said, "but when the agents changed the meet to Thursday, he wouldn't answer his phone. Mac, Dave, and I agreed not to meet with him until he contacted us with something worth collecting. Moped's intel has turned to shit. And he keeps wanting Mac and Dave to go out to Dujail to meet with him, anyway."

Commander Mitchell's eyebrows narrowed. "Absolutely not. I've been out that way, and it's too dangerous."

"I don't want to go out that far for so little," I said, "but I keep putting Moped up on the ops planning board in case he ever comes up with something worth a damn."

"Commander Mitchell and I have been talking about this a lot," Tom said. "Mac and Dave trust Moped too much."

"And they're not the only ones who've gotten too close to their sources," Commander Mitchell said.

Tom looked at me. "What do you think?"

"When it comes down to it," I said, "I don't trust any of the informants."

"We need to mix it up," Commander Mitchell said.

Tom rubbed his chin. "With Croft back in the States, and Cat here, and Huey out on R&R in Qatar, this might be a good time to switch AOs and sources for everyone."

Croft had finished her tour, and her replacement was Cat, an Asian-American agent who'd graduated from one of the most respectable forensic schools in Washington, DC.

"I don't think we'll get as much cooperation and information as before," I said, "but I think the bigger danger is agents believing in their sources too much. Their intel needs to be validated."

"We'll only swap out one agent from each pair," Commander Mitchell said, "and maintain some continuity."

"I get it," I said.

"Tom and I aren't running sources," Commander Mitchell said, "but you are, Kermit."

"We're on the outside looking in," Tom said, "but you're not. The agents will have a hard time hearing this if it comes from Commander Mitchell and me."

I thought about it for a moment. If I set the example of handing over my assets to another agent, the others were more likely to follow. "I'll let them know."

⊕　⊕　⊕

That evening, agents had a meet planned with a different source, but it was cancelled. Within minutes, Mac was at my office door.

"What's up?" I asked.

"Moped has new information about the insurgent who planted a bomb that killed the army EOD guy," Mac said, referring to an army Explosives Ordnance Disposal expert who died before I'd arrived at Balad Air Base. There was a conspicuous IED planted in the road, but the real bomb was carefully concealed in a secondary location. When the EOD expert moved in to defeat the obvious IED, the secondary bomb exploded, killing him.

"If intel on the planter is out there, we have to get it," I said. "I'll go talk to Commander Mitchell."

"I'll go with you, if you want."

"Nah," I said. I didn't want him to hear anything negative Commander Mitchell might have to say and be upset at him. Mac and the others could get upset at me, but I didn't want them to get upset at Commander Mitchell.

I walked down the hall and knocked on the commander's door.

"Come in," he said.

Tom was in his office. I told them about the mission.

"Let's do it," Commander Mitchell said before he turned to Tom.

Tom nodded in agreement.

I returned to my office and called JDOC about the mission.

Major Sherwood said, "We don't have any ops going on in that area, so it's a green light. By the way, there's a route clearance team going out tonight."

"What time?" I asked.

He told me, so I timed our mission to follow them out as far as we could before we had to turn off onto backcountry roads.

After our phone conversation ended, I went into the bullpen.

Mac and Dave looked up at me.

"It's a green light," I said.

Their faces lit up. They hustled to put together the mission with the other agents, except for Huey, who was still on R&R in Qatar. Then we all went into the briefing room, and Mac and Dave briefed the op. I noticed something, but I didn't want to bring it up in front of the other agents and embarrass Mac and Dave.

After the brief, I pulled Mac and Dave aside. "In your brief, you had Commander Mitchell driving the last vehicle. He can't lead as effectively if he has to drive too. If anything, you can make him navigator in the last vehicle."

Mac and Dave glared at me. They didn't like me messing with their mission.

In their brief, they had me driving the second vehicle. Typically, Commander Mitchell kept me in the navigator's spot in the second vehicle, so I could make tactical decisions if we got into something ugly. With Huey gone, we were down to nine agents tonight and having me drive made sense.

We agreed that Nate would drive the lead vehicle, Dave would navigate beside him, and Tom would man the machine gun in the turret. I'd drive the second vehicle with Mac navigating, Burl on the gun, and Ibrahim sitting in the back seat. Cat would drive the last Humvee with Commander Mitchell navigating and Orion in the turret.

I studied Mac and Dave's brief on the board, and I felt their eyes burn into the back of my head. As I looked at the board, I realized Nate was nearing the end of his tour and would be going home in a week or so, and he probably wanted to be in the same vehicle with Mac on what could be his final mission. Mac and Nate had been good friends since FLETC, and Nate had even lived with Mac and his wife at one time. I thought maybe I should switch places with Nate in the first truck so he and Mac could be together in the second truck—but Mac and Dave already seemed pissed at me for changing up their mission once, and I paused before making any more adjustments. *Nate knows the turnoff on that route better than anybody, and I don't want to be the one who blows past it and runs us into an IED or an ambush while we try to turn around.* After about twenty of the most important seconds of my life, I made up my mind. *No more changes.*

I turned around and looked at Mac and Dave. It was as if they knew I was contemplating a switch. When I didn't say anything more, they seemed relieved. That was that. We jocked up and went outside to the Humvees sitting in front of the porch.

Under the faint illumination of the compound lights, Tom looked at Professor, who was smoking a cigarette and asked, "Can I have one?"

Professor exhaled. "You smoke cigars not cigarettes—everything all right?"

Tom shrugged his shoulders and held out his hand.

Professor gave him a cigarette and lit it.

Tom took a puff. "Thanks."

The team joined the rest of us and loaded into the Humvees.

We started our engines with a growl. Professor and Shaky stood with Tex, a new terp who was Egyptian but claimed Texas as his home. With them was our analyst, Devil Dog, the former marine intel expert who'd replaced Doug. The terps and analyst stood on the porch to see us off as they always did when they weren't going out. We drove out of the EDet compound, and our three-vehicle convoy rolled through the base.

Nate swerved back and forth as if he were a NASCAR driver heating up his tires to optimum temperature at the start of a race.

"All right, Nate," I cautioned him over the radio.

Nate straightened out.

"Yeah, keep it between the lines, Jeff Gordon," someone radioed.

An agent laughed and another said something I couldn't decipher.

Commander Mitchell keyed the mic. "Okay, let's lock up the chatter."

The radio quieted down.

We exited the gate, locked and loaded our weapons, and test fired our crew-served machine guns. The route clearance team, headed by a Buffalo, passed us and headed in the direction of Dujail. We pulled out and followed the route clearance team for eight to ten miles, passing FOB Orion.

Nate's Humvee looked like a race car eager to leave the parade and overtake the pace car at the beginning of a race. We neared the area that looked like the entrance to an outpost. Nate found the turnoff—he was spot on. He steered onto a dirt road, and it was as if the green flag had been flown: *Boogity, boogity!*

I wanted to get on the mic and jump his shit for hot-dogging it, but we were almost on target, and I didn't want to be that guy who's always on everyone's ass. We turned off our headlights, and the guys went on their night vision while I stayed with my naked eyes. Hammer One passed between the six-foot-high barriers staggered to our left and the four-foot dirt berms lining the right. Something seemed off, but I couldn't put my finger on it.

Boom! A giant fireball exploded in front of me and shook my Humvee. It flashed so massively that it whited everything out, and I couldn't see. I slammed on the brakes. Steel ripped apart with a violent noise. Nate's vehicle had struck an IED. I clenched the mic: "Hammer One down, Hammer One down."

My vision slowly returned, and I spotted evidence of the source of the IED—an upside down compact truck bed lying beside the road surrounded by fire. I thought the enemies must've filled a truck with explosives, and when we neared the vehicle, it detonated.

I pulled off to the right shoulder of the road.

"Burl, cover our right flank," I said to my gunner.

I got on the mic again. "Hammer Three, block the road and hold security."

I glanced back. Cat whipped the rear Humvee around perpendicular to the road, and Orion pointed his gun at anyone trying to come at us from behind.

"What do we do?" Mac asked.

"We're going to get our guys," I said.

Immediately, I remembered Matt, a SEAL Team Four buddy of mine. He'd served in Operation Just Cause in Panama, where the SEALs' mission was to disable Dictator Manuel Noriega's jet to prevent his escape. Outnumbered and outgunned, the SEALs were caught in a horrible crossfire.

"How'd you not get hit?" I asked him. "What'd you use for cover?"

He pointed at the ground. "Everyone who stood up got shot."

I rolled out of the Humvee and hugged the ground. Bullets hissed from the darkness and made a *zipping* sound as they passed by my head.

Mac exited and hustled in my direction. "What's that?"

I reached up, grabbed him, and pulled him to the ground. "That's us getting shot at—stay low."

Small explosions continued from Hammer One as multiple zips passed above our heads. I didn't want to take all of us into the kill zone, so I moved out with Mac. We dashed several yards. Bullets cracked past us, and we dove to the dirt. Then we hopped up, hauled ass again, and dropped. Each time I was up I tried to make out what we were heading into, but it was all too bright and washed out by the flames.

I couldn't see our enemies, but I was angry as hell and wanted them to know we'd be shooting back. I couldn't fire in the direction of Hammer One without hitting one of our guys, and Burl had our right flank covered, so I blasted a three-round burst at our left flank in hopes the incoming zips would decrease.

The fire in the Humvee was ivory at its core with yellow, orange, and seismic red becoming a black cloud. Giant flames licked the sky. Ammo and grenades cooked off in the Humvee, causing more explosions. Blazing fuel sprayed into the field, igniting it. Mac and I hugged the ground. Soon we recovered and took cover behind a barrier.

I got on the mic, "Call for an air weapons team and a medevac."

Mac must've thought I was talking to him, and he took off back to the truck to make the calls. He ran so hard that his helmet fell off.

I turned my attention back to Hammer One. I pressed closer, and heat seared my nostrils and throat. The intense brightness of it partially blinded me, and the flames and heat distorted everything. There was misshapen metal, and I didn't know what I was looking at. I was about to try going into the fire on Nate's side when I noticed him lying near my feet. The blast had blown him out of the Humvee. He wore that blue outdoors shirt he loved so much. I became so numb that, for a moment, I couldn't move. Nate was dead.

Soon I heard the distant *thwop-thwop* of the air weapons team. As the lethal Apache gunships drew closer, the rounds cracking overhead decreased.

An agent radioed me: "The route clearance team saw the explosion, and they want to know if we need an assist."

I keyed the mic. "Hell, yeah, send them in."

The blaze stung my face, and I couldn't push closer on the driver's side, so I skirted the flames and went around to the passenger's side. The blast had thrown Dave out of the truck, and he lay dead on the ground too. More anesthesia filled my veins, and the monstrous inferno made me feel small.

The noisy rumble of the Buffalo and its tail of vehicles pulled up to our rear. Commander Mitchell and some soldiers dismounted and used the Buffalo for cover. The Buffalo peeled right and went around the far-right flank of the burning Humvee. Commander Mitchell and the soldiers dashed to cover behind a barrier with me.

Ammo and grenades continued to cook off sporadically from inside of Hammer One. The fire didn't seem quite so massive now, and my vision became clearer. Off to the right side of the road, I noticed the compact truck bed again—the source of the vehicle-borne explosives—surrounded by flames.

"What the hell's going on—who's shooting?" Commander Mitchell asked. In all the confusion, he must've lost his comms. The fog of war made the simplest of things incomprehensible.

"Hammer One is down," I said.

Commander Mitchell shook his head. "Holy shit."

Once more I looked at the truck bed surrounded by flames. Now I could see that it wasn't a truck bed. It was a gunner's turret. *If that turret blew off the top of Hammer One, maybe Tom was tossed free of the damage. Maybe Tom's okay.*

CHAPTER 27

EXTRACT

I ADVANCED SEVERAL YARDS TO the right of the burning vehicle. Several more yards away, I noticed Tom in the fetal position around the turret. I couldn't see if he was conscious or not. "Tom, are you okay?" I yelled.

He didn't respond.

An explosion erupted, and I felt a tremor in the ground, so I dropped in a charred spot of the field.

"Tom, can you hear me!"

Again, there was no reply, so I leaped to my feet. The ground between us was on fire. I ran through it.

A soldier's voice called out from behind me. "Your boots are on fire!"

Another explosion rocked the air, and I dove to the ground. I low-crawled to Tom. I reached out and grabbed the back of his Kevlar and shook him. "Tom, wake up! Wake up!"

He didn't move or say a word.

I looked around, and I was surprised that none of the soldiers had come with me. I was all alone and possibly surrounded by enemies. *Shit!*

I took a breath. *Screw it.* I ripped off Tom's Kevlar to reduce his weight, and I picked him up. Although I was fatigued, and Tom was unconscious and still weighed down with his other gear, he was lighter than I expected. I ran him through the fire and away from Hammer One.

Nearby was a three-foot high berm. I dashed to it and collapsed. The cover of that berm felt as if it were ten feet high. Tom's eyes were open. I checked his pulse. I thought I felt it, but I wasn't sure. Hope replaced the deadness inside me.

Army guys called out: "Hey, man, you need a hand?"

I sure as hell could've used a hand when I was alone out in the middle of that flaming open field. Even so, I was grateful. "Yeah. You guys got a corpsman?" In the navy and marine corps, we called medics *hospital corpsmen*.

"A what?"

"A medic," I said.

"Yeah." There was a pause. "Doc Cummings, quick up."

A medic hustled to our position on the right flank and knelt beside Tom and me.

"Doc, I think he has a pulse, but can you check it?" I asked. "I don't know if it's really there or if it's my own or if I just want it to be there. I'm pretty jacked up right now."

"Will do," Doc said.

The medevac helicopters' blades beat the air in the distance: *thwop-thwop-thwop*. Nobody was shooting at us anymore. Each beat of the chopper blades filled me with more hope. I bounced to my feet, whipped out my infrared strobe, clicked it on, and rotated it. Then I transmitted, "Marking my position, you identify."

"Cannot see your mark, but I see a big fire," a crewmember in the medevac helo said.

I paused for a moment. "That's us. We need a medevac ASAP. We have one wounded and two KIA."

"Roger."

The noise of the birds came closer. "Hear you at six hundred meters," I said.

"Roger."

"Three hundred meters."

Although I wanted them to land closer so I could get Tom out more quickly, they touched down a hundred meters away.

When I returned my attention to Tom, Doc shook his head. Army guys had gathered on one knee around Tom, and one handed me Tom's dog tags. "Sorry, man, your buddy didn't make it."

I was so focused on what I wanted to believe that I hadn't paid attention to what was real. The initial explosion killed Tom instantly. I'd hoped he was alive, but that didn't make it so. Now I had to face reality. Wretched paralysis replaced the last of my hope.

I got on the radio. "Call the medevac off." I could barely speak. "Three KIA. None of our guys made it."

There was a pause. "We're going to fly your guys out anyway," a crewmember in the medevac replied.

"QRF is on its way," came another voice over the comms. The Quick Reaction Force would soon arrive.

Meanwhile, soldiers from the clearance team put out the Humvee fire. When the QRF arrived, they assisted. I heard over the radio what sounded like the scrambling of A-10 Warthog jet fighter-bombers to fly overhead for close air support. Commander Mitchell, two soldiers, and I carried Tom on a stretcher while other soldiers carried Nate and Dave.

The IED explosion, decisions, fear, dodging bullets, anger, adrenaline, discovery of my downed buddies, sadness, shock, hope, and actions yanked the needle on my fuel gauge below empty. Endurance training was critical, but it wasn't enough. We carried our guys across a hundred meters of dirt clods and boulders and struggled to maintain our balance with each step. Then we loaded them on the helos.

The choppers rose into the night sky and soared away. We'd just lost three of our bravest and best. It's hard to explain to someone who hasn't deployed with a small unit. I'd spent 24/7 with them: eating, sleeping, working, and playing. We learned a lot about each other—sometimes too much. I spent more consecutive time with them than I ever had or ever would with my own family. They were my brothers.

Commander Mitchell, the two soldiers, and I returned to the convoy. A ground clearance soldier examined something—the hole left by the IED that killed our guys. I studied it with him. The hole didn't have the jagged edges and gouges caused by a homemade, Raggedy Ann, 120mm mortar round jerry-rigged to blow. This hole was cut clean, like a military-grade explosively formed penetrator (EFP). This was something new.

"I'm no EOD tech," the clearance guy said, "but I've done some training, and I've seen more than I care to."

I told him, "This wasn't command detonated—there's no wires going off to either flank of the road. This was victim initiated."

He nodded. "Some kind of pressure device." Instead of someone standing nearby to push a button attached to a wire that detonates the bomb, the pressure of the Humvee rolling over a sensitive device set off the explosive.

I nodded back at him, then I returned to my Humvee.

Before I reached it, Commander Mitchell approached me and said, "I can't believe this shit is happening to us."

I worried about returning to the base. My energy was sapped, and if we got hit again, I was going to have to dig deep to help us survive. Even so, we weren't quite done here yet.

"Sir," I said, "we need to gather up anything that's sensitive—comm gear and weapons that survived—and load them up in my truck."

The other agents and I rounded up anything we could find of importance. Then Commander Mitchell said, "The team is pretty shaken up, and we've spent more than enough time on this spot."

"Yeah," I said, "it's time to go."

Commander Mitchell found the QRF commander and told him, "We need to get back, but we're not supposed to roll through this area with anything smaller than a three-truck convoy, and now we're down to two."

"My men and I have to stay here," the QRF commander said.

Damn. With more than a quarter of our EDet wiped out, we had to drive back to base unescorted. Making matters worse, we'd been on the same site for too long, and the booger-eaters had plenty of time to set up a new EFP booby trap on the route back. It was a devastating kick in the crotch.

Commander Mitchell told us, "Load up. We're going back to the compound."

I spotted Mac's helmet where it had fallen beside the road and picked it up. I sat in the driver's seat of my Humvee. I handed the helmet to Mac, who was seated in the navigator spot beside me.

Mac took the helmet. "Where'd you find this?"

I was so damn proud of him. He went with me under enemy fire and explosions with no questions asked. I smiled at him. "You good to go?"

"Yeah. Just us?"

"We're lead vehicle now," I said.

"All right, let's go."

I got on the radio. "We're Hammer One now. Hammer Two are you ready?"

"Ready," Cat said.

I put the Humvee in gear, turned around, and took the lead. With only two vehicles, I didn't know if we'd survive another hit. It was easy to understand why the three-vehicle minimum outside the gate was set.

I couldn't remember the last time I was so nervous. With a lump in my throat, I radioed the QRF, "This is Hammer One—we're heading home."

Minutes later, two Apache choppers flew overhead, and a new voice said, "Hammer One, this is Gunslinger Two-Two. We'll be your escort home tonight."

I was so comforted to know that those guardian angels were watching over us that my eyes welled up with tears. I struggled to contain it.

"What area you most concerned about on the way back?" Gunslinger Two-Two asked.

I keyed the mic. "Where our AO splits with the FOB's AO. You know, that stretch of road where most of the IED's are planted?"

"Know it well," Gunslinger Two-Two said. One helo thundered ahead, and the other stayed with us. Soon Gunslinger Two-Two came back on the radio. "You guys are clear all the way home."

"Roger, we appreciate it," I said.

I turned near the entrance to the outpost and followed the main road.

Another radio call came in. It was from the QRF back where we were hit. "An Iraqi showed up. Says you know him as Moped. He's asking what's going on and where you're at. You want us to hold him?"

I was still struggling to process losing our guys, and thinking about Moped was beyond me. "Naw," I said. "Let him go and tell him we'll get back to him."

I drove through the base gate, pulled into the compound, and parked. We stepped out of the trucks.

Professor, Shaky, Tex, and Devil Dog were out waiting for us on the porch like they always did. "Where's the third truck?" Professor called out.

Our shoulders drooped, and we walked with heavy feet. It felt as if we carried the twisted, hollowed-out Humvee on our backs. Several of us shook our heads. Others had distant, wet stares. One of us said, "They're gone. Hammer One hit an IED—all three of them are gone."

Professor and Shaky teared up. Tex and Devil Dog were upset too.

The numbness returned, and my heart ached. Everyone stood still as if paralyzed. Then it dawned on me that we still had weapons to unload, sensitive comms to download, and other crap to put away. We needed some clarity in the here-and-now, so I said, "Everybody unload your weapons and put them on the racks. Then let's return the radios, get rid of the other gear, and jock down the rigs."

Commander Mitchell made sure they did their jobs and talked with whoever needed it.

The agents put things away, and the work seemed to calm them down a little.

Commander Mitchell leaned over to me. "I've got to go notify the air wing commander." The 332nd Air Expeditionary Wing commander was the air force one-star general in charge of our base. "And Qatar." Qatar was where our OSI regional headquarters was.

"I'll take care of the agents," I said.

The agents kept busy, but the usual buzz in the compound was muted.

They were visibly upset, but I seemed to be better off, and I wondered what was wrong with me. *Maybe I'm old.*

I slipped away, went to my office, and called the chaplain: "You might want to get over here. We've had a bad night—lost three of our agents. Some people's faith is stronger than others, but everybody could probably use your help right now."

"Sure thing," he said. He came over and did what he could.

Then I received a phone call at my desk from Tom's commander back in the States. Tom's wife wanted to know: "Did he suffer or was it quick?"

"It was quick," I said.

Months later, I'd be told that she grew weary of the look neighbors gave her—pity for the serviceman's widow. No matter how friendly they'd be, they always seemed to have that look. It reminded her of what she'd lost. She took her kids and moved.

After the brief call, I went to Commander Mitchell's office. His door was closed, and I knocked on it. There was a pause. "Come in," he said.

I walked in to find him behind his desk with tears in his eyes.

"You all right?" I asked.

"Took some time to myself," he said.

Maybe I should've taken a little time to myself. Maybe it would've helped me through the grieving process quicker, but I preferred to keep busy.

Commander Mitchell groaned. "I still have to call Huey in Qatar. I'll be okay. How you doing?"

"I'll be okay," I said. "Let me know if you need anything."

I left him alone and returned to my office. Minutes later, Commander Mitchell poked his head in. "Hey, Kermit, I've got to go to the morgue to identify our guys. I don't want to go down there by myself. Can you go with me?"

"Yeah," I said.

We went to the morgue, which looked like a wood shack inside. Commander Mitchell stood at attention in front of Nate and saluted him. Next, he faced Tom at attention and saluted him, too. Then he stood at attention and saluted Dave.

Commander Mitchell turned to me and said, "Those guys are fucking heroes."

Just hours ago in the field, his disposition was even-keeled as always, professional. Now, for the first time, I saw his raw emotions, tears in his eyes—his love for his men. I felt a spontaneous need to salute him but didn't. "Yes, sir."

We left the morgue, and on our way back to the compound, I said, "We've got to make sure everyone is squared away."

"Yeah, we got to talk with them and make sure they get to bed."

When we returned to our building, no one was ready to go to bed—everyone was moving about looking for something to do. I thought up as much work as I could for them.

By the time the wing commander came over, most of the agents had gone to sleep. He visited with Commander Mitchell and me, and we filled him in on what had happened.

"Anything you need, just let me know," he said.

"Thank you, sir," we said.

At 03:00, only Orion and one other agent were still up.

"You got more stuff that needs to be done?" Orion asked.

I couldn't think of more things for them to do. "Look, you two just got to go to bed. It's all going to be the same tomorrow. You got to get some sleep."

They went to bed.

CHAPTER 28

In Memoriam

THE NEXT DAY OR SO was a blur, and events slipped in and out of space and time. Two OSI officers—a major and lieutenant colonel from DC—flew out from OSI headquarters in the States and conducted after-action interviews with each of us. They came to my office last.

"What kind of training did you and the agents do?" the major asked.

I told him about training the agents how to shoot, move and communicate, prisoner handling, patrolling with and without Humvees, what to do if a vehicle went down, and physical training.

They nodded politely as if I was speaking Martian to them. They didn't seem to comprehend that the army was stretched so thin in Afghanistan and Iraq that they couldn't provide us with tactical security teams as they had before. Even artillery soldiers were doing infantry soldiers' work. For us to do our jobs, we had to adapt. Instead of sending out two agents with an interpreter, we had to send out our whole EDet.

"Well," the lieutenant colonel said, "what'd you guys do for medical training?" I'd heard that they asked the same question to each member of our EDet.

This line of questioning pissed me off because I was sure it was related to another attack on agents working north of our location in Kirkuk. An agent who arrived there after the fact stirred up an accusation about whether the agents killed in action were medically treated in time. I guarantee that those agents did everything in their power to save their teammates. Later, the investigation would validate this. All the same, what a slap in the face to that unit and OSI by a guy who wasn't even on the mission with them.

These two officers struck me as office commandos who understood what happened in the past but didn't understand what was happening now. I felt as if they were afraid they'd somehow receive blame for something, and they were accusing us of negligence in our guys' deaths so when any shit rolled towards headquarters, they could redirect it towards us. I couldn't keep the irritation out of my voice: "What'd we do for medical training? The training you guys gave us before we deployed."

"Oh," the lieutenant colonel said.

I added, "An army medic, Doc Cummings, helped us when we were hit."

The major took notes. Then he asked, "After your men were hit by the IED, you were shot at, but did you see any enemies?"

"No," I said.

"Did the attack helos find any sign of enemies?" he asked.

"No," I said. I second-guessed myself: "We were receiving rounds, but the shots were probably cooked off from the fire in the Humvee."

The two officers finished my interview and didn't stick around the compound much longer after that.

Later, I reflected on it. The incoming rounds were way too accurate for random cooking off, and when the attack helos neared us, it was as if the bullets zipping past mine and Mac's heads came to an abrupt halt. The best position for an enemy to fire at us with good cover would've been behind the cement pump house. It was located about a hundred yards past Hammer One. Or maybe they could've been firing from further away, like the night we were there to meet Moped.

Now all that mattered was tracking down who hit us. I decided to talk to our new intel analyst and headed down the hallway. I had to pass Tom's now silent office on the way. I stepped inside Devil Dog's office. Names of insurgent organizations and factions with branches that led to individuals in geographic areas covered his wall.

I told him about the bomb and the cleanly cut crater it left, which was similar to shape charges I used in the SEAL Teams.

He nodded. "Iran has had close relations with the Shia in Dujail since the eighties. A precise explosive like the one that hit your team was probably supplied by Iran, but that's a high-demand, low-density weapon. In other words, the Iraqi Shia militias want as many of those weapons as they can get their hands on, but the Iranian government knows the weapons can be traced back to them, so they'll be careful about which Iraqi Shia militias they give them to. Iran will consider whether or not the target is worth the risk of being discovered. Also, there has to be a high likelihood of the weapon actually being used because the Iranians don't want pictures of their unexploded bomb showing up all over the internet. Permission for using such a bomb has to come from high up the chain of command."

"That means it wasn't planted with the intent of hitting some random target," I said. "Someone was targeting us."

Devil Dog bowed his head in agreement.

"Thanks." I left his office.

I returned to my office, joined by Orion and Professor, with whom I shared the information. We handled it like an investigative case in the States. I wrote the names of the victims on my whiteboard—Nate, Tom, and Dave—and drew a circle around them. "Who have we been running that might be trying to target us?" Orion and Professor rattled off some possibilities, and I drew branches from the circle and connected them to the names of the bad guys. We discussed primary and secondary actors, but we didn't focus on any one individual yet. Professor seemed to be deep in thought, but he didn't say what was on his mind. He was close to Nate and had translated for most of his meets. More than Orion or me, Professor was probably beginning to get an idea of who set us up, but with the memorial ceremony and loading our guys on the plane still ahead of us, we were simply taking a moment to spitball some ideas.

Soon after, we agents gathered together our guys' belongings, put them inside olive drab colored plastic bags, and locked them in a separate room, not to be touched until they could be sent home to the families. Officers from outside our organization would come later to take care of the items and ship them.

A lot of us continued to walk around like mindless zombies. Mac seemed to suffer the most. Since the attack, I hadn't seen him with dry eyes. He shut down and rarely talked. Nate had been like his brother, and Dave had been his partner. Making matters worse, Mac was nearby when I discovered they were dead.

The chaplain returned and spoke with Mac, but he was still a wreck.

I went to Commander Mitchell's office and asked, "Can we send Mac with our guys to escort their bodies all the way home?"

"Yeah, he may not be of much use to us in the near future," Commander Mitchell said.

I left and told Mac that he'd be ending his tour in Iraq and escorting the bodies home.

When I returned to my office, Major Sherwood called. "Hey, man, I'm really sorry about your guys."

"Thanks," I said.

"If you need anything, buddy, just holler."

"I appreciate it."

My email inbox flooded with messages. One was from Agent Croft. I WISH I WOULD'VE LISTENED TO YOU MORE THE FIRST TIME. YOU WERE RIGHT. KERMIT, I'M SO SORRY.

Yes, and maybe next time you deploy, you'll consider this. She'd been a civilian agent on her first deployment, and she did an incredible job. She just didn't have the experience. It'd been hard for her to fathom the dangers—until now. I wasn't angry with her. Now, there was nothing I could do about it. I didn't know what to say, and thinking about it was too much of a burden. I had other things to do, so I didn't reply.

Orion showed up at my office. "Mortuary Affairs called about the ceremony for boarding our guys on the Angel Flight back home," he said. "We told them that we don't want an honor guard to perform the ceremony—we want to learn it and put our guys on the aircraft."

"Okay, let me tell Commander Mitchell."

I went to Commander Mitchell's office. His eyes were red, and he looked beat.

"The agents want to learn the ceremony for loading our guys on the plane, sir," I said.

He looked down for a moment. Then he looked up at me with tears in his eyes. "I'm not going to be able to do that." His voice cracked. "Can you handle it?"

The underlying responsibilities of a commander for typical daily ops is a heavy load in itself. Now, he was not only communicating answers to leadership but also family members of our fallen. I couldn't imagine the weight of it all. "Yeah, I've got it."

"Thanks," he said.

Commander Mitchell continued to field questions from our base and different parts of the world. He received a phone call from Colonel Gray, the OSI regional boss whose command included all the EDets in the Middle East and Afghanistan. She controlled all the resources, including agents, vehicles, and money. She'd be flying out from Al Udeid Air Base, Qatar the next day.

Back in my office, my Ranger vest, boots, and other gear sat in the corner smelling like fire, blood, and death. I couldn't get that odor out of my nose. Showering didn't help. It seemed to last forever. The smell was a sad reminder that I carried with me.

The hours disappeared, and I lost track of where one day ended and another began. OSI officers came from Baghdad for the memorial ceremony. Colonel Gray arrived from Qatar with her Command Chief master sergeant and a psychologist. General Dana Simmons, the top boss of OSI, flew out from headquarters at Quantico, Virginia. He brought citations and medals for Nate, Tom, and Dave: a Purple Heart and Bronze Star for each. General Simmons and the other bigwigs met with our commander.

Later, the psychologist came to my office. "How are you holding up?" he asked.

"I'm doing fine," I said. "Some of these other guys are a lot younger and probably more affected than I am, so you might want to talk to them first."

He left me to speak with the others.

◇   ◇   ◇

We attended the memorial ceremony to honor and respect our guys. First Cav troops, 101st Airborne paratroopers, pilots, mechanics, doctors, nurses, OSI agents from other parts of the world, and others—hundreds—filed into a large Quonset hut and filled rows of metal folding chairs. I sat in front facing them with Commander Mitchell and General Simmons beside me. Behind us on a makeshift field stage was a battlefield cross for each man: a pair of combat boots at the base of a rifle pointed down with a helmet placed on the top of the rifle butt. Dog tags rested on each rifle. Behind the three battlefield crosses was the American flag.

The national anthem played, and we stood at attention and faced the flag. Afterwards, we took our seats, and the chaplain said a prayer.

General Simmons stepped up to the podium and spoke about each agent,

"Master Sergeant Thomas Crowell deployed to the Middle East in support of Operations Desert Shield and Desert Storm. Later, he served in Africa to support Operation Restore Hope II. Recently, he served as the Superintendent of the Air Force Office of Special Investigations Expeditionary Detachment 2411 here in Balad, Iraq, to support Operation Iraqi Freedom. And I am told that he will be awarded his bachelor's degree in criminal justice from Park University in Missouri. Agent Thomas Crowell exhibited among the highest levels of leadership, team building, and mentorship.

"Also in EDet 2411 served Staff Sergeant David Wieger, who joined the air force in 1999 as a Visual Imagery and Intrusion Detection System Apprentice. Through his outstanding work, he later specialized in technical surveillance countermeasures and supported all air force installations on the West Coast, including Hawaii and Alaska. Here in Balad, he provided his expert investigative and technical skills to his fellow agents, and he displayed the highest values of integrity, service, and excellence in all he did.

"Serving with them was Nathan Schuldheiss, who earned his Juris Doctorate before becoming a civilian agent for the Air Force Office of Special Investigations. He volunteered to deploy here to OSI EDet 2411 to support

Operation Iraqi Freedom. Recently, Agent Nathan Schuldheiss was selected above his peers as the Civilian Special Agent of the Quarter.

"All three of these agents bravely identified, investigated, and neutralized insurgent threats to personnel and resources of the United States Air Force and the Department of Defense, protecting the national security of America. They were on a mission to gather intelligence about insurgents when they were hit by a roadside bomb. They will always be honored and never forgotten."

The general paused. "And we will get the people who did this. That's what we do." He returned to his seat.

Commander Mitchell took his turn at the podium. He spoke about his personal relationship with the men and about the important work they did—and I couldn't listen so closely anymore. I didn't want to break down—I still had to present their awards. Commander Mitchell's words floated in the air of a dream that I faded in and out of. He mentioned his friendship with Tom, who truly cared about his agents and was among the finest leaders he'd known. Commander Mitchell recalled Dave's infectious smile and selfless service. Then he highlighted Nate's lust for life, his mischievous smile, and the aggressive way he went after insurgents. "Tom, Dave, and Nate actioned many missions, which captured over a dozen insurgents and stopped dozens more threats to all of us here on this base. They're all heroes." Commander Mitchell talked as much as he could without it getting to him. Then he steeled himself and forged his way back to his seat.

Tim McGraw's song "If You're Reading This" played, accompanied by a slideshow tribute projected on a big screen off to the side: Nate and Huey working out together in the gym; Nate presenting gifts from his sister's elementary school in the US to Iraqi schoolchildren; Nate striking a hipster commando pose; and in the evening, up on the EDet rooftop, Nate drinking tea with Professor. Dave and I making Hulk poses with the kids in the village; Dave and Mac working at their desks in the bullpen; Dave doing tricks with a soccer ball. Tom and Commander Mitchell sharing a smile in Tom's office; Tom anxiously opening a package from his wife; Tom smoking a cigar on the porch with Doug and me.

My chest tightened up, my eyes watered, and I couldn't watch anymore. I had to keep myself together. So many people in the audience wept; I couldn't spot a dry eye in the building. I busied myself thinking about the awards I was about to present.

When the slideshow tribute ended, I stood and made my way to the podium. "Attention to orders," I called.

Everyone on the floor smartly stood to attention and snapped out of their tears.

I read the Bronze Star citation: each agent's job to protect air force and DOD assets, how many missions they'd been part of, and combat operations they participated in.

Then the chaplain gave the benediction.

Finally, "Taps" was played.

Commander Mitchell, our EDet, others, and I lined up and waited our turn to take a knee before the battlefield cross of each of our fallen friends. Some said a prayer or held a moment of silence.

Some of us lingered and talked. I overheard an agent say: "Nate replied, 'You don't know, I could be gone tomorrow.' It's like he knew."

I remembered the hair standing on the back of Dave's neck in Kaiser Soze's village and Tom not being a cigarette smoker but smoking that cigarette before he mounted up in the convoy that terrible night. It was like all three of them knew death was near. They didn't know exactly when or where, but they knew it was coming.

We departed the building. I wanted to figure out who did this. This was personal.

Back in my office at the compound, Commander Mitchell appeared in my doorway.

"Sir?" I asked.

"You should call your wife," he said.

"Shit," I said. I'd forgotten to call the people who meant the most to me—my wife and kids.

Commander Mitchell explained, "People back home know agents in Balad were killed, but a lot of them don't know who. Your home detachment thinks it was you."

"I'll call her."

Commander Mitchell left.

I exited my office, picked up the iridium phone, and went up on the roof to make the call.

"Hello?" my wife said.

"It's me," I said.

She became unusually silent. I didn't know if she was crying or what. There'd been other times when she was worried, but this was different.

"I'm guessing you heard what happened to us," I said.

"Yeah." There was a long pause. "I thought it was you."

Her words caught me by surprise. "The days here blended into one long day," I said, "and I don't remember sleeping much."

She was quiet.

I shook my head. "I'm sorry I didn't call earlier."

I could hear her breathing.

I told her what I could about what happened that night. Then I whined about how *maybe I should've done this*, and *maybe I should've done that*.

"I don't know what to think," she said.

"We're going to get the people who did this to us. I don't know how long it's going to take, but we're going to get them."

"You're not a cat," she said.

"What?" I asked.

"You don't have nine lives."

I thought about her words and other close calls I had.

"I'm on my way to pick up the kids from school," she said.

"Be safe," I said.

"You too."

⊕   ⊕   ⊕

The Mortuary Affairs honor guard trained the other agents and me to do the ceremony to send our guys home. The next day, we did it for real wearing our downrange gear. The entire air force wing—pilots, medical and support personnel, and others—stood in ranks beside the runway where a C-130 sat.

My fellow agents and I carried Nate, Tom, and Dave's remains in aluminum caskets draped with American flags. I gave the commands, and we marched each one up the ramp onto the back of the C-130, where we laid each one down and gave him our final salute. Then we marched off the plane.

The ceremony ended, and I helped Mac load his things on the plane. We shook hands and I said, "Please tell Nate's family I'm sorry."

"For what, man?" he said.

I fought hard to keep my eyes from watering up. "Tell them I tried."

Mac had tears in his eyes. "Man, it's not your fault."

I hoped my words might somehow comfort them. "Just tell them I'm sorry."

Mac boarded the plane, and they closed the hatches. Then the C-130, now designated "Angel Flight," lumbered down the runway. Soon it lifted into the air. Higher and higher our friends flew.

I'd spent a lot of time with them, and it affected me. I recalled when I was making changes to Mac and Dave's mission for that night. In a matter of seconds, I thought about switching places with Nate in Hammer One so he could be with his buddy, but I made a tactical choice instead. As a leader, I felt responsible for their deaths. I couldn't fathom how hard it must've hit Commander Mitchell.

In the distance, Angel Flight continued to rise higher and higher, becoming smaller and smaller—until my buddies were gone.

CHAPTER 29

BAGHDAD BOB

BACK AT THE RANCH, WE swiftly went to work trying to figure out who'd done this to us. Meanwhile, talk filtered down that, due to the circumstances and us being short four agents, powers above were considering sending a whole detachment to relieve us. I was too busy trying to figure out who killed our guys to worry about it. Our agents didn't want to be replaced; they wanted to finish the job. Word must've gotten back up the chain of command, and we were allowed to stay.

OSI's Anti-Terrorism Specialty Team (AST), created years ago by a former army Special Forces major turned OSI agent, sent four agents from their base in San Antonio, Texas, to help us out. Orion had served in the same unit. I was ordered to train at a couple of their schools to audit their courses to see how they compared to schools I attended in the SEAL Teams. When the AST agents arrived at our compound, Orion knew four, and I recognized two of them. One was a Hawaiian guy called Maui, and the other was Del, with whom I'd trained at a shooting school in Las Vegas and a defensive driving course in Richmond, Virginia. Maui had served in Balad previously, and he already knew the area. Del had started out as an enlisted OSI agent before leaving the military to come back as a civilian agent. He had a big family with lots of kids. The ASTs were in their early thirties and experienced, and I was happy to see them—but I harbored some concerns.

Five months earlier, in Kirkuk, Iraq, OSI agents Matthew Kuglics and Ryan Balmer were killed when their vehicle hit an IED. Afterwards, when ASTs flew out to assist, one of them stirred up rumors that one of the fallen agents hadn't received the medical attention he needed soon enough, causing his death. Both the detachment commander and the superintendent of the EDet in Kirkuk came under scrutiny, and their unit was investigated. The findings were that there was nothing more anyone could've done with the training they had. My commander, the other agents, and I worried that one of the incoming ASTs would put us through the same ordeal.

"No, these guys aren't like that," Orion assured us. "The AST who went to Kirkuk was an outlier—I don't know why he did that."

I brought Maui and Del into my office, and I got right to it: "We don't want any of you guys to do to us what was done in Kirkuk."

Maui leaned back and said, "This is the first I'm hearing of it."

Del raised his eyebrows and said, "Don't compare us to that AST."

"Okay. I didn't think so," I said, "but I had to clarify."

Another AST, the senior of the four, came to my office and said, "I was wondering if you might brief me on your sources here, so we can figure out how to help."

"Sure." I showed him photos of the confidential informants.

He pointed to one of the photos. "I used to run that guy in Baghdad," he said. "He's a professional source."

"Our codename for him is Baghdad Bob," I said. "He's probably already killed people, and I don't trust him."

"He did kill someone," the senior AST said calmly. "Baghdad Bob shot a dude in the face while he was sitting in his car."

"Nate trusted him too much, and I don't like him," I said.

❖　❖　❖

I couldn't sleep at night, so I worked. When daylight came, I pulled aside Devil Dog, Professor, Orion and other agents for help. We sent out word to our sources to contact us if they knew anything about the attack. One by one, we crossed off names from the suspect tree on my whiteboard.

We called Moped to come meet us on base, but he wouldn't. He insisted that we meet him off the base, but we weren't ready to go out on patrol yet. Some of our agents were still working on installing comms, a machine gun, and other equipment on our replacement Humvee.

One day, Professor stopped by my office and said, "Remember that asset of Nate's who ran with Sunni insurgents so he could get more intel on them—then he was arrested and imprisoned in a holding cell at FOB Orion?"

"Baghdad Bob," I said. "You and Nate told Captain al-Hakim that Baghdad Bob was one of the good guys. Nate asked Captain al-Hakim to free Baghdad Bob, but he refused. Then you and Nate got in the captain's face."

"Yes," Professor said. "Later, Nate got Baghdad Bob sprung."

"I remember."

"Well, Baghdad Bob was beginning to report to us that Captain al-Hakim was into something bad, but he needed more information."

I thought about it for a moment. "You know, Captain al-Hakim is the only one with the autonomy to be out and about at night in that area. Maybe it was him who took the potshots at us during that evening meet with Moped—trying to prevent any information from being passed on about him. Let's see what Devil Dog has on him."

We went over to Devil Dog's office and asked.

"I already have a file on the captain," Devil Dog said. "Let me find it." He searched the files on his computer. "This is it: both Captain al-Hakim and Moped are Shiites from the city of Dujail. Within two years, Captain al-Hakim was promoted from an E-3 to O-3. In the short space of two years, he jumped over six enlisted ranks and four officer ranks to get where he is now. His connections go all the way up to the Minister of the Interior, who is also a Shiite."

"Wow," I said.

"There's more," Devil Dog said. "He was suspected of killing his former commanding officer. Now everyone, including his new commanding officer, is afraid of him."

I turned to Professor and said, "You and Burl need to talk with Baghdad Bob."

Professor nodded and said he'd set it up with Burl.

Later that day, Baghdad Bob came and met with them.

"You took so long to call," Baghdad Bob said.

"We got busy with other things," Burl said.

"I heard what happened," Baghdad Bob said. "Everyone between the base and Dujail heard. Nate was my friend, and I'm madder than hell about what happened to him. I wanted to find out who did it, and I've been listening to people talking. Now I know."

"Know what?" Burl asked.

"Who did it."

"Who?" Burl asked.

"Captain al-Hakim," Baghdad Bob said. "He was so angry that Nate released me from jail and that I'd been spying around in his city. He was worried that he'd be outed."

"Are you sure?" Burl asked.

"Yes, I'm sure. This captain killed his own commander—a colonel. Another time, he threw a grenade into the house of a Sunni family. It killed all the people inside except for a little girl who ran out the back. He spotted her and shot her in the back. That's the kind of animal he is."

After the meet, Burl and Professor briefed me and Devil Dog.

"We need to have Captain al-Hakim come in for a visit," I said.

Professor called him. "We need to talk to you."

Captain al-Hakim said, "I'm not afraid to talk with you."

"Why would you say that?" Professor asked.

"Say what?" Captain al-Hakim asked.

"Why would you say you're not afraid to talk with us?"

"I have to go." He hung up.

Minutes later, Moped called and said he'd meet us on the base. It was highly unusual, as if Captain al-Hakim had ordered Moped to show up in his place.

We prepared for Moped's arrival by going over how we would interview him. Most meets on base were conducted in a different location than our compound, but we were pretty sure Moped wouldn't be leaving too soon, so we prepared the trailer in our compound.

In the aftermath of the attack, lots of people asked if there was anything they could do to help. One of those people was with OSI: Agent Smith. He worked with a unit across the base focused on strategic impacting missions or missions that can affect US goals throughout Iraq. Our missions were tactical, focused on the immediate areas around Balad Air Base.

Now I decided to take Agent Smith up on his offer and called him. "We have a suspect coming in to talk to us. We call him Moped. He might be connected to some people you'd be interested in. After we finish with Moped, you guys want to take a crack?"

"Hell yeah. We'd love to," he said.

I wondered if his people could administer a polygraph, too. "Can you poly him?"

"Sure," Agent Smith said. He came over and briefed me on what questions to ask and how to word them.

"Thanks." He left, and I went to the bullpen to share the information with Orion.

Meanwhile, Professor tried to call Captain al-Hakim, but he didn't answer his phone.

Moped arrived at the base gate. Orion, Maui, Agent Smith, and I met him there. After the soldiers searched him, Orion, Maui, and I searched him again and seized his belongings.

Then Orion, Maui, and I escorted Moped back to our compound, where we took him around back and into our trailer—the same place where Hollywood had stayed.

Moped strutted inside the trailer like a peacock and sat down at the dining table with his legs spread wide.

Huey had returned from his R&R, and he and Orion interviewed Moped. Professor translated.

Huey and Orion started out being nice.

I didn't like it, but I'd played good cop before, and I understood their strategy.

Moped pushed out his chest and cocked his head. He probed us with his eyes as if he owned us.

Orion talked to him about the meet where we hit the explosive. Orion purposefully gave a false narrative about the explosive, hoping that Moped's arrogance would kick in and he'd correct him: "It was a common IED made from a 120mm mortar round wired to a detonation device. Someone initiated it by flipping a switch," Orion said.

Moped's eyes lit up, and he cut off Orion. "How do you know it was that kind of IED? How do you know it wasn't a more sophisticated IED? How do you know it wasn't pressure activated?"

Moped had taken the bait and hooked himself. Now we knew he was involved.

Huey stood up. "I've heard enough. I hope you burn in hell." Then he walked out.

Professor continued to translate.

Moped sneered. "What? What's his problem?"

I was angry. I flipped the dining table, and it almost landed on top of him.

Moped gasped and jerked back, closing his legs.

I stared at him.

His body stiffened.

A knock came at the door. I stepped outside to see who it was. Agent Smith stood there with a big black bag and a smile.

"Come on in," I said. He entered, and I righted the table so he could set up his equipment.

Orion stepped out of the room.

Moped scratched the back of his hand. "What's that?"

"It's a lie detector," Agent Smith said.

Moped continued scratching. "What for?"

"To detect lies," Agent Smith said. "But you have nothing to worry about if you're telling us the truth. You're telling us the truth right?"

Moped cleared his throat. "Right."

"All right then. Let's do it."

Agent Smith attached a cuff to Moped's arm to measure blood pressure, a fingertip device to check his pulse rate, and a chest band to record his breathing.

"How accurate is this machine?" Moped asked.

"Real accurate," Agent Smith said. "It's a lie detector." He turned on his laptop, connected the arm band, fingertip device, and chest band to it. Then he gave a thumbs up. "Okay, I'll start with an easy question or two."

Moped couldn't stop scratching his hand.

"Don't do that," Agent Smith said. "You might give a false reading. Don't move. Simply answer the questions."

Moped stopped scratching. "Okay."

"Are you on a US military base?" Agent Smith asked.

"Yes," Moped said.

"Did you have an appointment to meet with agents on the evening of November 1?"

"Yes."

Agent Smith reeled him in. "Why were you late to the meet?"

Moped paused. "My moped wouldn't start."

"What was wrong with it?" Agent Smith asked.

"I don't know. That's why I was late."

"You must've figured out what was wrong with it. You came later. What was wrong with it?"

"Battery."

Agent Smith studied his laptop monitor. "You were late because of your moped battery?"

"Yes."

"Did you have anything to do with the agents being killed?" Agent Smith asked.

"No."

"Did you kill them?"

"No."

Agent Smith observed his monitor as he continued the interview. Then he stopped, stood up, and walked over to me. "Can I speak with you outside?"

I nodded.

The two of us stepped out of the trailer and closed the door. The sun fell out of the sky and took its light with it.

"That's your guy," Agent Smith said.

"Are you sure?"

"I've been doing this for a long time, and that's him."

Agent Smith's cell phone rang. "Just a minute." He turned away from me and answered it. "Yeah, what's up?" Then there was a pause. He turned back to me and said, "Can we have Moped?"

"Yeah, if you can answer who he's connected to, who set us up, who planted the EFP—all that shit."

"No problem," Agent Smith said. He relayed my words to whoever was on the other end of the phone.

We went back inside, and Agent Smith disconnected the lie detector from Moped, then packed it in his carrying bag.

Moped scratched his hand. "Did I pass?"

We didn't say anything.

"What?" Moped asked.

"Just shut up and wait," I said.

I'd wasted half of my day with this shitbird, and I couldn't wait to get rid of him. Then I received a phone call from Jimmy Stewart.

I went outside and answered it. "Hello?"

"Got two people who claim to be the mother and brother of Moped," Jimmy Stewart said. "They're asking where he is."

"Tell them to leave their contact information, and I'll get back to them." I went back inside the trailer.

Minutes later, I heard the sound of a vehicle. I looked outside, and a white van with no windows backed up to our trailer. I opened the door. Two men hopped out of the van and rushed inside our trailer. I pointed to Moped.

"What—what's going on?" Moped cried.

They put a black bag on his head, cuffed him, and scuttled him outside.

"No!" Moped shouted.

They tossed him in the back of the van, slammed the door shut, and spun off in a cloud of dust.

Professor and I secured the trailer and debriefed with Orion and Devil Dog in his office. After we finished, I retreated to my office.

Several hours later, Agent Smith showed up at my door with a white guy and a Muslim woman. "These are the two interrogators," Agent Smith said.

The male interrogator said, "Moped told us that Captain al-Hakim had already been thinking of hitting your men with a roadside bomb, but he had to get permission from higher ranking Shia, which he did. That night, within an hour after Moped called you, Captain al-Hakim, two of his soldiers, and Moped planted the explosive device in the road. Moped also gave us information about some other people we're interested in."

I was curious. "What the hell did you guys do to Moped to get all this information?"

The Muslim woman answered. "Oh, we only isolated him. They don't like to be isolated."

I shook my head in disbelief. I didn't give a shit what they did to him. I had the information I needed. I didn't care how they got it.

CHAPTER 30

THE TRIAL

THE NEXT DAY, MOPED WAS flown to a prison in Baghdad to await trial by the Central Criminal Court of Iraq (CCCI). There, they investigated and judged suspected insurgents, terrorists, organized criminals, and corrupt government officials.

Meanwhile, back at Balad, I talked with Major Sherwood and others in the First Cav: "What do we have to do to get the green light to go after Captain al-Hakim?"

"He's an officer—an ally who belongs to our host country. It'll take a lot of proof and a lot of paperwork," Major Sherwood said. "We can't action him until you put all that together."

It was as if Captain al-Hakim was untouchable. Despite the challenge, the other agents and I put our noses to the grindstone to build a package to nail him. We interviewed sources and recorded what he'd been involved in.

Soon the CCCI summoned Orion, Burl, and me to Baghdad to testify against Moped. We needed a strong case against him in order to line up evidence against Captain al-Hakim. I packed my bags and rode out of the EDet compound with Orion and Burl to the helo pad, where a Black Hawk's helicopter blades spun. We climbed aboard and buckled ourselves in.

A cute little blonde pilot with aquamarine eyes spirited us away from our base. As she flew near the Tigris River, her gunners fired their weapons.

Burl sat up straight. "What the hell—already?"

I leaned back and breathed easy. "They're just test firing."

The odor of helo fuel and steel was comfortingly familiar. My seat rumbled, and vibrations pulsated through me. Blades chopped the air above with a throbbing sound that lulled me into their rhythm. The pilot bent the throttle, and I closed my eyes. For a moment, I blew out the bad of Balad.

When I opened my eyes, we descended into Baghdad. Below, a black Suburban SUV rested near a helo pad. As the Suburban grew larger, I recognized the man standing beside it—Major Jones—an OSI agent whom I'd gone through pre-deployment training with. Now he worked with a joint military intelligence group that synergized intel for all of Iraq. More agents came out of the SUV and joined him.

The pilot gently touched down the bird. I unassed the helo with Orion and Burl. The wind of the whirling blades whipped at my beard and T-shirt, and I put a hand on my baseball cap to keep it in place.

Major Jones held out his hand. "Been awhile."

I shook it. "A lot has happened."

"I heard about some of it." He motioned for us to load up in the black beast, and we did. Then we sped away.

We veered onto the Qadisiyyah Expressway and picked up speed. Iraqi shops, a TV station, mosque domes, and a hospital marked with the star and crescent moon symbols floated past.

Minutes later, we slowed down. Up ahead, barbed wire fences and twelve-foot-high concrete blast walls came into view—the Green Zone. We paused at a military checkpoint, and the driver flashed his ID. The checkpoint guard waved us through. Our SUV rolled into the protective bubble of the international zone.

We cruised past the Italian embassy. Beyond it flowed the turquoise waters of the Tigris River. On the opposite side of the road stood the Iraqi Supreme court. We passed between Babylon College and the US Embassy. After several mosques, we reached the center of the city, marked by the bronze Freedom Monument.

We turned into a smaller checkpoint, and the driver flashed his ID before he parked in the lot of a building with a porcupine of antennas on the roof.

I dismounted the vehicle. Being a federal agent, I openly carried my Sig Sauer pistol on my rigger's belt and displayed my badge on my cargo pants. Orion and Burl were outfitted similarly. We must've appeared a cross between Wild West gunfighters and a modern posse.

We split up. Major Jones led me upstairs and escorted me onto my floor. There, a charismatic agent laughed with a curvy gal with cinnamon-colored hair and a brown-skinned beauty with an inviting smile.

"How's it going?" the agent said in greeting.

His breath had a hint of alcohol on it.

"This is Jack Treadway, the EDet ops officer in Balad," Major Jones said.

The agent's smile faded, and he nodded politely.

We left them.

Major Jones escorted me to a simple barracks style room with a bunkbed. "Would you like to see or do anything right away?"

"Nah, man. I only want to sleep," I said.

He handed me a business card. "Okay. If you change your mind, call me."

"Thanks." I settled in and was preparing to go to bed when a knock came at my door. I crossed the room and opened it.

It was the charismatic agent from the hall. "Would you like to come over and join us?" he asked.

It was the last thing on my mind. "I appreciate you thinking about me, but I really want to get some sleep."

"Well, have a good rest," he said kindly. "If you change your mind, you'll be welcome."

"Thanks."

⊹ ⊹ ⊹

The next morning, I went downstairs and joined Orion and Burl in Major Jones's office, and we waited for our ride.

Major Jones asked me, "Do you know a SEAL officer named Bomber?"

How could I forget my former officer in charge who got sick so easily—on the sea puking on the back of my neck, passing out at the sight of the needle sticking out of his arm, and blowing chunks during our roller coaster ride over the snowy mountains of Korea. "Yeah, I served in two platoons with Bomber at Team Five. He's a good officer and takes care of his guys."

"Yeah, he was here working with us, and he left yesterday. He slept there on that couch you're sitting on."

I grinned. "Small world."

Our ride arrived and shuttled us to the edge of the Green Zone. Two giant bronze hands held curved swords, weighing twenty-four tons each, forming Saddam Hussein's Victory Arch. Below the swords lay thousands of helmets.

We continued to the offices of the US Judge Advocate General (JAG), where we passed another checkpoint before entering a resort-like compound marked by palm trees, a swimming pool, and a cabana. Military servicemen and servicewomen from various branches as well as civilians walked between the office buildings.

"These people are really living it up here," I said.

"Yeah," Orion said.

Our driver parked, and he hopped out with us. We strolled over to a cluster of buildings.

A thin-necked guy in a polo shirt approached us. His eyes went to the pistol on my hip and he halted, blocking our path. "Who are you guys?" he asked.

Our driver explained.

Thin Neck shook his head. "You can't come in here without ID badges."

I thought about punching him out and taking his ID badge, but I kept my Wild West fantasies to myself.

Boom! The ground shook, but I couldn't see where the explosion came from.

Thin Neck ran away from us, and others scattered too.

Orion, Burl, and I simply stood there and looked at each other.

"Really? Again?" I said.

"We can't escape this shit," Orion said.

Burl hung his head.

Later, we'd find out that an army Stryker vehicle was hit with an IED—another EFP—killing one soldier and wounding another. The blast was on the road just on the other side of the barriers protecting us.

Our driver led us into one of the buildings. There the JAG met us. He brought us into his office one at a time and took our statements.

I was last. I thought I was only going to testify about Moped, but the JAG said, "I want you to recount everything that happened the night your men hit the IED." His interest seemed morbid and unnecessary.

I didn't want to, but if there was a chance it would help make the case against Moped and later Captain al-Hakim, I would. Uncomfortable, I told him about the fireball and finding Nate's body; the intense heat on the driver's side and having to go around to find another way to rescue my teammates, only to discover that Dave was dead too; the hope that Tom might somehow have survived the blast, only to find out he hadn't; loading my three friends into body bags—and every painful detail in between. I could smell the fire and the blood and the death again. The darkness and the numbness returned. I became furious at the JAG for asking me to tell him more than he needed, but I hid my anger. The recounting of events made my chest tighten and gave me a strange dizzy feeling, as if everything around me was in slow motion.

After I left his office, I told Orion and Burl, "He made me tell him more than I think he needed me to."

"What did you see that night?" Burl asked.

"You know what I saw," I said.

Burl leaned forward and raised his voice. "I don't know. I didn't go in with you!"

"I told you and the others," I said.

"I want to know more."

Burl seemed odd to me. "Dude, I'm not telling you all the details," I said. "That's morbid. Why would you want to know? I could've gone the rest of my life without seeing that."

Burl became angrier and persisted: "I want to know everything that happened!"

The irony didn't escape me. Burl was the most experienced agent in our EDet, but he was the least competent and showed the least bravery. Now, he was showing the least respect for the sacred sacrifice of our guys—and he attempted to trample on my grief to satisfy his own freak curiosity.

"If the details were so damn important to you, why didn't you switch places with Mac and stand by my side that night? That's just sick!"

Much later, after I returned stateside, Commander Mitchell would tell me that Burl requested that he be awarded a bronze medal. "What for?" I asked. Commander Mitchell had the same question. I didn't understand Burl, and he disappointed me.

Soon the JAG's assistant escorted us through the halls of what seemed like a giant headquarters out of Washington. In another part of the building, we filled out paperwork.

We ate lunch before riding to the CCCI with our legal counsel in a couple of SUVs. The courtroom wasn't like any I'd seen in the States. Two Iraqi judges sat behind desks facing us. Off to the side sat a defendant in a white jumpsuit with his back to the wall. The witnesses and their team were seated in the two front rows facing the judges. The JAG, Orion, Burl, and I waited our turn.

When the case before us ended, we moved up to the seats in front. Moped was brought in and sat to the side wearing a white jumpsuit. He had a dazed look on his face.

Orion, Burl, and I gave our testimonies. We mentioned how Moped was involved with Captain al-Hakim, but we walked on thin ice accusing an Iraqi military officer who was supposed to be on our side.

The two judges' reactions seemed strange. They didn't appear to give a shit one way or the other. One turned to Moped and asked, "What do you have to say to this?"

Moped spoke Arabic and the courtroom interpreter translated. "I didn't do anything. I didn't have anything to do with it." He gave no explanation for his actions. His defense seemed to be ignorance.

After the trial finished, I wasn't sure what would happen next, but I felt as if I'd accomplished something—we all did—and that something would be done.

CHAPTER 31

PSYCHOLOGICAL

WE RETURNED TO BALAD, AND I wanted a green light to kill or capture Captain al-Hakim. Secretly, I hoped we'd go in after him, he'd attempt to fight his way out, and we'd kill him. We discussed who would go capture him and how, but we got ahead of ourselves. First, we needed statements and a solid case to gain authorization to go after a military officer—a supposed ally.

In my office, I labored on it along with several other missions while rocking out to an internet radio channel that played Foo Fighters, Staind, and Nickelback. I was typing up a coordination with the First Cav guys and the 101st when a knock came at my door.

"Door's open," I said.

Dr. Blackwell, an OSI psychologist came in and took a chair.

I stopped typing.

Dr. Blackwell's eyes fixated on my stereo speaker. I hadn't been paying attention to the lyrics, but he seemed to be.

Creed sang about burning, survivor's guilt, holding out for sunshine, and no time for mourning. It was a random song, but the timing was so wrong. I didn't want to be analyzed.

Ah shit.

"What song is that?" Dr. Blackwell asked.

"'My Own Prison,'" I said.

"Oh."

"Some random song—I'm good, man. No worse than anyone else. What do you want us to do?"

Dr. Blackwell studied me. "What do you want to do?"

I gestured at the work on my desk. "Keep working."

"Okay."

"You don't remember me, do you?" I said.

197

"I'm sorry?" he said.

"We spoke over the phone about a case in Florida—some other agents and I worked a case to catch a serial rapist who met guys in bars and spiked their drinks with GHB, then kidnapped and raped them. I asked if you had any ideas for interviewing someone who underwent a traumatic experience. You told me some things to do before I interviewed the victim."

"How'd that go?" he asked.

"He's doing fifty years in Leavenworth."

We chit-chatted a little more before he left.

Later that evening, I met with my commander in his office. With him was Dr. Blackwell and the command chief master sergeant from our base in Qatar.

"Have a seat," Commander Mitchell said.

I felt an ambush coming. Slowly, I sat down.

"I'll get right to it," Commander Mitchell said. "I need you to go with Dr. Blackwell and the chief to Qatar to take three days R&R." All the agents who'd served in Balad were encouraged to take R&R in Qatar for three days during their six-month tour.

In the Teams, a six-month deployment was no reason for R&R. "No, I don't think that's what I want to do. Taking R&R with all this stuff going on doesn't seem right, and missions we have on the board here are what I need to do."

The chief piped in. "We knew you were going to be against this, but it's an order from Colonel Gray."

There was no use fighting it. This was coming down from our boss in Qatar. "Roger," I said.

"After you pack your bags, you can leave them by the front door," the chief said. "You'll leave with us tomorrow morning."

"Will do," I said.

I left Commander Mitchell's office, told the other agents, packed my bags, and dumped them outside the door of my office as instructed. Then I returned to my desk.

An agent from Qatar emailed me. I knew her from FLETC, where she'd been a good friend to Nate, Mac, and me. I read her email: WE'RE GOING TO PUT YOU UP IN AN EXCELLENT HOTEL WITH A POOL AND EVERYTHING. WHAT DO YOU WANT TO DRINK? WE'LL STOCK YOUR REFRIGERATOR. She was really cool about it.

About that time, one of our sources fingered a Shiite man in Dujail who was involved in setting the IED that we hit. He seemed to be part of the hierarchy that gave the materials and the green light to Captain al-Hakim. Commander Mitchell wouldn't sign off on a mission to bag the guy until we had a decent-sized army contingent with us, so we planned for troops from the

Third Infantry Division to escort us with APCs and tanks. It was Burl's area, so he'd take the lead on this. Maui, two more ASTs, Professor, and another agent from our EDet would accompany him. The mission was planned for the next morning. I told the agents that I'd been ordered to leave the same morning to fly out to Qatar for R&R.

Morning arrived, and I made final preparations for my trip.

Burl trudged into my office jocked up and apprehensive as all hell—reasonably so, given that this was one of the first missions after we'd been hit. "Where're you going?" he asked.

"It's like I told you and the others yesterday. They're making me go to Qatar for three days."

He shuffled a step back and had a shocked look on his face.

I tried to reason with him: "This is your op, your area, and you're the most experienced agent. This mission is yours," I said.

His body stiffened, and he squeezed his eyes shut.

"You want me to go with you, don't you?" I said.

He opened his eyes. "That'd be great!"

I didn't want to go to Qatar anyway. I jocked up, grabbed my helmet and rifle, and stepped over my bag. I marched over to Commander Mitchell's door. It was cracked a quarter of the way. I knocked. "Sir?"

"Enter," Commander Mitchell's voice called out from inside.

I went in. Dr. Blackwell and the chief sat in front of Commander Mitchell, who was at his desk. The three of them looked up at me.

"What's up, Kermit?" Commander Mitchell asked.

"Burl wants me to go on this mission with them, and I think it's a good idea," I said.

Dr. Blackwell and the chief turned their heads as if to see Commander Mitchell's reaction. He didn't say anything.

"Guys?" I said.

The three of them fixed their gaze on me.

I cleared my throat. "This is better for me than going to Qatar and sitting on my ass."

It was as if I'd dropped a stun grenade in the room. Nobody said a word.

I eased out of Commander Mitchell's office. Then I caught up with Burl and told him, "Get the rigs ready to roll."

Burl hopped to it.

Dr. Blackwell came out and walked up to me.

"Yes?" I asked.

"I talked it over with your commander and the chief. It's probably better for you to keep working. We understand."

I put on my helmet. "I appreciate what you guys are doing—really."

I mounted up with Burl, Maui, and the others in two Humvees. We drove across the base and linked up with the Third ID convoy.

When I met with the patrol leader—an army lieutenant I hadn't worked with before—I was shocked to see only four Humvees and an APC. "Where are the other APCs and tanks?" I asked.

"They got pulled for another mission," the lieutenant said matter-of-factly.

I shook my head in disbelief.

We lined up our Humvees and the one APC and rolled out of the gate. I dreaded the sixteen-mile drive—each an opportunity for booger-eaters to plant IEDs on that route.

We traveled southeast on the highway. Military traffic came from the opposite direction. *If they're safe, maybe we'll be safe too.* I breathed a little easier.

A little over half an hour later, the bland sprawl of Dujail came into view, and my heart rate increased. It looked like a mini-Mogadishu from *Black Hawk Down*. It was a Shia city, and I always felt the Shia were more dangerous than Sunnis or al Qaeda because the Shia had the Iranian government backing them. I took deep breaths to try to calm down.

Our convoy drove clockwise around the perimeter until we reached the east side, where we entered. We turned left then right, probing deeper. I searched for landmarks in case everything turned to shit and we had to get the hell out—a pharmacy, a clump of trees, and a row of five identical stucco houses. We pulled up to our target house and formed a perimeter.

People came out of their homes and shops and from off the street to see what we were doing. Soon there was a swarm of them around us.

"Stay back!" a soldier warned.

Infantrymen cleared the target house. Then our agents did site exploitation, searching for and gathering intel—nothing. I didn't want to come all the way out here just to end up empty-handed, so I thought I'd send a message. I told Professor to ask the crowd if they knew our target and where he was. I didn't care if they answered.

One guy seemed especially interested in us and what we were doing. He spoke to Professor in Arabic.

"This one says he has something," Professor said.

I turned to the man and asked, "Do you know where the owner of this house is?"

"Yes, I can help you. Will you pay me?" the man said.

"Yes," I said.

The man stepped closer and said quietly, "I know his uncle. He's normally with him. But you have to make it look like you're arresting me and taking me away. These people around here are his friends."

"Fine." I kicked his feet out, put him on the ground, and cuffed him.

He twisted and yelled, "Hey, I'm innocent! I don't know anything!" He put on a performance.

We shoved him in the Humvee, I called the lieutenant, and we convoyed the hell out of there. The Performer gave directions, and within minutes we reached the far west side. The uncle's house was on a busy street next to a sporting goods shop with discounted clothes displayed out on the sidewalk. His home and the others in his neighborhood were two- and three-story buildings. We stopped and all the turret gunners in our convoy scanned inside and outside our perimeter.

I jumped out and passed through a gate behind two entry teams. The first team cleared the courtyard. The second examined the front door—it was unlocked. They penetrated and cleared the first room. I followed. They split into smaller teams, and the one in the room ahead of me rounded up a man who was a Saddam lookalike who wore jeans and a sweatshirt. With him was a woman and two girls. They looked like a father, mother, and two daughters. There was a stairway to the right, a closed door to the left, and another room in the back containing nothing but furniture.

Soldiers held the stairs until Maui calmly arrived and signaled for them to proceed. He followed them upstairs. It was comforting to have Maui, Del, Senior, and the other AST with us. They'd done this work many times before, and they handled tasks from muscle memory, freeing cognitive space to focus on other things, thus creating greater situational awareness.

In OSI leadership, there were officers who focused on stateside investigations for most of their careers, and they didn't see the need for ASTs, but for agents like me working downrange, yeah, there would be a bad apple or two, but as a whole, the ASTs were worth every penny.

Another soldier held his weapon on the door to the left while I tried the handle—it was locked. I told Professor, "Ask Saddam what's in this locked room."

"An old woman rents that room," Saddam said.

"Open it," I said.

"I can't," Saddam said. "She's not here, and she has the key."

"You're full of shit." I turned to a tall, young, black army soldier and said, "Kick this door in."

He took a step back then kicked with his long leg. The door burst open. Inside were AK-47s, ammo, and grenades. *Some old lady.*

Maui came down the stairs carrying a box of grenades and IED initiators.

We departed the house, and I told the lieutenant, "Hold this guy until we can take him in for more questioning."

Maui and I passed through the gate.

A teenage Iraqi called out in English, "Hey, Maui."

What the hell?

"I'll be damned," Maui said. "He used to be one of my sources."

The Iraqi teen spoke English slang as if he'd seen a lot of American TV and movies. "What up, man?"

"Hey, Kid, chill," Maui said. "Is your contact number still good?"

"Yeah, man, yeah," Kid said.

"I'm busy right now, but I'll get a hold of you."

"Okay, later." Kid took off.

A white van drove by with the side door open. I looked up at an AST in the turret of one of our Humvees. "Yeah, that's the second time," the AST said. "That van's got military-age males in it."

"Roger," I said, "we're spending too much time on this target."

I turned, and the soldiers who were supposed to be helping were shopping in the sporting goods store next door. "What the hell are you guys doing?"

"There's a sale," one said matter-of-factly.

"I was getting a T-shirt for my girlfriend," another said.

"You don't know how bad this area is," I said.

They were oblivious.

Maui put his box of grenades and initiators in the back of his Humvee. "We need to grab Saddam."

"Yeah," I said.

We returned to the courtyard, but I didn't see Saddam. "Where's our suspect?" I asked.

"We asked him for ID," a soldier said, "and he told us he had to go into the house next door to fetch it upstairs."

I lost it. "Holy shit, are you kidding me!" Not only had we lost a bad guy, but he'd now had plenty of time to call his buddies to tell them about us. "Show me where he went!"

The two soldiers took me down an alley on the side of the house, but Saddam was nowhere to be found. We could've gone searching some more, but there was no telling where he'd gone in that city of a hundred thousand people, and there was no telling which doors might open and feed us bullet sandwiches.

Shots fired from about a block away. It reminded me of that night with Moped when we'd first heard the potshots.

I turned around, and the soldier and I hurried back to the convoy. "That's it, guys, we're getting the hell out of here. Take all the AKs and grenades and shit with us."

I found the lieutenant and said, "Tell your guys to wrap it up—we got to get out of here."

"Hey, I'm sorry my men lost him," he said, "but if you let me use your terp, you can stay out here, and I'll go back in the house with his wife and daughters and find out where he's at."

"That's not happening," I said.

"I don't want to get in trouble for losing your prisoner," he said.

"That's the last thing on my mind right now. We need to get the hell out of here."

"But my boss…"

Normally, if we arrived safely at our target area, we knew there were no IEDs or other dangers on that path and we would go back out the same way—safe in, safe out. Even if an ambush was sprung, we'd know how to get back. Still, I worried that given as much time as we'd spent on the target and that our prisoner was probably running around telling all his friends about us, there could be an IED waiting for us on the route back. In addition, our Humvees were already pointed in the opposite direction from where we'd come in. "Is there a quicker way out straight ahead than going back the way we came?" I asked.

"Yeah, we can go a mile or so straight," the lieutenant said, "take a right and be back on the main drag to return to base."

"Let's do it."

We loaded up into the convoy. Scrunched in the back with Professor and me was the Performer. Our convoy rolled.

A hundred yards down the road, Professor said, "That's him."

"Who?" I asked.

"There," Professor said.

"Where?"

Professor pointed. "Right there."

Sitting in a truck pulled off to the side of the road and facing us was Captain al-Hakim and one of his henchmen. One of his henchmen was missing. The hairs on the back of my neck stood up.

"Can you believe that smug son of a bitch?" Professor said.

Captain al-Hakim seemed surprised, as if he'd expected us to go out the way we came in.

I didn't know why, but our convoy stopped, and we idled. Angry as hell, I stared at Captain al-Hakim. All kinds of shit crossed my mind about how to kill him, like throwing a grenade in his truck.

My temperature boiled, and I reverted to the mindset of an aggressive young SEAL running and gunning in a platoon. I might've gotten away with it in the old days, but now, as an older law enforcement agent, I rationalized myself out of it. I could be court martialed and thrown in Leavenworth. As a busted federal agent in a federal prison, a big bullseye would be painted on me, especially from guys I'd put in that jail. My family would be devastated.

I've replayed seeing Captain al-Hakim in his truck a thousand times to this day, and it still fills me with anger.

Our convoy moved out again, and we passed Captain al-Hakim.

Soon the Performer told us, "Let me out here."

We stopped once more. The Performer exited the Humvee and disappeared into the city. Then we took off again. We reached a shack with a policeman manning a checkpoint on the outskirts of Dujail. He gave us a double take, and his jaw slackened. We blew past him.

We turned onto the main highway and gained momentum—faster and faster. Soon Dujail shrank behind us.

Inside the gates of our base, I sighed. We'd survived.

About an hour later, I found out that an Iraqi convoy traveling the same road we'd used to enter Dujail hit an IED. Captain al-Hakim had to know that our investigation was closing in on him, and I knew in my gut he'd intended that IED for us.

CHAPTER 32

THE CHOICE

MY DEPLOYMENT REACHED ITS TWILIGHT, and various forces, seen and unseen, tugged at me to return home. NCIS's protective detail leader showed up at my EDet compound in Balad and said, "I'm losing two guys from my team, and I'd like you to join me full time protecting the marine corps commandant." OSI had trained me to do protective service details—advance team planning, driving in a motorcade, shooting, and so on—similar to what the Secret Service does. "You can become a civilian agent for NCIS and live in Washington, DC."

Because DC was so crowded, I wasn't keen on living there. To live somewhere affordable, I might have to commute for up to two hours one way. Besides, there was more I wanted to do in OSI, especially here in Iraq. "No thanks," I told him.

Several hours after sunset, I picked up an iridium phone and stepped outside of my building to call home. I walked across the gravel to the Humvees.

My wife answered, and we chit-chatted a bit.

Then I came around to the topic that was on both our minds. "I'd like to extend my deployment," I said.

She stopped talking and there was a long pause.

Then my daughter's voice came on: "Hi, Daddy. When you coming home?" It felt like someone had reached into my chest and flipped my heart like a pancake.

Oh crap. If I extend, my family might not be there when I get back. I had to choose which was more important, my job or them.

I remembered SEAL Commander John Koenig's words to me when I was thinking of leaving the Teams and doing something different, such as becoming an air force officer. "Don't worry about letting your brothers here down because someone will replace you as soon as you're gone. A husband or father can't be replaced." His words stung.

My daughter waited for an answer.

My voice cracked as if it was someone else's. "Soon, honey, soon."

My wife had played a dirty trick on me—and it worked. When she took back the phone, I told her, "I won't extend."

I could hear her breathing heavily. "Don't let us down," she said.

She'd taken care of the kids and home while I was gone. She was a strong woman to have stuck it out with me this long. Her father should've shaved *her* head and sent her to BUD/S.

"I won't let you down," I said.

Tom had put the idea of going to graduate school in my head, and I thought about it again. For OSI agents, the air force had three tracks to choose from: a master's in forensic sciences at George Washington University, a master's in accounting with a concentration in financial fraud examination and management at Xavier University, and a master's in security studies at the Naval Postgraduate School in Monterey, California. The latter was closest to a counterintelligence focus and what I wanted to do more of, so I applied to the Naval Postgraduate School. If accepted, I'd learn about a world region and a language from that area. I put in my application and told them I wanted to specialize in the Middle East and study Arabic or Euro-Russia and Russian. I didn't do it as a favor to Tom; rather, I did it because he'd convinced me that it was the right thing to do.

Commander Mitchell backed me with a hell of a write-up, which led to me being recognized as company grade officer of the year. His boss, Colonel Gray in Qatar, approved. Back in Florida, my detachment commander, Chris Jameson, supported me too. I was supposed to take the Graduate Record Examination—an SAT for graduate students—but it wasn't available to me in Balad, so I submitted my paperwork without it. It probably didn't help that I put my application in at the last minute. Then I waited to hear if I'd been accepted or not.

As I made plans to go home, my window of opportunity to kill or capture Captain al-Hakim was closing fast.

CHAPTER 33

Night Crawler

After we lost our guys, I attempted to go out with each agent the first time they went outside of the wire. I remembered losing Johnny Lancaster and my own experience of nearly getting chopped up by an SDV propeller in the Teams, and I knew how traumatic experiences could shake people and throw off their rhythm—I'd forgotten my dive mask. Chief LaConte had helped me regain my balance and rhythm. Now, it was up to me to help the agents regain their balance and rhythm.

We mounted the Humvees for one of these missions, and I said over the radio, "Check yourself head to toe and make sure you have your personal gear and the gear we need in the vehicles." I hadn't had to tell them this before, and they probably wondered why I did it now. Sure enough, as we pulled out of the compound, one of the agents realized he forgot to bring his weapon. Before another mission, an agent forgot his comms.

We all struggled, but I did my best to make sure we had our shit together. The only agent I didn't try to go out with was Commander Mitchell. He had enough on his plate, and I wasn't going to push him.

We tried hard to recover from our loss, but I felt we needed a boost. Back in the bullpen, I said, "Even though we're investigating who killed our guys, we still have other missions. You still have to run your sources and go after the targets who're doing bad things to Iraqis and US personnel. Those targets are your responsibility. When the First Cav lost some guys, it affected them, but they knew what their job was, and they went right back out there and did it."

Cat was unusually quiet during meets with confidential informants, and her partner Orion was concerned about whether she was aggressive enough. *Is she actively listening or being passive?* Cat was the first agent to leave the wire without me. It happened one day when the rest of us split up to work on various other tasks. She grabbed her terp to go collect intel.

Cat and her terp rolled out of the wire with the 101st Airborne. The paratroopers hadn't bothered to tell her that they wouldn't be driving up to the target. They parked a couple klicks away and patrolled in on foot. At five-foot-seven, Cat was tall for a woman, but she was thin, only weighing a hundred and twenty pounds. Wearing a heavy Kevlar vest and helmet and carrying her rifle, pistol, ammo, and comms, she humped the two klicks across uneven terrain in enemy territory and kept up with the paratroopers. She did what she had to do and inspired the rest of us.

✧ ✧ ✧

For some time, the army badly wanted one insurgent, codenamed Night Crawler after the worm that feeds off of living and dead organic matter. The four AST agents, Huey, the new terp, Tex, and I linked up with the 101st Airborne and convoyed through the black night to the target area. There, we parked our vehicles and set up perimeter security.

The paratroopers hopped out of their trucks and moved in to breach the target building. They wore night vision goggles (NVGs) and carried infrared laser sights on their rifles. The lasers were invisible to enemies and anyone else without night vision. The soldiers could simply point the laser at their target and pull the trigger, more like a video game than traditional shooting—except this was for real. Their breacher carried a shotgun to either blast open the lock and latch of a door or blow out the hinges. These tactics were more advanced than the First Cav's artillery soldiers used, and this way of running and gunning was beyond what I'd been able to share with my fellow agents in the limited training time we had.

I waited for the paratroopers to clear the building.

"Hey, Kermit," Huey asked, "are those of us not on the turret guns going to join the shooting train and clear the house?"

"Nope," I said.

"Why not?"

"These guys don't need us. We'll stay right here and wait until they call us in." I thought for a moment. "Maybe a couple of us can go around to the other side and help watch the perimeter on the back of the building."

Boom! Boom!

"Are they shooting already?" Huey asked.

"No, they're breaching. And they're using night vision. We didn't train with these men, and we don't want to be part of that without NVGs and without knowing where to line up for a breach."

Del rolled out and went to the back of the building. Soon, he radioed: "I got movement in the cemetery behind me."

I pushed to join him back there. It was dark, and all I could see was a field of tombstones. I was in no hurry to join the corpses and the maggots. "I'm pretty sure that whoever is out there knows that area better than we do. I don't think we need to go after him by ourselves."

"I concur," Del said.

I radioed the 101st and told them.

"The cemetery is out of our way," a soldier replied. "Target building is clear, and we have a suspect."

I moved into the house, and the other agents joined me with their terp. We conducted site exploitation, searched for intel, and interrogated the suspect, who looked nothing like Night Crawler.

"I'm not who you're looking for," the suspect said. "He stays down the street with a family member."

A paratrooper said, "Hey, let's head down the street to visit this family member. You guys want to roll with us?"

"I do," I said. I exited the building and grabbed Tex from my vehicle and took him with me, leaving Huey, Del, the other agents, and their terp to finish questioning the suspect and searching his house.

The paratroopers patrolled a block ahead of me. *Boom-boom-boom!* I saw muzzle flash from the shotgun. When I arrived, the door was blown off the hinges, and the paratroopers had already entered and had a man lying on the floor in a wide pool of water. A busted water container lay nearby, and the man's wife and daughter screamed.

A baby-faced paratrooper sat on the man lying on the floor and was about to beat the shit out of him. His buddies were almost as young as Baby Face, and they looked like they wanted to put the hurt on the suspect too. One paratrooper held a confiscated AK in his hand.

"Hang on," I said. "Let me talk to him a second."

"Hey," Baby Face said, "when we came through the door, he grabbed an AK rifle!"

"Hey," I said, "think about it. If you were at home asleep in the middle of the night with your wife and daughter and somebody shotgun-blasted your front door open, what would you reach for if you had it?"

Baby Face scratched his head. "Oh, yeah."

Tex translated what I said.

The man on the floor looked up as if I was his new friend.

I sincerely empathized with him. The good cop routine came naturally to me. "Who are you?"

He said his name.

"We're not looking for you," I said. I told him who we were looking for.

"This is not his house or his family," the man said. "We're not related. We're not even friends. I don't like what he's into. He hangs out with insurgents."

Shit, we breached the wrong house. "I need to find out where he is," I said.

"He lives with his sister," the man said. He pointed his nose to the street we arrived on. "Go down this street, make a left, and pass three houses to a two-story building. That's where he lives. That's his sister's house."

"Thanks." At that time, each house was allowed to have one AK, so I motioned for the paratrooper holding the man's AK to hand it to me.

He did.

I took the magazine out, put it in my pocket, and racked the weapon to make sure the cartridge chamber was empty. Then I laid the empty weapon down beside the man on the floor.

The paratroopers and I exited, patrolled back out on the street, and followed the man's directions. Baby Face and another paratrooper walked point, and the others followed behind Tex and me. The green lights in their NVGs glowed, and it appeared as if we were aliens traveling in a formation. It was pretty cool.

Tex, on the other hand, couldn't see the coolness in this. Nervously, he jerked his head from side to side. "I didn't know that I signed up for all this."

"Oh," I said.

"Why can't I have my own gun?" he asked.

"That's not the way it works."

"What if something happens?" he asked.

"I've taken you to the range, and you've practiced. You can grab the pistol on my hip if something happens to me."

We turned left, and Tex pointed at a house. "I saw some feet under that door."

I pointed my weapon in the direction of that house and went to a knee. Then I rose up and shook my head—*nobody.*

He smiled and seemed glad that I listened to him.

We continued past three homes until we saw the two-story house on a corner to the left. Its back bordered the cemetery. A gust of wind howled. I looked for movement but didn't see any.

Up on the second story of the house, something was spraypainted on the wall in Arabic.

"What's that say?" I asked.

"The guy we're looking for," Tex said.

"What?"

Tex's voice became anxious. "That's Night Crawler's real name."

"Why is it painted up there?"

Tex shook his head. "I don't know."

Baby Face overheard us and asked, "Is that Night Crawler's name?"

"Yep," I said.

"What the hell?" he said.

"How'd they even get up to the second floor to write that?" another paratrooper said.

I shrugged my shoulders. It was the weirdest thing.

I took a position on the perimeter, and the paratroopers cleared the house.

Then I went in with Tex. Sure enough, it was Night Crawler's sister's house. The sister's eyes shifted while she avoided the truth: "I haven't seen him in a couple days."

We hit a dry hole.

Later, I told the other agents about the graffiti on the sister's wall, and we figured that the villagers didn't like Night Crawler. Insurgents like him brought trouble. They told people how to dress and how to act. They attracted American soldiers, who busted down doors in the middle of the night and questioned people. The insurgents threatened innocent civilians and killed them. The sheikhs had grown to dislike the insurgents, too, especially those linked to al Qaeda.

CHAPTER 34

UNBELIEVABLE

WE NEEDED TO GATHER MORE information about who'd helped Moped plant the IED, and if possible, have them sign a written statement. We were short agents, and I was too busy helping run meets in Balad to fly out to Baghdad again, so I talked with Commander Mitchell about the problem.

"Burl is our most experienced agent," Commander Mitchell said.

"Yeah, let's send Burl to Baghdad to interview Moped," I said.

Devil Dog and I sat down with Burl and went over the details that we needed from Moped and how those details would help us build target packages on Captain al-Hakim and the others involved. We gave Burl comprehensive maps of Dujail, so Moped could point out where our suspects lived.

"This interview is important, and you're our most experienced agent, so I'm counting on you to do this," I said. "Commander Mitchell is counting on you too."

"Okay," Burl said.

I drove Burl to the helo pad myself. "The intel you gather will drive many more missions to get justice for our guys," I said.

"I understand," Burl said.

I parked the SUV. "Good luck." Then I escorted him to the Black Hawk helicopter and saw him off.

During the two days he was gone, the anticipation was intense. I met him at the landing pad when he returned.

He stepped off the Black Hawk, and wind from the rotors whipped us.

I shook his hand. "How'd it go?"

Burl gave me a puzzled look. "He wouldn't admit to doing it."

"What?" I said. "What the hell are you talking about?"

"Moped argued the whole time about his involvement."

"Who cares what he wants to admit to," I said. "He's already cooked. Your job was to get him to talk about the others involved. All you had to do was get him to blame others. C'mon, you know the deal. Minimize his part enough to get him comfortable and pull the rest out of him."

"Yeah, but he kept arguing that he didn't do anything."

"You were gone for two days—how much time did you sit with him?" I asked.

"A few hours," Burl said.

"A few hours and all you did was argue with him? What a waste!"

I left Burl and reported to Commander Mitchell.

Commander Mitchell smacked his desk. "Unbelievable!"

CHAPTER 35

OLD MAN HAJIB RETURNS

Our two newest agents, Dee and Jay, had been with us several days. Dee was a low maintenance gal, and Jay was cleverly resourceful at finding what we needed, like Hank had been. Jay was the one who'd done the most work getting our new Humvee up and ready. Hunting season officially opened.

In the afternoon, as I drove across base, I spotted a man in a navy uniform poking around some army vehicles, so I pulled over and said, "What's up?"

He pulled his head out of a truck and gave me a strange look.

"I used to be in the navy," I said.

He held a screwdriver in his hand. "Guess you don't see many sailors around here."

"I don't. What're you up to?"

"I'm redoing the frequencies on the Humvees." He put his head back inside and resumed tinkering.

"I don't understand. Why do you have to redo frequencies?"

His voice was muffled from talking inside the truck. "They're changed on a regular basis; otherwise, they don't function."

"Nobody told us that," I said. "We haven't been changing ours."

"Yeah, there's a schedule."

"Nobody ever told us there was a schedule."

He came out of the vehicle and closed the Humvee door. "Guess the army left stuff for you without telling you about it," he said.

"Can you come work on ours?" I asked. "Show us what to do?"

"Sure, let me take a look."

I escorted him back to the compound and grabbed hold of Jay. The sailor looked over our Hummers and said, "Yeah, all your frequencies are old."

He went to work showing Jay how to reset them and gave him a schedule for doing it.

✦   ✦   ✦

The next day, around lunchtime, a Special Forces unit out of Baghdad called me up. I wasn't sure how they got my number, but I guessed the guys from the Tenth Special Forces must've shared my package on Kaiser Soze. This Baghdad team was a counter-terrorism unit that hit targets all over Iraq. The voice on the other end of the phone sounded like that of a young surfer—he was an intelligence analyst in his twenties: "Were you the one who put this target package together?"

"Yes," I said.

"What's your background?" he asked.

"I was a Team guy."

"SEAL Team?"

"Yep."

"That makes sense," he said. "This package is bone-brilliant. Hey, we're flying out to take down a target, and we thought we'd stop by and hit Kaiser Soze on our way back."

I chuckled. "Dude, this isn't like a drive-by. It's not going to be that easy. You better be ready."

He was nonchalant about it. "Naw man, we're good. We got it."

"I guess you guys don't need me to go with you," I said.

"No, we do this all the time," he said.

"Okay."

"There's enough space in front of Kaiser Soze's place for our helos to land and everything," he said.

"All right, man," I said. "Let me know what goes down."

The next morning, I stepped out of the gym, and I got a call from one of the Special Forces guys from Baghdad: "Last night we landed at Kaiser Soze's place. When we unassed the helos, he came running out of the front of his house shooting at us with an AK. He shot one of our Iraqi scouts in the chest, but it struck his Kevlar and only knocked him on the ground. Another round knocked the night vision goggles off my buddy's face. Then Kaiser Soze squirted out the back into the orchard."

"Did you go after him?"

"We called in two F-16s from your base, and each dropped a five-hundred-pound bomb on the orchard. No one could've survived that. Kaiser Soze is no more."

I smiled. "I told you guys it wasn't going to be easy."

Dee and Jay came out of the gym too. "What's going on?" Dee asked.

I gestured for them to wait a minute.

The Green Beret continued. "Now I got fifty paratroopers and a hundred Iraqi soldiers in the orchard searching for what's left of the dude."

"Thanks for the update," I said.

"Later." He hung up the phone.

I told Dee and Jay.

They got fired up and full of piss and vinegar. "Hey, man," Jay said, "let's go help them."

"Yeah," Dee said.

"Are you serious?" I said. "What're three agents going to do with fifty paratroopers and a hundred Iraqi soldiers? All we'd be looking for is to hit another IED on the way there."

Their jaws slackened.

"Good point," Dee said.

The greatest trick the Devil ever pulled was convincing the world he didn't exist. Two weeks later, Kaiser Soze resurfaced.

I received an intel report that in a nearby town, an al Qaeda insurgent got into a shootout with a police officer. In the crossfire, the insurgent shot a mother and her daughter. The policeman wounded the insurgent before the insurgent killed him and escaped.

That same day, my phone rumbled, and I glanced at the caller ID: Jimmy Stewart.

"How's it going?" I asked.

"Your little old man, the dirt farmer, is here at the gate wearing his red-and-white keffiyeh, dishdasha, and flip flops. His AK scared the hell out of my guys."

"Hajib," I said.

"Yeah, we're holding his AK. He's saying something about an insurgent being shot, and he's on our base."

"What?" I asked.

"I don't know, but he wants to talk with you."

"All right," I said, "I'm coming down."

I took Huey and Tex, and we met with Hajib in the trailer.

The old man leaned forward. "A police officer shot an al Qaeda insurgent, but he killed the police officer and ran away. Now he's in the hospital here on base."

"Let's go take a look," I said.

We hopped into my Suburban and drove to the hospital parking lot. I turned to Huey and said, "I'm going in and taking a picture of him. I'll be right back."

"I'll take Hajib to get a bite to eat and a drink, and we'll meet you back here," Huey said.

Tex interpreted our plans to Hajib before Tex and I exited the Suburban. Tex and I entered the hospital and stopped at the reception desk, where I asked the woman sitting behind it, "Do you have an Iraqi in here with a gunshot wound?"

A nurse who stood nearby said, "Yes, I can show you to him." She escorted me down the hall. "He's in a room with a mother and daughter who were caught in the crossfire as he was shooting at the police."

I walked into the room and saw a man wearing bandages. He moaned in pain.

"What's your name?" I asked.

He told me. Then he added, "I already know that you know I work for al Qaeda. I'll tell you everything you want if you'll put me in the same prison as my father." His father had worked for al Qaeda too.

"Well, we can work that out," I said, "but we need to talk some more."

A medic worked on the mother and child. The medic turned to me and said, "He's the one who shot these two."

A doctor came in and saw me questioning the man—I wasn't even going hard at him.

"Hey, you can't talk to him right now," the doctor said.

What the hell?

"He's getting ready to go into surgery," the doctor said.

"I really don't care, this is a bad guy," I said.

"Well, I have to do my job," the doctor said.

"Go ahead, I got what I came for." I left the room.

Tex followed me into the hall. We departed the hospital and returned to the SUV. Huey and Hajib were in the vehicle munching out.

I showed Hajib the picture.

He swallowed a bite of cheeseburger. "That's him—the al Qaeda insurgent!"

I handed him some money. "Good job."

Hajib smiled. For him, it was never so much about the money; it was more about the satisfaction of cleaning out another dirtbag from his village.

I pulled out my cell phone and called the 101st Airborne major who'd taken Major Sherwood's place at JDOC. The major told me he'd send over some men to guard the insurgent until he finished surgery. Then they'd arrest him. I put my phone back in my pocket.

After Hajib washed his cheeseburger and fries down with a soda, I drove him back to the gate. There, Jimmy Stewart handed him back his AK. Hajib cradled his weapon and strolled off the base. The wind blew at his white dish-dasha as he passed Iraqi teenagers wearing colorful Nike knockoffs and blue jeans. The little old man walked tall between a pair of yellow taxi cabs and kept walking.

Huey and I returned to our compound. Later, it was *Groundhog Day* all over again. The 101st major sent a guard detail over to the hospital. After our prisoner underwent surgery, the army released him. Again, this seemed like part of the Sons of Iraq program—insurgents were given a second chance to return to their communities and protect them from violence. This worked well in cities like Fallujah and Ramadi, but here it seemed ill-conceived and poorly executed.

Once again, I couldn't believe it. Once again, Huey was pissed and wanted to give the new battalion commanding officer a piece of his mind.

I started to reason with Huey. "Look, man—"

Huey cut me off. "I'm not a colonel, and I'm not going to tell the colonel what to do—I get it."

I was chafed too.

CHAPTER 36

JUSTICE

WHILE I PREPARED TO GO home, the other agents and I maintained contact with the Combined Joint Special Operations Task Force (CJSOTF) about how to build a case to action a mission to kill or capture Captain al-Hakim. Nate's source, Baghdad Bob, continued to run with the insurgents and report back to us on their activities. When the insurgents planned a mortar attack, Baghdad Bob told us where it would be fired from and who would fire it.

One day, Baghdad Bob visited the base and spoke with Professor, who translated for Burl and his AST partner.

Baghdad Bob began: "Captain al-Hakim is king of Dujail because of his connections with people who are connected to the Iranian backed militias. His superiors in the military fear him, so he controls them too. Even the police are in his hand."

"What evidence do you have?" Professor asked. "We need evidence."

"I know where he keeps his munitions and bombs," Baghdad Bob said.

Later, when provided with a map from satellite imagery, he pointed out where Captain al-Hakim stashed his stuff.

Shortly after that, Burl, a few AST agents, and Professor rolled out with the Third ID in Humvees and APCs. They entered Dujail and raided a small warehouse. It was empty.

Is Baghdad Bob full of shit?

It frustrated me that Captain al-Hakim was still out there, yet I was packing my bags to leave.

Baghdad Bob returned for a meet with Professor, Burl, and the AST. They asked him why there was nothing in the warehouse.

"You went to the wrong place!" Baghdad Bob said. "You were supposed to go to the warehouse a block away on the opposite side of the street! You hit the wrong place."

On a crisp, sunny day, Burl and an AST agent hid Baghdad Bob in their Humvee and rode with paratroopers out to Dujail. This time, he directed them to the correct building.

The paratroopers breached the warehouse and cleared it. Burl and the AST followed. The place was stockpiled with pistols, rifles, ammo, explosives, and RPGs. It wasn't a police or military facility, and Captain al-Hakim wasn't supposed to have a cache like this.

While the agents gathered intel and the paratroopers stood watch, Captain al-Hakim swaggered in. He yelled at them in Arabic.

"He wants to know what we're doing on his property," Professor said.

"Can you believe this jerk?" a paratrooper sergeant said.

The AST turned to Professor and asked, "Is he admitting all this is his?"

"This is mine," Captain al-Hakim shouted. "What're you doing on my property?"

The paratrooper sergeant pulled out his flex cuffs. "You want us to wrap him up?"

"Yes!" the AST said.

Burl nodded.

The sergeant cuffed Captain al-Hakim.

"You can't do this!" Captain al-Hakim shouted. "You can't do this to me!"

The paratroopers hauled him outside.

"Let me go. Let me go!" Captain al-Hakim demanded. "You can't do this to me."

The paratroopers stuffed him into an APC. Then paratroopers and agents carried him back to base, where they locked him in a prison cell. Within a couple days, he was flown to a jail in Baghdad to await trial.

Around the same time that Captain al-Hakim checked into the jail in Baghdad, Moped checked out. Moped received judgment and was hanged by the neck until dead.

I hoped Captain al-Hakim would hang too.

CHAPTER 37

FNGS

ALTHOUGH THERE WERE ONLY A couple thousand OSI agents, we were in high demand all over the globe. After losing Nate, Tom, and Dave—and two additional agents in Kirkuk—all in the span of five months, OSI couldn't afford to lose another agent. OSI couldn't continue to endanger agents by sending out entire EDets on meets and other missions.

The air force called on its security forces for assistance. Stateside, security forces primarily served as base cops. Overseas, their primary job was air base defense. Chuck Norris served as an air policeman in Osan Air Base, Korea, where he learned the martial art Tang Soo Do. Especially in a war zone, security forces manned Mark 19 grenade launchers, .50 caliber machine guns, sniper rifles, and other weapons in towers and other fighting positions. Increasingly, these airmen would be called upon to backfill traditional army jobs, especially in Iraq and Afghanistan. More and more, they pursued threats outside of the wire. Now the air force wanted some security forces personnel to run a Tactical Security Element (TSE) for our EDet and others.

To create the TSEs, security forces turned to their airmen who provided high-risk protection in austere locations: the 820th Contingency Response Group. On the cutting edge of land warfare, many of the 820th had attended airborne, air assault, Ranger, army sniper, and similar schools. In addition, they responded to contingencies in war zones and pursued threats outside of the wire.

The 820th called me from Moody Air Force Base in Valdosta, Georgia: "What's the terrain like there? How many patrols per week? What kind of comms do you use? Weapons? Other gear?"

I told them what worked for us and what we wished we had.

Then they asked, "Could you advise TSEs for deployment to EDets all over the globe?"

I thought about it. "What works in Balad may not work in a more urban area like Baghdad. I can tell you some of the foundations you'll need, but you might want to talk to the EDets at each specific location."

Trailers were installed behind our compound, and soon after, the new Tactical Security Element arrived, led by a senior NCO. The new TSEs appeared physically fit, excited to be here, and eager to work.

Part of their job was to lay the foundation of standard operating procedures and equipment to be used for future security forces from other units who'd relieve them. Other agents, including our ASTs and I, helped them set up, showed them our gear, pointed out our areas of responsibility on maps, and so on. I offered up some ideas of how to run things, but they already had a game plan of their own, so I stepped aside and let them do their thing. They asked questions, without being too intrusive, as to what happened that terrible night. We were still licking our wounds a bit. The air force made our EDet pause operations until we brought the new TSEs up to speed. Gone were the days when our whole EDet would go out to support a pair of agents at a meet.

In early January, my relief arrived. He was a younger OSI agent who'd done bodyguard work. I first met him back in the States when he visited my home Det in Hurlburt Field, Florida. A four-star general arrived, and I assisted Agent Bodyguard with his responsibilities. Most four-star generals had a protective service detail, depending on their command. At PSD training, I'd learned that the number of agents required for details depended on location, venue, and length of stay of the principal. For this trip, me and Agent Bodyguard were enough.

In Florida, Agent Bodyguard seemed to think he ruled the roost, cruising around with a four-star general. I drove the general, his wife, and Agent Bodyguard around in an SUV. The general's wife said, "This car is too high off the ground. Can you get me a stool?"

"Yes, ma'am," Agent Bodyguard said.

I drove to a nearby store, where we bought her a stool.

Is this the kind of crap a PSD agent has to do?

Later that evening, I shuttled them to a banquet event at a fancy hotel. After the general gave a speech and handed out some awards, he ate dinner with his wife and others. Agent Bodyguard and I sat at the table beside them. Soon a marine captain, who was in charge of the general's secure communications, walked up to the table carrying a comms briefcase. "Sir, there's an urgent phone call for you."

The general appeared red-faced. "Now?"

"It's from the Pentagon, sir," the marine said.

Agent Bodyguard and I escorted the general out of the banquet hall and into a secure hotel room that had been prepared earlier.

The general gave the marine the stink eye before answering the phone. "Hello?"

After the phone conversation, the general didn't seem too pleased.

Then I thought, well, maybe they shouldn't call him about trivial matters. Later, I found out that the phone call was intel regarding an al Qaeda plot to detonate liquid explosives disguised as soft drinks on aircraft flying from the UK to the US and Canada. The suspected terrorists were arrested before they could launch the attack. Because of that threat, passengers in the UK and other countries would be limited as to how much liquid they could carry onto a commercial flight.

Although Agent Bodyguard had never served with an EDet in a war zone, now he would be the operations officer for one. He didn't seem to be there because he wanted to chase bad guys downrange; he seemed to be there to get promoted from captain to major. This assignment could tick an important box for him. He was a sharp guy, and I considered him a friend, but after I showed him around a bit, it became apparent he was in over his head.

"I don't know how I'm going to do this," he said.

"Look, we did between eighty and a hundred missions in the months I've been here, and nearly every agent had to go out on nearly every mission," I said. "But now you have a Tactical Security Element, and that means only two agents and a terp need to go out each time. You'll only have to go out on a fifth of the missions."

I took him to an operations brief at the JDOC and introduced him to the 101st Airborne major who was in charge of ops. Then I connected him with the Signals Intelligence guys, showed him the Predator feeds to video, base camera surveillance, and other JDOC resources.

Agent Bodyguard remained mute for most of the time. He turned to me and quietly said, "Holy shit. This is what you do?"

"Yep." I took him back to my office in our compound, and we sat down. I described how we scheduled missions.

He seemed overwhelmed.

"Look," I said, "Now that you have TSEs, all you have to do is let them know when and where. You're not going to have to map out the infils and exfils—they're going to have to do that. You don't have to coordinate with the JDOC—the TSEs will."

He fidgeted, and his eyes darted around my office.

"What's up, man?" I asked.

"Dude, I can't do this."

I stood up, walked over to the door, and shut it. "Yes, you can."

"The agents and the paratroopers and everyone else—those guys aren't going to listen to me like they listened to you."

"What else are you going to do? You can handle this. Grow a beard, man, and you'll fit right in."

"I can't grow a beard," Agent Bodyguard said.

I wanted to laugh, but I didn't. I felt bad for him.

I would later hear from Commander Mitchell that Agent Bodyguard turned out fine. The Tactical Security Element saved him.

CHAPTER 38

GOODBYE

MY EDET HAD A CURIOUS tradition for saying goodbye. Late at night on my last working day, I finished up some emails in my office. My job was done. Then I turned out the lights and walked out of my office for the last time. I made my way across the building to where several agents sat. One of them said something. Then all the agents came out of the woodwork. I was astonished that they were all awake—including the newly arrived TSEs.

They hesitated. It may have had something to do with the fact that I was benching 385 pounds and running six-minute miles.

Commander Mitchell nudged a TSE.

"Hell no," the TSE said. "I'm not going to touch that guy."

"Pizza," Commander Mitchell said. "Lots of it."

A muscular TSE came out of the comms room and rushed me low. I sidestepped him and bounced his head off the wall. Another TSE came at me high and grabbed me. *Game on.* Then their whole team mobbed me. They groped at my wrists and arms, but I thrashed them off.

Two held my legs and another taped them like a mummy. I struggled to free myself without hurting anyone—at least, not permanently. I lowered myself to the ground, so I wouldn't injure myself with a fall.

Someone snapped a handcuff on me, and I had to be careful not to sling the other metal cuff into someone's face and take his eye out. I especially worried about injuring Cat or Dee.

The senior AST was addicted to jujitsu, and he turned to Maui and said, "I'm going to put a chokehold on him." The senior AST stepped forward.

The needle on my fun meter dropped, and the needle on my ass-kicking meter popped up. I gave him a hard stare. "Really?"

"Okay, okay." The senior AST backed off.

I held my hands behind my back, gesturing that I was ready to be cuffed. "Do what you got to do."

"Ah shit," Commander Mitchell said. "He's going to let you guys do it."

Agents joined in and handcuffed me and taped my arms to my sides. Next, they hoisted me into a chair and tied me to it. They blindfolded me. Then all of them wheeled me through what sounded like the back exit of the building.

"I just want you to know," Commander Mitchell's voice said, "this cost me a lot of pizza."

I knew what was coming next—a frogman's nemesis—cold water. This would come in a huge vat filled with ice.

Someone poured a little cold water on me. "Ah!" I yelled.

Agents laughed.

Then a flood of frigid water came down on me. "Ah!" It knocked off my blindfold.

They howled with laughter.

I sat there shivering. Mercifully someone cut loose the tape on my legs. I thrashed around until I loosened the rope that bound me to the chair. Then I stood up and wiggled, trying to break the tape off my arms. I walked on the slippery ground and people backed away from me as if a monster had escaped.

I wanted to free myself before some jackass could take a final dig at me. I headed to the building. My hands were still cuffed behind my back, but my arms were close to breaking through the tape that bound them to my sides. Something was still attached to my legs, and I stopped in the doorway of the building and looked down to see what it was—tape. I kicked it off. When I brought my head back up, I slammed my arms out to break loose of the tape that bound them. Someone was nearby, and my sudden movement jacked their head into the steel frame of the door—*crack*!

It was Cat. She looked as if she was about to cry.

"Oh!" Commander Mitchell shouted as if he were a spectator at a football game.

Oh no.

Beside Cat stood Dee, who gave me a dirty look as if to say, *We were coming to help you.*

I felt horrible.

Cat held her head and turned to me. Her eyes seemed to ask, *How could you?*

Commander Mitchell roared with laughter.

I gave him a stare: *Dude, this is not funny.*

After I was free, I said my goodbyes. The agents I was closest to had all pretty much departed already. Nate, Dave, and Tom were gone. Orion, Huey, Mac, and a few others had returned to the States.

Maui said, "See you around." The other ASTs had the same attitude. We'd crossed paths before, we crossed paths here, and we'd cross paths again. I gave my farewell to most of the other agents. Burl was there, but I didn't say a word to him. After the doorway incident, I never saw Cat again.

I retired to my living quarters, stripped out of my wet clothes, toweled off and changed into dry clothes. A knock sounded at my door.

I opened it.

Commander Mitchell stood there.

"Come in," I said.

He took a seat.

"These TSEs from the 820th are going to take good care of you, sir," I said.

"Yeah, I've served with security forces before," he said.

"And the ASTs are still here to help—Maui, Del, and Senior."

"I just want you to know that we did some good things here even though the cost was so high. Each month, regional headquarters emailed us a PowerPoint showing the performance of each EDet: number of intelligence reports, ops, captures, and kills. Baghdad and Bagram came close, but they couldn't beat us. That's saying something for Balad, where it isn't as populated. In Baghdad, you can't swing a cat by the tail without hitting an insurgent. Each month, we had a string of pictures on our EDet report of bad guys killed or captured. It wasn't like that before you came. Thanks."

"We did it together, sir."

While I was there, our EDet identified nine hundred and fifty-five threats and produced seven hundred and twenty Intelligence Information Reports— reports that affected the battlespace. We'd disrupted or neutralized insurgent cells, removing more than a hundred insurgents from the battlespace around our air base. We smashed two high-value individual al Qaeda financier rings and crafted two packages leading to the capture of its leaders. IED, mortar, and rocket attacks dropped significantly.

"I'm putting you in for a medal," Commander Mitchell said.

"I'm not worried about that. The guys who deserved it and paid the price received theirs. I get to go home."

✧   ✧   ✧

In the cold, dark morning, I walked out of the EDet building one final time and tossed my bags into the back of an SUV. The agents had gone across the base with the new TSEs to practice patrolling and shooting in low-light conditions. The compound was unusually quiet.

Devil Dog hopped into the driver's seat, and I sat beside him. He started the engine and shifted into drive. I checked my side-view mirror, taking one final look at the lights of the EDet compound. Smaller and smaller they contracted until they disappeared into the morning gray.

Devil Dog stopped at the tarmac. "Thanks for everything."

I opened the SUV door. "You too."

"Good luck."

"You too."

I carried my bags and gear onboard the C-130 cargo plane. I remembered the last time I was on a C-130, loading our guys on it. I remembered when they were alive. The memories were bittersweet.

I stowed my gear and took a seat. The cabin was remarkably empty and quiet. The C-130 lumbered down the runway, then its nose lifted, and it rose into the air. We were within range of a shoulder-fired missile, and I could hardly wait until we picked up speed and climbed out of that range. I'd never heard of any shoulder-fired missiles being smuggled into our area, but I didn't want to be on the first plane shot down by one that slipped through.

The C-130 continued to ascend and banked into a turn. The sun peeked over the horizon and shone on the fields below. Once more, I was reminded of the homesteads in San Joaquin Valley. The Tigris sparkled through the valley. It could've been a farm resort if it wasn't for the assholes who stirred up trouble.

I had plenty of space, so I stretched out my legs and leaned back. The weight of the job was gone, and thoughts of home lifted me. I was thankful to be able to go back home. I looked forward to seeing my wife and holding my kids. Nothing else really mattered.

PART III

AFTER THE HUNT

We must be willing to let go of the life we've planned
so as to have the life that is waiting for us.

-JOSEPH CAMPBELL

CHAPTER 39

HOMECOMING

ALTHOUGH I WANTED TO GO straight home, the military made me stop at the air force base in Ramstein, Germany, for processing. A group of OSI agents were my receiving team. They picked me up and took me to a hotel room, where I dropped off my bags. Then we went out to dinner at a Chili's Grill and Bar on base. The agents acted as if this duty was a vacation for them. Those who weren't busy partying said nothing to me—as if they knew where I'd come from and what I'd been through. I disengaged. With time on my hands, I remembered some of the bad times from Balad. For the first time, I realized that stuff may have affected me more than I thought.

A support guy who was also there for processing sat next to me. He seemed disconnected from the others too.

A female agent I recognized from FLETC came over and said, "I'm sorry about what happened."

"Thanks."

I ordered Monterey chicken—skinless chicken with barbecue sauce, crisp bacon, and a blend of Monterey jack and cheddar cheese. It's my favorite Chili's meal.

The support guy ordered something, too, and we ate without saying a word.

The next morning, a contracted psychologist, Dr. Kennedy, took the support guy and me on a long drive through the snowy German countryside to a castle. In the freezing cold, we walked around the outside of it, but it appeared to be closed. *What the hell?*

The support guy looked at me and shook his head.

We found a door that opened, and we entered a café with only a few tables. Dr. Kennedy motioned for us to sit at one of the tables.

We did.

Inside the castle it was cold, and I was hungry. "What sandwiches do they have here?"

"None," Dr. Kennedy said. "They don't serve food here."

I looked over at the support guy, who shrugged his shoulders.

Dr. Kennedy faced me and asked, "Did you see anyone die while you were over there?"

I couldn't believe he was interviewing me on such a personal matter in front of a stranger. "Yeah. I lost three of my teammates."

Dr. Kennedy leaned back as if surprised. Then he straightened up in his chair. "Well, what happened?"

I told him.

"Your life is like a tree," he said, "and when a tree grows, it makes rings inside of it—rings around rings around rings. The experience you had in Iraq is like that tree, and you're going to build rings around it."

What the hell? He seemed to need a psychologist more than me.

"Would you like a drink?" he asked.

"I'll take a beer," I said.

He stood up. "I have to make a phone call." Then he left.

"Who's paying this guy?" I asked.

"That's the same shit he said to me yesterday," the support guy said.

Dr. Kennedy returned. Despite the frigid temperature, he was sweating. "Nobody told me you were coming today," he said.

"That's okay with me," I said. "This isn't going to slow down my return home, is it?"

"No, you should be fine. If you ever feel like talking to someone, on the backs of those grocery bags in the commissaries are 1-800 numbers to call."

I couldn't believe the military was paying this quack. Even so, as long as he didn't hinder me from going home, I didn't care.

That was my transitional briefing. We went back to our rooms and prepared for the next day's flight home.

Someone must have given some honest feedback about how these contracted psychologists were conducting the transitions. Later, the air force would use active-duty officers as their psychologists, and OSI set up a more robust system for screening and helping agents in transition back to the States.

◈   ◈   ◈

I was hoping it would only be my wife and kids at the airport, and we could jump in the car and leave. My plane landed, and I stepped off wearing hiking boots, khaki cargo pants, a black polo shirt, and a full beard. I looked military and not-military. I walked through Florida's Fort Walton Beach Airport terminal humping a three-foot-by-two-foot tactical gear bag strapped to my back, pulling a big black bag with one hand, and carrying an olive drab US military duffle bag in the other—each weighing seventy to a hundred pounds. I was used to pumping a lot of iron, and now I was super pumped to reunite with my family. I advanced through the terminal like a tank.

I turned a corner, and a little boy told the woman beside him, "Mom, I want to be like that when I grow up."

I grinned.

The channel opened up into a sea of people. Many agents, including good friends from my unit at Hulbert Field, waved signs, cheered, and took pictures. Agents I didn't know had come over from Eglin Air Force Base and welcomed me home too. My wife's posse surrounded her and joined in the celebration. Civilian strangers saw what was going on and clapped and said thank you.

My daughter shouted, "Hi, Daddy!"

I went down to a knee and hugged her. When I stood up, she locked onto my leg.

My oldest son seemed torn between shaking my hand and hugging me—he shook my hand, and I hugged him.

Then my wife handed me my youngest. He'd been a bald-headed, squinty-eyed baby when I left, but now he was a toddler with hair and wide eyes. I expected him to be standoffish to this stranger, but quickly he put a tight squeeze around my neck. For a little guy, he was strong. He knew who I was right away.

My wife cried and hugged me, and I stole a quick kiss. I sensed that she wasn't going to let me go to a place like Balad ever again. She'd experienced my comings and goings before, but this had been a close call.

Agent Sperry Linger helped me carry my bags. "When we heard the news about the ambush, we thought it was you," he said.

"We're so glad you're home," another said.

More agents said that they thought I'd been KIA, and they were glad I was home. The mob followed us out of the airport. Although I hadn't wanted anyone other than my family to come, and though it embarrassed me, I was happy they were there.

Originally, my wife didn't want a minivan, but we'd bought one—a gold-colored Chrysler. After a couple months, though, she fell in love with it. I tired of the color, and I hated how sluggishly it responded. Before my deployment to Iraq, I couldn't wait to get rid of it, but she wouldn't let it go. She and the kids called it the Mother Ship. Now, it felt good seeing the Mother Ship in the lot. We loaded into it and drove away. When we pulled into our driveway, a few neighbors and their families came out of their houses to welcome me home.

My wife opened the door, and Bill, our 140-pound American bulldog met me enthusiastically. Normally, he was mellow, but when people saw him in our front yard, they walked on the other side of the street. Bill had guarded my family while I was away. He wasn't much of a tail-wagger, but now he wagged his tail and rubbed his face against my leg. His greeting energized me.

For dinner, my wife made my favorite homemade dish, chicken Marsala. The aroma of chicken, pasta, mushrooms, garlic, and Marsala wine was hungrifying. She'd always wanted to be a mom, and she loved cooking. She kept repeating, "They're so happy you're back; they're so happy you're back." I thought she was saying that about herself too.

"I missed them too," I said. "And I missed you, honey."

Being at home and eating dinner with my wife and children seemed surreal—a dream within a dream. Going to Iraq I expected to have to adapt. I forgot that I'd have to adapt to coming home too. The sight of my wife and kids sitting with me at the dinner table made me want to relax, but my mind kept wanting to prep for tomorrow's patrol. There was no smell of the burn pit or the rumble of jets flying overhead through the night. Even the humidity in the air felt alien, and the drinking water didn't taste the same. I was delighted, but I couldn't register all of it at once.

I'd changed while I was gone, and things at home had changed too. An older Team guy once told me, "When you go home, you can't expect everything to be the way it was. Your wife had to figure out a way to accomplish all the things that you did and all the things that she had to do. So when you return, if you don't take these things into consideration and bitch and complain about it, it can spiral into a bad thing. You may see this or that out of place, but you have to think, hey, she had it all to herself and did the best she could." When we retired for the night, it felt like sleeping in someone else's bed.

I was so exhausted that I slept like a rock, and when I woke up early, I felt a bit like Rip Van Winkle, having slept for twenty years and finding out how much my neighborhood and the country had changed. I returned to my unit to in-process: check stuff back in, fill out paperwork, and so on. Then my unit gave me a couple weeks to spend with my family. I shaved my beard clean off and cut my hair short and tight.

My mother-in-law flew in and took care of the kids and the house while Sharon and I went on a cruise to Mexico and the Caribbean. It was affordable for us because of a special deal the cruise line had for military personnel recently returning from deployments in the sandbox. During the cruise, time slowed down. The military seemed far away, and Sharon didn't have the home and kids nearby to worry about so much. Our favorite port was Cozumel, Mexico. There, we left the ship and explored ancient Mayan ruins. Then we window shopped in Playa Mia for watches and jewelry we couldn't afford.

We strolled along the beach and stopped at a couple bars with grass awnings over them and drank a bucket filled with ice and mini-Coronas. Later, we waded in crystal clear waters. The saltwater felt good. Watching tropical fish swim around the reefs relaxed me. A breeze played with Sharon's white see-through cover-up dress that she wore over her bikini. I fell in love with her all over again. I was home.

CHAPTER 40

RUMORS OF WAR

Although I'd returned to the States, a part of me was still in Balad. It was hard to let go. A couple times agents there contacted me officially and unofficially via phone calls and email messages. The air force purchased Mine-Resistant Ambush Protected (MRAP) vehicles for my EDet in Balad. Their V-shaped hulls could deflect the explosive force of an IED, providing superior protection. I advised Jay and the other agents in Balad, "On a wide road, the MRAP would be a good vehicle, but on narrow roads, there's no way you'll be able to turn these around. You'd have to go off-road in a field, and they're going to get stuck in the mud. If one of those falls into a canal, forget about it. Don't let anyone take your Humvees away. Keep them because there are some missions where you're going to want them."

Later, I received an email from Jay: "Hey, Kermit, exactly what you said was going to happen happened to us. We tried to turn around in an MRAP at a meet, and it got stuck. We called for a QRF."

After the team radioed for the quick reaction force, a reply came back from the base, "The QRF is on its way, but be advised that our eyes in the sky spot insurgents with weapons moving in on your position."

Fortunately, the QRF arrived before the insurgents did and scared them off. Soldiers and agents towed the MRAP out of the mud.

While I was in Iraq, Florida's Hurlbert and Eglin OSI detachments had been combined into one humongous field investigative squadron. I briefed the agents on what kind of missions we did in Balad. Later, my former commander from Hurlbert, Chris Jameson, asked me to brief some new OSI officers as part of a leadership conference he held monthly. I briefed the new officers about the new MRAPs and Tactical Support Elements. I explained how my EDet coordinated with the JDOC, conducted our meets, went on raids, and so on. Then the officers asked questions and I answered. I ended with what happened that terrible night and how we investigated it. After my brief, Chris came up to me a bit choked up.

He said, "That brief took me back to when I visited you guys for the memorial in Balad." I remembered how it hit so many agents so hard at my EDet, including me."

"Yes, sir. I remember there wasn't a dry eye at the memorial while Commander Mitchell spoke about Tom, Dave, and Nate."

He added, "You and I met briefly in your bullpen in Balad where you were throwing a football with one of your team. Watching your interactions with your team stuck with me. Your team clearly wanted to get back to work chasing down the killers. I remember flying my team back to Kirkuk and wanting to get them back in the saddle and not let their minds dwell on the attack."

After the brief, a group of us went to a bar on base and had a couple beers. A major in the reserves showed up late and started running his mouth about what happened in Balad. The agents who'd arrived with me from the conference became quiet and looked away from him.

Among other things, the reserve major said, "The EDet Commander didn't go out on that mission. If he had, maybe those agents would still be alive today."

I tried to stay quiet and let him hang himself, but I'd heard enough.

I called over to the reserve major, "Who told you this?"

He stuck his chest out. "My buddy in headquarters."

"How does he know?" I asked.

"Because my buddy was sitting in the EDet Commander's office with him when his team got hit."

"Well, I'll just tell you—I was actually there that night when my friends were killed, and your buddy is full of shit. Commander Mitchell was right there with me. So how could your buddy have been in his office when it happened?"

The reserve major froze with a dumb look on his face. His chest deflated.

"I'd work for Commander Mitchell again any day," I said. "He has his shit together. Major Mitchell is one of the finest officers I've ever worked with, and that includes my SEAL officers. Like I said, your buddy is full of shit."

Major Jameson and I continued to drink and discuss our recent experiences and what was next for us in OSI as the rest of the agents began to thin out. He was a scotch and cigar guy. I was happy with a beer and an occasional shot. Later in the evening, his wife would arrive to pour us into her car and get us home.

Commander Mitchell and I only emailed each other once after I left Iraq. I think we didn't want to remind each other of what happened to Nate, Tom, and Dave. It was an ugly elephant in the room that neither one of us wanted to disturb.

◈ ◈ ◈

The air force selected Orion and me to fly out to the Joint Base McGuire-Dix-Lakehurst in New Jersey, more commonly known as Fort Dix. A mix of airmen, soldiers, and sailors were stationed there. Here in the States, if shit went down, I didn't know who had my back. It was scary and lonely, but I knew Orion had my back, and I was excited to see him. We shared a brotherhood—a deeper connection than friendship. It was unconditional. We'd agreed to put the safety of our EDet above our own—to love each other more than ourselves. I didn't miss people dying, but I missed the camaraderie.

At the US Air Force Expeditionary Center, Orion and I helped prepare conventional security forces to relieve the 820th airmen as tactical support elements. More recently returned OSI agents briefed TSEs training to work where the agents had served—Iraq, Afghanistan, and so on. Orion and I showed our group of TSEs how we patrolled and our standard operating procedures.

After work, Orion and I went out to a bar. Orion drank a lot, and he didn't look well. Not only had he suffered the loss of our three guys, but three months earlier, he'd lost a friend with whom he'd served in the ASTs back in Texas—Agent Matt Kuglics, who was killed when his vehicle hit an IED in Kirkuk, Iraq.

Orion talked about the night when Nate, Tom, and Dave were killed. His eyes teared up, and he looked like he was going to fall apart. "That meet wasn't necessary."

I didn't know how much of this was the alcohol talking or Orion, but it caused me to put down my beer. "What do you mean?"

"Moped didn't have anything for us."

"Who told you that?" I asked.

He shook his head. "I think it was a couple guys from headquarters."

"Orion, you know that's bullshit. They weren't there. You were there with me when the other meet for that night got cancelled and when Mac received the call from Moped saying he had intel about who planted the IED that killed the EOD soldier. It was a last-minute decision to meet him that night because of the importance of the intel."

Orion took a drink. "Oh, yeah, that's right."

"You got to be careful, man. People run their mouths about what they heard from someone who wasn't even there, and then those rumors spread like wildfire. You can't let the gossipers and conspiracists into your head."

"You're right."

The rumor mill wasn't limited to OSI or the air force. I'd heard SEALs talk about Operation Red Wings and *Lone Survivor* SEAL Marcus Luttrell: "They shouldn't have done this. They shouldn't have done that." I didn't say anything because my friends were doing the talking. No matter which branch of service, if guys weren't there, how could they know what painful decisions had to be made? The critics who run their mouths the most seem the least likely to put their knees in the breeze and do what needs to be done. If they weren't there, and they weren't doing it, they needed to shut the hell up.

I returned to Hurlburt, Florida, and was assigned to an OSI Special Mission Unit (SMU) in the Air Force Special Operations Command. From there, I supported OSI agents who went out to different parts of the world to provide force protection and counterintelligence to US Air Force units who advised our allies on flying, fighting, civil engineering, and so on—Foreign Internal Defense.

An agent friend of mine and his partner flew out with a group of these air force advisors to Islamabad, Pakistan. There, agents greeted and shared notes with the local police, military intelligence, and government intelligence officers. Also, they met with assets and developed new ones. Soon chatter arose that terrorists were targeting Westerners in the area where embassies and government buildings stood—the same place where the agents and the air force advisors were staying. When the agents told the advisors about the imminent danger, the advisors didn't want to listen to it and said they could take care of themselves. The more the agents provided new intel and tried to persuade them, the more the advisors ignored them. Making matters worse, the advisors seemed suspicious of the agents' federal law enforcement role and were concerned that they might investigate some of their partying. The agents tried to explain that they were there to protect them and provide intel for force protection, not to investigate them. Bottom line, the advisors didn't want federal agents around. After several weeks of trying, the agents emailed and phoned me that they were unappreciated, and they wondered what the hell they were doing there. The buzz of threats increased, and the situation became more dangerous.

I showed our lieutenant colonel—an experienced leader who'd served in Iraq—what the agents had been reporting.

"What do you think we ought to do?" he asked.

"You're asking me, sir?"

"Yes," he said.

"It's ugly there, and the advisors don't appreciate the work our guys are doing for them. We ought to bring our guys home—now."

Our two agents came home. A couple weeks later, on September 20, 2008, a dump truck filled with explosives drove in front of the Islamabad Marriott Hotel—the same hotel our two agents had been staying in—and detonated. Fifty-four people were killed. Most of the casualties were Pakistanis. One of the air force advisors was among those killed. Two hundred and sixty-six people were injured. The blast left a crater in front of the hotel that was twenty feet deep and sixty feet wide. The deaths and casualties saddened me, but I was thrilled that my buddy and his partner had made it home safe.

With SMU agents coming and going from various hot spots around the world, I knew that my turn would come soon. I hadn't been home a year yet, and I was already itching to venture out and do something again.

CHAPTER 41

NAVAL POSTGRADUATE SCHOOL

IN THE BULLPEN AN AGENT asked me, "Are you going to be attached to us permanently, or are they going to send you someplace else?"

Almost on cue, an email popped up on my computer monitor, and I opened it. I read it aloud: "Congratulations on your selection to Naval Postgraduate School. Your area of specialization will be Far East Asia, and you will learn Korean." I turned to the agents and said, "What the hell?"

"Korean—holy shit," an agent behind me said. "That's one of the hardest languages."

Although I'd applied for Arabic or Russian and knew Spanish, I was now going to learn Korean. The agents laughed their asses off.

I told my wife about the acceptance letter. She enjoyed being stationed in and experiencing different places, and she was excited to go.

In September, we packed everything up and moved to Monterey. It was October when school started.

OSI Colonel Keith Givens came out visiting OSI Detachments in northern California, and he stopped by to see those of us at Naval Postgrad School. He'd heard about me and wanted to meet me.

"Have you learned the one thing that's really important since you've been here at Naval Postgraduate School?" he asked.

"What would that be, sir?"

"Never pick a navy school. Because they're really hard."

Colonel Givens would go on to become the general in charge of OSI.

At another time, Admiral Michael Mullen, Chairman of the Joint Chiefs of Staff and the highest ranking officer in the military, came out to the King Auditorium and spoke to all the students and faculty. He said something that meshed with what Colonel Givens told me: "I earned my master's of science in operations here because I wanted to learn something that would help me solve

241

real-world problems in my career. Strong institutions can make a significant difference in our lives, whether they be here at the Naval Postgraduate School or a personal institution, such as one's family. Fortunately, I had both. I struggled here as a student. This is a tough school, but stick with it—it's worth it."

Then Admiral Mullen's wife spoke at the podium. "Mike didn't exactly tell you all of the story—he wanted to quit."

There was laughter.

She continued, "I had to tell him that if he quit this school, his career would be over."

Givens and the Mullens were right, Naval Postgraduate School was a kick in the nuts. One of my professors also taught international relations at the Hoover Institute at Stanford. Faculty came from Yale, the military academies, Johns Hopkins, Brown, and other top universities. Over two dozen astronauts, numerous generals, and many admirals graduated from Naval Postgraduate School.

Many of my classmates seemed sharper than me, and I didn't know how a knuckle dragger like me was going to survive. It took me so long to read the hundreds of pages of homework, and I had to hunt and peck on the keyboard to write each of the many papers I was assigned. Fridays there was no class, and while some of my classmates took the day off, I went straight to the library and studied.

When we had discussions in the classroom, though, I realized that several of my classmates weren't as bright as I thought they were. Although they handed in their assignments, when asked questions or engaged in conversation, they showed little mastery of the subject matter. They passed the classes, but it was the students who worked hardest that seemed to gain the most.

Postgraduate grading wasn't like undergraduate grading. Now a B was considered average and B- was failing. Many of the lectures were two hours long. I never drank coffee before, but during breaks, my classmates and I bolted to the barista on campus. I started with a foo-foo drink—café mocha. As time went on, I could practically inject black coffee directly into my veins. *Anything is better than Professor's chai.*

On Friday evenings, I'd come home with a stack of books and papers and sit down with my laptop, but my wife and kids were already out the door. They visited my parents in the Sierra Foothills more than I did. My folks had year-round passes to Universal Studios, and my wife and children always seemed to be out enjoying themselves. They'd come back on Sunday evening, and I'd still be slugging it out with my homework. I'd continue working while they went to sleep. They loved Monterey.

During my days at Naval Postgraduate School, the Supreme Leader of North Korea, Kim Jong-il, was still alive, but he was old, and his health had deteriorated. He had three sons, and the salient question was: Which would be the successor? In my seminar on Northeast Asian Security Studies, I gave a presentation on who I thought it would be. All my information told me that it was going to be Kim Jong-un. Near the end of my presentation, I said, "The National Defense Commission leads North Korea's military and domestic affairs, and there are only thirteen seats at that table. If Kim Jong-un takes a seat at that table, this will confirm that he will be the one to take his father's place as head of North Korea."

Dr. Clay Moltz taught the seminar, and he was one of my favorites. I enjoyed the subject matter and how open he was to discussion. He disagreed with the thesis of my presentation, but he enjoyed my reasoning. He also appreciated one of my visuals—a night satellite photo of the Korean peninsula. Korea (also known as South Korea) was a sea of lights, but North Korea was dark. It was as if the Yellow Sea merged with the Sea of Japan, and there was no land where North Korea should exist—only a sparkle in Pyongyang where North Korea's supreme leader partied. Although such photos would later become common on the internet, at that time, I had to dig up the photo at the library. Dr. Moltz liked it so much that he printed it out. Later, on the Naval Postgraduate School's website, under his National Security Affairs Department webpage was a photo of him at his desk smiling and holding that photo.

Soon after my presentation, Kim Jong-un *did* take a seat at the National Defense Commission.

After two years of postgrad, I was almost finished. If I had a choice between doing a master's degree all over again or doing Hell Week, it'd be a hard choice to make. Hell Week only lasted five-and-a-half days, and it was more fun than Naval Postgraduate School. Then again, Hell Week happened so long ago that I've forgotten how much it sucked.

Instead of writing a final thesis paper like other students, all I had to do was study a language across the street at the Defense Language Institute—easy day—or so I thought. The military, in its infinite wisdom, decided to chop the sixty-four-week Korean course down to fifty weeks for my class. Because officers were supposed to be academically stronger than enlisted men, two other officers—an F-16 pilot and a marine corps major—and I were the first to experience the condensed curriculum. The three of us were the most Neanderthal language learners they could've chosen to experiment on. The teachers became frustrated. They ran out of time to teach us material, but they tested us on it anyways. We were frustrated too.

While I was at language school, Kim Jong-il died and his son, Kim Jong-un, became supreme leader of North Korea. My prediction had been right.

We were told that, based on our scores and recommendations from our teachers and military unit superiors, the three of us had been selected to be sent to Korea University in Seoul for six weeks as part of an immersion program. In both the US and Korea, the F-16 pilot was a spring-butt who jumped to answer questions before the marine and me. He seemed smarter than us, and I guessed that's the way a guy had to be to become a fighter pilot. Outside of class, he'd often be the first to hop on a train. More than once he looked back at us and wondered why we didn't follow him. He was on the wrong train.

After one of our university field trips, the marine major and I got lost trying to find our way home. We got off at the wrong subway stop, walked up the stairs, and stepped onto a main street where Middle Easterners were every-where. We walked farther in hopes of finding our way, but we were lost. For as far as we could see, these Middle Easterners literally ran the place. I may have stood out as military, but the marine major had a high and tight haircut, and he stuck out like a turd in a punchbowl. The Arabs gave him the evil eye. Then they gave it to me too. These weren't run-of-the-mill Middle Easterners—they glared at us as if they wanted to kill us. I hadn't seen anything like this when I was in Korea with SEAL Team Five in the nineties, but I saw those faces on insurgents in Iraq. The marine major and I watched our backs as we navigated our way out of there. Luckily, we found another subway without incident.

On a personal note, I knew that if I graduated language school, my family would accompany me to my next duty station at Osan Air Base, Korea. While I was studying at Korea University, I took a trip out to visit my new com-mand, but an officer I met with said, "We don't have you coming out here with your family."

"I was told I'd be doing an accompanied tour," I said.

"We weren't aware of that," he said.

Because of the time difference, I had to wake up at 1:00 a.m. to call my detailer in Washington, DC. I pleaded my case: "You have to fix this because I'm going to Osan with my family. That was the agreement."

After several nights of 1:00 a.m. calls, I found out that two people at Osan hadn't done their jobs. I didn't think my detailer in DC was doing his job either. Then I was told, "The quickest your family could join you in Korea would be after eight months."

For me, it was unacceptable. I'd already spent time in Korea as part of SEAL Team Five; now I was here on the language immersion program, and I wasn't excited about spending more time here, especially without my family. I'd been out of my wife's and children's lives for too many years.

I called my wife, and she was disappointed too. We figured that if we had to spend eight months apart—which could actually end up being longer—we may as well get my twelve-month unaccompanied tour out of the way during this assignment. Everyone was required to do one.

I completed the immersion program in Korea and returned to Monterey, California. Soon, I received an email from Dr. Moltz about an upcoming seminar. I attended, and an expert with a fifty-five pound brain on his shoulders gave a lecture. He was bald on top with red hair around the sides that made him look like Friar Tuck. Most of the content of his seminar I already knew from my studies. Near the end of his lecture, he said, "Does anyone have any questions?"

I raised my hand. "When I was in Seoul, I noticed an area that appeared to be controlled by radical Middle Easterners. Their attitude was anti-military. Have any Middle Eastern radicals attempted to immigrate to Korea—either legally or illegally?"

"That's nonexistent," Friar Tuck replied.

"Oh," I said. I didn't want to argue with him in front of everyone. *What the hell?*

After class, I told my professor about it, but he said, "I haven't heard any reports of radicalized Middle Easterners in Korea. Anything is possible, but it's hard to believe."

"Okay," I said. *These guys in the think tanks must have their heads in the sand.*

I returned to the Defense Language Institute across the street. We had to score a certain level on the Defense Language Proficiency Test to graduate and receive our orders. The marine and I passed. The pilot didn't.

I moved my family into an apartment near my wife's folks in the Piedmont Crescent of North Carolina, and I flew out to Osan Air Base in Korea—unaccompanied.

CHAPTER 42

INSURGENTS IN KOREA

My new unit, the Fifth Field Investigative Squadron (FIS), had failed their most recent evaluation. My new boss, Commander Brass, was one step away from having the first red mark on his stellar career.

Normally I wore a suit, but once a week I donned a camouflage uniform without rank insignia but with *Special Agent Treadway* written on my name tape. Whether in suit or camouflage, I carried a concealed pistol, as agents were required to do.

I parked at Osan Air Base in an asphalt parking lot and walked through the one entrance of a fenced-in compound. Inside were three buildings: Leadership and Counterintelligence, Criminal Investigations, and Training and Resources. Our FIS oversaw air force counterintelligence and criminal investigations at three detachments: Detachment 611 here at Osan, Detachment 613 at Kunsan Air Base on the west coast, and Detachment 614 in Seoul. We were also in charge of smaller units in the Korean Peninsula.

On my first day at Osan, I entered the Leadership and Counterintel building, where I met with Commander Brass in his office. After greeting each other and some small talk, he said, "In three months, an operational readiness inspection is coming up. I want you to lead training and resources—prepare us for the inspection. And I need you to oversee our counterintel agents and their day-to-day collections on the Korean Peninsula—synergize information between agents and review it before we publish anything to the broader intelligence community."

He provided me with an office in the Sensitive Compartmented Information Facility (SCIF) of our building. This enabled me to securely reach out to agents within the SCIF and all over Korea. I could coordinate weekly tactical training and oversee counterintelligence and force protection operations.

I quickly learned who had a passion for what. Some agents wanted to work the insider threat of air force personnel—those with classified jobs who went out into town and leaked secrets, whether it be unknowingly for sex, money, blackmail threats, or whatever.

Other agents wanted to work force protection counterintelligence in the less built up areas of Korea—finding out who was collecting intelligence on us. The agents had a variety of talents and interests in an assortment of areas. Soon it became apparent that there was a mismatch between their talents and passions and their actual jobs. It looked like a football team where the star quarterback was told to become a wide receiver and catch the football, the MVP receiver was sent to the front to become a lineman and block, and the Pro Bowl lineman was pulled back to play quarterback and throw the ball. It made no sense. They were doomed before the football was snapped.

I visited Commander Brass in his office and told him, "I'd like to put Hoganski and Fritz to work doing what they do best, sir."

He scratched his jaw. "What they've been doing best is screwing up this unit."

"How so, sir?"

"Ivy says so." She was Commander Brass's second in command. "The man you relieved said so too."

"I understand that they disliked Hoganski and Fritz. Ivy and my predecessor didn't seem to listen or pay attention to the talented agents we have here because the summary they gave me on the quality of these agents isn't what I see. For instance, Hoganski and Fritz are two of the most experienced and talented agents, but Ivy switched them to jobs they hated, and it's no wonder they want to quit the air force."

Commander Brass leaned back, and his body stiffened for a moment. Then his body relaxed, and he leaned forward. Despite the pressure he'd been receiving from HQ and the new information I was giving him, he remained even keeled and kept his cool. "You want to do what now?"

"Put Hoganski and Fritz to work doing what they do best, sir."

Commander Brass studied me for a moment. Then he took a deep breath and exhaled long. "Okay."

I was excited to have his support, but I worried about the upcoming operational readiness inspection. Our unit was already failing, and if we didn't turn the situation around, Commander Brass would probably get the boot. He'd had an all-star career to that point, but he was being misled by his officer and senior enlisted staff—the same people who dropped the ball on my family accompanying me to Korea.

I talked with Hoganski and Fritz at their desks, trying to figure out how to motivate them again.

Hoganski was built like a Slavic lumberjack and strong as hell. He could bench four hundred pounds without needing to lift on a regular basis. He was only a staff sergeant in rank—an E-5—but he was highly intelligent and worked in the SCIF. After this assignment, his goal was to flex his skills in a more classified unit in OSI, but given the recent situation, he wanted out of the air force altogether.

I sat down with him at his desk and said, "I need you to pick someone to help you put together counterintel training—you know, refresh agents on how to receive intel and write reports so they're prepared for this operational readiness inspection."

He scribbled on a notepad. "Ted would be good. He used to operate in an SMU." Each special mission unit was made up of top performers who conducted clandestine missions in austere locations. "Ted was stationed in Okinawa, Japan, and flew out of Kadena Air Base a lot, so he's quite familiar with East Asia. His Korean is great too. He's especially knowledgeable about Korea and the units here."

"Sounds good. I know you've already been through several of these inspections, but if you have any questions, let me know."

"Yes, sir."

I left him and went to see Fritz, who had a shaved head and wore glasses. He wanted to be stationed in Ramstein, Germany, but now he was aching to leave the air force too.

"I'd like you to help me prepare for the upcoming inspection," I said.

"No one listens to me," he said.

"I'm listening to you."

"We've got outdated gear that we don't need any more," he said. "There's advanced equipment that we should be training with and using on a regular basis, but we don't have it."

I leaned forward. "I need you to oversee training and resources. Get someone to assist you and make it happen. If you need any help, just let me know what you need."

"I have someone in mind," he said. "But..."

"But?" I asked.

Fritz hesitated. "There might be a problem."

I waited for him to explain.

Fritz took a breath. "Romeo got in trouble on Halloween. It involved alcohol and a pretty girl dressed up like Madonna. They'd been partying out in town, and when they and their entourage returned to base, Madonna had forgotten her ID, and things escalated from there. The general of OSI was ready to pull Romeo's badge and gun and kick him out of OSI."

I couldn't resist grinning. "Put Romeo to work and keep him out of trouble."

Meeting with Hoganski and Fritz seemed a simple thing, and it was odd that it hadn't been done before. They were like the perfect pieces to a puzzle—they only needed to be placed in the right spots.

Later, I pulled Hoganski and Fritz and their assistants into a room just outside of the SCIF. We sat at a large staff table, and I briefed them: "I want you to prepare us to crush the operational readiness inspection. We'll need a training schedule too. There's a strong chance that the inspectors will give us a scenario where the base is overrun, and we'll have to take it back. We need to be ready for that and whatever else they throw at us."

There were nods and smiles all around the table.

In the following weeks, they reviewed writing and sharing intel reports. They trained our agents on chemical warfare: wearing chemical warfare suits, giving epinephrine shots, using decontamination stations, and recognizing different sirens and what each one meant.

I taught patrolling and building-clearing tactics.

My day-to-day job of running counterintel on the peninsula was challenging. Going to Seoul every other week and briefing Operational Forces Korea on what we were working on wasn't the tough part. Talking with the US Navy's NCIS, army intelligence, and other intelligence agencies throughout Korea wasn't the most difficult part either. The hard part was communicating with the air force OSI agents immediately outside my office door.

I was still a captain, and Ivy outranked me by one notch. She required me to go through her before talking with the counterintel guys. She complicated this further by rarely communicating with agents. When she did, it was mainly with one person—the senior noncommissioned officer, Sophia, who functioned like a manager. Sophia didn't like Ivy or her one-way style of communication. It was a comedy of errors, but no one was laughing.

I could listen to problems the agents were stuck on, but I couldn't help them. I was the ear, Ivy was the mouth, and Sophia was the mouthpiece—our connection was circuitous. This was made worse because Ivy was also in charge of criminal investigations, which split her time away from counterintelligence. She made it a point to be in control, but her leadership style was a failure. Whatever her reasoning, it made no sense to me.

On the training side, I met twice a week in the same room with Hoganski, Fritz, and all the people we needed to support them. I broke them into groups—

counterintel, insider threat, training and resources, and so on. I asked what each group was working on and what they needed, such as personnel and capabilities. Then I'd provide them with the support they required. At the next meeting, I asked what they'd done. We'd discuss what they'd do the next week. In my office, I kept a schedule board and tracked our progress.

For our real day-to-day operations, we improved at coordinating intel with our air base leadership, security forces, other US military intelligence units, and our Korean counterparts.

Once a week, we shut down to do practice drills. In one exercise, we simulated receiving intel about a security weakness at a gate. We shared that with the air base leadership and security forces, and they tightened up security at that entry. We role-played enemy forces attempting to infiltrate a section of the fence, so the base and its security force responded by adding a heavy weapons team to that area. Both in training and reality, our intel drove the base's defense posture.

In times of war, criminal investigation agents would shift to working counterintelligence, so we trained them up for that too. During peacetime, counterintel agents might have to pitch in to assist a criminal investigation—which is exactly what we were called on to do. Five US Army reserve soldiers on our base became involved in a drug ring to smuggle "spice," a synthetic marijuana, through the mail from the US. Then they'd go to other US bases in Korea and sell it. Though they were arrested at night, we didn't wrap up interviews with the soldiers until 05:00 the next morning. I was partnered with Fritz during interviews, and we elicited a key confession from the ringleader. The soldiers were discharged from the army.

Not long after, the operational readiness inspectors departed their Pacific headquarters in Hawaii and flew out to Korea. They put our whole base, including air force, army, and the Korean air force into low-level alert. We donned chemical warfare suits and performed mock missions. I didn't mind wearing the chem warfare gear outside in the winter weather, but inside, I sweated my butt off. Before coming to Korea, when I deployed to other parts of the world, I hadn't taken chemical warfare seriously, but now that I lived in close proximity to Kim Jong-un and his chemical weapons, I made sure I had my shots and two good chem warfare suits.

The evaluators observed our tactics and took notes. They graded us on individual performance, unit performance, how well we worked with other units, and the base's performance as a whole. Then the evaluators escalated the scenarios into a full scale attack from North Korea—with infiltrations and assaults hitting the base twenty-four hours a day for several days. Even though we worked in shifts, we still got little sleep.

In one scenario, our compound was overrun, and we had to retake it from North Korean soldiers. The evaluators separated me from the other agents, who were worried because I wasn't going with them. I'd trained them the best I knew how, and I knew they could do it. They did.

I felt a lot of pressure because Commander Brass had put his trust in me. If our unit scored poorly, he'd be in jeopardy of being fired—and it would have been my fault. We rated a C1, the highest score possible. We blew it out of the water.

The whole attitude in our FIS lifted. In the past, some agents talked trash about others, but after seeing everyone perform at such a high level, the trash talking died down. Agents were proud of their unit and themselves.

Commander Brass called me into his office. We chit-chatted a bit, but I didn't understand what the real point of me being there was. Then Ivy walked in, and I became uncomfortable. I felt an ambush coming on.

Commander Brass said, "The air force is reducing its number of officers. They've been combing through records for our credentials and accomplishments." Then he focused on Ivy and held his gaze. "Ivy, you just don't have the kind of record that would rack and stack you high enough to keep you around. You need to start making plans to leave."

Ivy swallowed hard. "Leave Korea, sir?"

"Leave the air force," Commander Brass said.

Her eyes and mouth opened wide.

Commander Brass was an excellent boss who'd been terribly misinformed by his top two officers. He not only kept his job, but he was promoted to full bird colonel and shipped off to his next unit.

The new commander arrived, and with Ivy out of the way, it was time to kick day-to-day counterintelligence ops into high gear and crank the throttle. Sophia, who had been Ivy's mouthpiece, was in charge of counterintelligence, and my perception was that she had problems with me.

I sat down and talked with her. "Now we work together," I said. "You don't work for me—we're partners. If I did something that you're not happy with, I want to know. Feel free to tell me. We're both professionals."

She leaned back in surprise. "I didn't want to tell you because you and Ivy were both officers. I thought the two of you were an impenetrable wall. She made me mad a couple times, but I didn't want to make waves." She explained what I already knew. Ivy never took the time to find out what Sophia was upset about. Being unable to communicate directly with me worsened matters. After that conversation, Sophia and I became good friends.

Hoganski reported on observations from security forces that Middle Easterners in Western clothes were conducting surveillance on our base. I remembered the hostile stares of the Middle Easterners who ran that place in Seoul when I was in the language immersion program. No matter how far people stuck their heads in the sand, a storm was coming. We conducted counter-surveillance to find out who they were, where they lived, and who they were working for.

When I reported it to my new commander, his reaction was, "What!"

He took me to see the commander of all the air forces in Korea—a three-star general—and his reaction was similar. After the commander's initial surprise, he said, "I need more evidence."

I put Sophia and our agents to work on it, and they sniffed out the terrorist threat further. They discovered terrorists on the US watchlist and exposed one as a financier. Furthermore, these terrorist surveillance activities extended beyond Seoul and throughout the peninsula. When my commander and I briefed the three-star general with our latest evidence, he took us to his boss at US Forces Korea—the four-star general in charge of all air, naval, marine, ground, and special operation forces on the peninsula. "I need you to brief us on this regularly," he said. "We need to shut this down."

As the four-star general requested, I regularly briefed his man in charge of intelligence, a one-star general. I had to bring in more agents to support our investigations. One terrorist link led to another, and the names of known terrorists popped like popcorn. Without my family there, all I did was work cases and work out—even on Saturdays—from the crack of dawn and into dusk.

When we'd figured out as much as we could, we passed the information to the Koreans, who joined us on some surveillance operations. The Koreans put in the time necessary to understand what was going on and the connections. In their country, we didn't have powers of arrest, but the Koreans did, and they used it. They also expelled several people from the country. We'd mitigated the terrorist threat.

◈   ◈   ◈

In a separate incident, our base planned to put on an air show where we would display some sensitive aircraft. Our enemies have professionals who travel from air show to air show and get as close as they can to the planes and take photos with hidden cameras to gather intelligence. We were concerned that these people were collecting information about our aircraft. One of my agents picked up intel about a group of these folks, and we contacted other US Air Force bases to see if they could tell us more. A base in Paris gave us pictures and identities. We passed that to our security forces. When the air show began, visitors were screened at the gates. Three of these guys showed up, and security forces turned them away. They tried to come in at another entrance, and they were rejected again. Because we had no powers of arrest, the most we could do was deny entry.

I was fortunate to conduct the rare debrief of a North Korean Special Operations Forces defector. Generals and other agencies praised our work. The details remain classified, but we enhanced our assessment of North Korea's war plans.

After more than half a year, I returned home for a month and enjoyed time with the family, but when I returned to Korea, I injured myself. I'd continued to lift weights in the mornings, and during a normal workout, while bench pressing, I heard a *pop*! I was getting older and used to hearing more pops, but never this bad. I pressed the weights back up, and I felt a tearing in my chest. I couldn't push the bar all the way up. *Damn.* "I need some help, here!"

A couple guys hurried over and racked the weights for me. My whole arm felt like it was hanging to my knee.

I dragged myself out of the gym and into the parking lot. It was cold, and there was ice on the ground, so I tried not slip. I made it to my car and drove myself to the emergency room. They took off my shirt. I was black-and-blue from my throat down to my waist. They shot me up with Toradol for the pain and notified my commander. The doctor tried to do an MRI, but there was so much blood and torn up tissue inside that they couldn't get a good read.

The military didn't have anyone in Korea who was experienced in operating on my type of injury. They could fly me to Hawaii for the operation, but I'd be in the hospital awhile. If I did that, it would end my tour prematurely, and I'd have to do it all over again. The eight months or so I'd already put in wouldn't count for my remote. I'd still have to do a full year without my family. *To hell with that.* I'd let it heal without an operation.

A couple days after, I wasn't feeling well and went back to the doctor. "I'm feeling lightheaded," I said.

"Yeah, you probably bled about a liter," he said. "The internal hemorrhaging is most likely what's making you lightheaded."

Later, I'd find out that I'd torn my largest chest muscle off the shoulder bone. I was determined to recover without surgery, and the doctor supported me.

Two weeks after hurting myself, my wife came out to see me. Of all the places I'd been in the world, Korea was the closest to like being on another planet—even more so than the Middle East. The people, food, language, and culture seemed alien. My wife loved it, and I loved being her personal tour guide, even if my arm was in a sling. I showed her Busan and places I used to hang out when I was there with SEAL Team Five.

I introduced her to Sophia, and the two quickly became friends. My commander promoted me to major, and we had a brief ceremony. My wife and Sophia pinned my new ranks—oak leaves—on me. Then I invited everyone over to the bowling alley, and I paid for an open bar. My wife was happy to meet the agents in a relaxed atmosphere. We had a pitch-perfect time. Then I took her out into town, Pyeongtaek, to celebrate. Eventually, she flew back home.

Colonel Gray, the same boss in Qatar who was in charge of EDets in Iraq had been transferred to Hawaii and now oversaw all OSI agents in the Pacific, including my field investigative squadron. Her command chief master sergeant followed her. When the two of them came out to Korea, I introduced them to Sophia, Hoganski, and Fritz, and I bragged about how awesome they were. Both Hoganski and Fritz were near their time to apply for promotions, and I secured them achievement medals for their outstanding work.

Hoganski got his wish and transferred to a more classified part of OSI, and he and Fritz each earned a commendation medal. Afterwards, Fritz transferred to his dream duty station: Ramstein, Germany. Both Agents Hoganski and Fritz stayed in the air force.

Although I'd only recently been promoted to the field grade of major, I was selected above all the other OSI majors and lieutenant colonels to be Field Grade Officer of the Year for the Pacific region. I'd worked hard, but the main reason I received the award was because I had two commanders who trusted me and talented agents who made me look good.

CHAPTER 43

BACKDRAFT

MY PLAN WAS TO GET promoted to lieutenant colonel before I retired. Well, that was the plan. My wife and children accompanied me to my next duty station, Field Investigative Region Three at Scott Air Force Base in Illinois. I became the operations officer—the number three man in charge of OSI detachments in thirteen states. As I had in Korea, I found myself swimming in the waters of a drowning unit. Our performance ranked seventh of eight OSI regions across the globe.

Scott Air Force Base had been Tom's home station, and I was surprised to learn that the whole base had started an annual run in his memory. Beginning on Friday afternoon at the base track, anyone could join the memorial run at any time and run for as many miles as they wanted to. The memorial run would last for twenty-four hours. Before the run, someone asked, "Would you like to do us the honors of starting the run?"

I was happy they were doing this for Tom, but I didn't want to grieve again—especially in public. "I don't think I'd like to."

Before the run, my whole OSI detachment took a group photo together. Then we went out to the track. I was scared, but I went. The colonel pointed to a woman fifteen yards away and said, "That's Tom's mother."

I looked at her, but I couldn't bring myself to go and talk to her. The colonel went over and greeted her. He said something, and she looked my way. I had the impression she didn't want to talk with me either. If she was like me, she didn't want to remove the scab from the wound. We didn't close the space between us. Each hour, the group of runners changed. After a couple hours, I went home.

Late in the evening, I sat in the living room and watched TV with my wife. I looked at the clock. It was almost midnight, and soon the group of runners would change again. I felt a fire under my ass. "I'm going to head out there and run."

"Really?" my wife asked.

"Yeah. It'll only be a mile."

I changed into my running clothes and shoes.

"I'll go with you," she said.

"Okay."

We drove out to the track, lit up by field lights and the moon. Runners gathered for the midnight group. I stood off to the side and stretched. At midnight, they took their turn, and I slipped in with them. The cool air felt good.

I recognized that the guys were from the communications squadron, which had two of the fastest guys on the base. Even so, I figured that I could keep up for a mile.

"What unit are you with?" one of them asked.

"OSI."

"Oh, really? Did you know Tom?"

I told them about him and our missions. They asked questions, and I answered them.

The first mile went by, and they kept running. We kept talking. Finally, I asked, "How far are you guys running?"

"Six miles."

Shit. I forced a smile.

They asked more questions, and I told them some more. When we reached the fifth mile, I thought we could take it easy in the homestretch—but they kicked it in the ass. I couldn't swallow my pride, so I sped up too.

We finished our run, and each of them thanked me. "This was the coolest," one said.

"I never would've guessed I'd get this much out of this," another said.

"Me neither," I said. "I wasn't expecting to do six miles."

My wife overheard me and laughed.

I left them and walked over to her.

"That was a long mile," she said.

I groaned.

She laughed again.

⊕ ⊕ ⊕

Like some of my mentors—SEALs who'd set foot in Vietnam for the first time—I crept through the office jungle and watched and listened, day after day.

What I heard was that my agents in the FIR were disconnected from the agents out in the field—they were literally detachments. After enough stalking and observing, it was time for direct action.

I told my guys, "You're responsible for those detachments out there. If they're failing, you're failing. I want you to visit your detachments monthly and help them out."

"That's gonna take some time," an agent complained.

"You got something better to do?" I asked.

The agent and other personnel sat up straight in their chairs. Shit just got real—and I think they liked it.

The famous army general, Colin Powell, said: "Leadership is solving problems. The day soldiers stop bringing you their problems is the day you have stopped leading them. They have either lost confidence that you can help or concluded you do not care. Either case is a failure of leadership."

On the investigative side, Washington, DC, pushed hard to stop sexual assault in the military, so I aligned our goals with the powers above and put sexual assault cases on the front burner. I gathered my team, including a tough little Irish-American agent who specialized in investigating the cases of minors who'd been raped. She was so skilled at her job, agents from all over the United States requested her assistance.

One of our cases involved a merchant marine who raped at least eighteen victims in different parts of the world before setting sail to his next port and doing it again. His movement was so hard to track, agents had given up. We told the agents at Travis AFB to dust off the case, and we put them in touch with the Navy Criminal Investigative Service, experts at tracking ship's movements. NCIS caught up with the suspect in a port in East Asia and interviewed him. He was a serial pedophile. He was arrested.

We also identified two rapists that local police departments had missed.

On the counterintelligence side, we worked with the FBI's counterintelligence agents on six cases. Because my FIR had a direct link with OSI headquarters, we called on Washington to send us whatever experts we needed—surveillance, forensics and so on. We mitigated four terrorist threats and six Foreign Intelligence Security Service threats.

Our unit quickly shot up from second worst to second best. I was awarded field grade officer of the year for our region—again.

The good news was, the air force offered me a slot at an air force graduate school—an opportunity to earn another master's degree and accelerate my promotion to lieutenant colonel and beyond.

The bad news was, the air force offered me a slot at an air force graduate school. I hated graduate school. My superiors tried to persuade me, "It won't be as bad as Naval Postgraduate School. You'll get some credits for your NPS degree."

I wasn't having it.

I talked it over with my wife. More promotions meant more transfers. Our oldest son was in high school, and soon he'd be in college. He'd attend a nearby university. Then we'd pack up and leave him. Our daughter would be next to attend college. Then we'd pack up and leave her. Wash, rinse, repeat. Our family would become spread out, and we didn't like the thought of it.

We decided that I'd retire at my current rank of major, keep the family together, and move close to my wife's folks. I would earn about 70 percent of my major's pay in retirement, but that wouldn't be enough to put my kids through college and to do all that we wanted to. How could I earn more income?

I flirted with the idea of becoming a history teacher. Over the years, I'd coached my son and other kids in baseball and loved it. History was a favorite of mine too. Combining that with teaching made sense—but the itch of law enforcement was still strong, and I had to scratch the itch.

I applied to two major police agencies in the Piedmont Crescent of North Carolina, and both accepted me. I retired from the air force and became a police officer at the closest agency to my wife's family. I worked late hours on my work days, and on my two days off, it seemed I was always in court testifying at some trial. I spent less time with my family than I had when I was in the military. Foot chases and wrapping up bad guys, which was what I wanted to do, happened less often than domestic disputes and car accidents.

One night while I was still a rookie, I responded to a domestic violence complaint. During dinner, an argument arose, and the wife threw a bowl of spaghetti at her husband. His uncle, who had recently been released from jail, called the police. I was required by law to arrest her. I didn't like it, but I escorted her out of the house and helped her into the patrol car. Then the children came out and stood in the snow.

I rolled down the window and asked, "What's going on?"

"I'm going to my daddy's house," the little girl said.

"I'm going to my daddy's too," the little boy said.

Both had the same mother, but their fathers were different—and neither was the stepfather at the dinner table.

The oldest put her hands on her hips. "I'll stay with my sister and her boyfriend."

"Why?" I asked.

"They kicked us out," the oldest said. "They're calling friends, and they're going to have a party."

I was pissed. "No they're not."

I stormed my way to the house and knocked. The husband answered the door with an open beer in his hand.

I leaned toward him. "You're going to take care of these kids." I motioned for the kids and they went back inside.

When I got back in the patrol car, my trainer told the wife how she could apply for a restraining order against her husband. Police officers don't get paid nearly enough.

It's not surprising that more car accidents happen in bad weather, but I hadn't thought about working those accidents in the wet cold. One night I came upon a burning car. It torched so brightly that it whited everything out, and I could hardly see.

I keyed the mic and reported the flaming car.

My vision returned, and I found the shoulder of the road to pull off on.

I looked around for possible threats.

Patrol cars rolled up behind me and stopped.

Instinctively, I crouched low and advanced to the blaze. The fire crackled and popped. Its sound angered me.

I searched the darkness for enemies, but no one was there. I pushed closer, and hot air singed my nostril hairs. The brilliant light took some of my eyesight, and the massive flickering heat distorted everything.

I checked the driver's seat, but no one was there. I looked down at my feet. Nothing.

Police officers and dispatch called out over my radio, but it was all garbled to me.

The heat hurt my skin as I circled around to the passenger side. The numbness inside me came back, and I became small again.

Firefighters and others arrived.

I looked away.

A big numbness enveloped me.

"Is anyone in there?" a firefighter asked.

I wanted to cry but I held it together. "No."

"Are you okay?" the firefighter asked.

"I'm okay." My police uniform, shoes, and other gear smelled like fire, blood, and death, though some part of me knew they didn't really smell like that. I was pretty damn far from okay.

For months, I tried to drink my demons away, but alcohol only plunged me deeper into despair. I compared myself to Nate and Dave, who were younger than me, and I wondered why their lives were cut so short, and why I was allowed to live so long. They didn't have a chance to do a lot of things I did. It seemed horribly unfair.

On the other hand, I thought about Tom. His kids were the same age as mine. Why him and not me? It made no sense, and I felt guilty for surviving.

The first time I visited Tom's burial site in Arlington, I asked my wife to wait for me on a nearby street because I was worried I might cry. Instead, anger consumed me.

I paid my respects to Nate, Tom, and Dave at the National Law Enforcement Officers Memorial in DC. I hoped it would get easier. It didn't.

More than anything, I blamed myself for not being able to save my team-mates and not taking revenge on their killer. I was angry and haunted that I had not killed Captain al-Hakim. My hate for him created its own mental prison.

The guilt and anger changed me for the worse. I withdrew from the rich social life my wife and I enjoyed. I put my wife and family through dark times. I distrusted people around me. I disconnected from the life I was so fortunate to live. At first, I thought it was because of all the negative stuff I'd seen as a federal agent. I tried to deny that it was related to that horrible night, but it was. As a frogman, I thought I was mentally tougher than that—but I wasn't. I thought it affected other agents and not me. *Bullshit*.

CHAPTER 44

UNICORNS & RAINBOWS

I BITCHED AND MOANED ABOUT this and that, and I wanted to quit. I *did* quit alcohol. I thought going to a SEAL Team reunion might help me, but the booze and war stories summoned up old demons, and I quit going to the reunions too—but I didn't quit on life. My wife was my greatest support. I put one foot in front of the other and sucked it up until I could find something that motivated me again. None of this happened overnight, and I wasn't completely out of the funk, but I was moving forward again. I was living again.

One spring, while I was coaching a youth baseball team, a parent mentioned a job opening as a Junior Reserve Officer Training Corps (JROTC) instructor in high school. I became excited at the prospect of teaching kids about the military, national objectives, patriotism, self-discipline, team building, communicating, and physical fitness. I looked around at other job availabilities, and a JROTC teaching position opened up at a high school close to me. I interviewed for it, and the district interviewer on the other side of the table seemed to know a lot about my time in the Teams—so much that it made me uncomfortable.

"How do you know so much about me?" I asked.

"Uncle is a SEAL, and I asked him about you. Told me all about you."

"Oh."

"If we hire you, you can have your choice between teaching military science or global affairs. Which would you prefer?"

I smiled. "Global affairs."

It was a competitive job, but I got it. I hung up my badge and gun and put on my military uniform once more.

I dug teaching high schoolers. I helped the assistant principal break up fights in the halls. The chief, my teaching partner, was also retired military, and together, he and I provided stability and role models to kids from broken homes. One girl called us after hearing gunshots at her apartment complex at night while she was alone with her younger brother and sister. Their single mother was away working. Chief and I advised her to get low and get in the bathtub. "Don't come up until you hear the police arrive." After an increased police presence, her apartment complex calmed down.

We trained our cadets to become good citizens and leaders. Those who volunteered to join the military were better prepared.

In my first year, one of my students wanted to become a marine. He was an easy-going guy, intelligent, and the commander of one of my drill teams. He had a smooth way of keeping the other cadets in line and motivating them, and they loved him. Despite his strengths, he struggled to pass the state's End of Course Test to graduate, and the military's Armed Services Vocational Aptitude Battery (ASVAB).

I noticed that he didn't take notes much and seemed to prefer memorizing what I said. During one of my classes, he wrote something with the letters in his words all messed up.

"When you read, do you keep jumping to the end and coming back to the beginning of the line?" I asked.

"All the time," he said.

"Nobody's ever tested you for that?"

"No."

I talked to my principal about him, and he gave me some colored films to put over his reading materials.

I took them back to him and let him try reading using the films. "How's that?" I asked.

"That's way better," he said.

"Really—it makes a difference?" I asked.

"Makes a huge difference."

Later, he took his test and passed, enabling him to graduate. He also scored high enough on the ASVAB to enter the marine corps, which he did.

After boot camp, he returned for a visit wearing his camouflage uniform. He was in such hardcore physical shape that I hardly recognized him. I let him come to the front of my classroom and speak to the cadets. Although he'd experienced hardships in the marine corps, he was able to joke about it and tell the class how worthwhile it was for him. I was happy to see him overcome his dyslexic challenges, make a plan for his future, and execute it.

In another instance, we had a tough girl who loved PT. She and a cadet from the varsity football team helped lead other cadets in PT. She saw things in black and white—there was rarely middle ground with her. I thought she'd be a good fit for the marine corps. I told her, "Your ASVAB score is so high, you might consider working intelligence in the marine corps. I think you'll like that." She met with the marine recruiters and PTed with them and others who were joining, and she beat a lot of the guys. She recently graduated basic training and is attending the navy and marine corps intelligence course.

One of my freshmen seemed nervous and was extremely quiet. Chief and I had to go out of our way to involve her. It took some time for her to figure out where she fit in. She picked up drill quickly.

In her sophomore year, she snuck up on us, and in her junior year, she blossomed—like a nuke. She liked to do her nails and hair nice when she was in civilian clothes, but once a week, when the cadets wore uniforms, she set aside her civilian style to be a military example, especially for the freshmen. She came in early and helped them with questions they had about how to wear the uniform properly. She also assisted in the morning with marching out to the school's flagpole and raising the US and state flags. She joined all three of our drill teams: color guard, armed regulation, and advanced.

Our color guard was made up of four young women, including her. She had us order pumps and alter the skirts, so they looked just right. Their appearance was impressive. She carried the American flag, and the girl next to her carried the state flag. Flanking them on each end was a cadet carrying a rifle. They presented the flags at open house, school sporting activities, graduation, city events, and so on. In competitions, her team had to perform a sequence of twenty to thirty movements like: uncase colors, carry the colors, perform right wheels and left wheels, colors reverse, and present the colors. She led her color guard team against other schools to first in regions and second in state.

She was mature for her age, maybe partly because her parents were divorced, and she had to work full time to pay her way at home—food, housing, clothing, car, and car insurance. Chief and I talked to her about working more in the summer before her senior year and less during the school year so she could focus more on academics and become cadet commander of our program. She made a plan and stuck to it.

As our cadet commander, she set up ceremonies, coordinated events with other schools, and put together community service activities. That same year, we had a headquarters military inspection of our whole program. If the cadets did poorly, the military could shut us down. She gave a PowerPoint brief in the auditorium, led all 130 cadets out on the parade field in drill, and was interviewed by the inspectors. It lasted all day, and only her cadet leadership team could assist her. Chief and I weren't allowed to help. Our unit earned the highest possible score—outstanding. Our cadet commander and our unit appeared in the newspaper. She'd found her place in JROTC.

JACK TREADWAY AND STEPHEN TEMPLIN

Some previous graduates talked her into going into the marine corps. Chief and I both had the same reaction: "Are you kidding me?"

"That is not you," I told her. "You don't like to PT every day. Your fashion sense doesn't fit the marine corps either. If you were my daughter, I'd recommend you join the navy or the air force."

She discussed it with one of her friends who was in the marine corps, and his comments validated what we told her. We helped her break off with the marine corps, which pissed them off, and worked hard with the air force recruiters, who helped her get a job. Since then, she has received an air force top performer award at her last two assignments.

I had to practically look over a young man's shoulder to make him apply for an army scholarship. His mother brought him in, and I sat him down and took him through a practice interview. He talked about what he wanted to get from the army, but I helped him focus on what he could give. Later, the officer who interviewed him said, "That was the best interview I've ever given." The young man received a full ride scholarship to the army ROTC program at a state university.

A few of our cadets also joined the navy. One of the best programs going for our cadets who score well on the ASVAB is the navy's nuclear program. For cadets that don't come from much, this program's signing bonuses and guaranteed education opportunities are life-changing.

Representatives from various colleges and technical schools came out and talked with my students. A few organizations have started a fully paid scholarship program for students to earn their commercial pilot's license. Economically challenged areas like mine have to compete with more affluent areas. Three thousand kids apply for this scholarship, and only about a hundred are selected. I encouraged two of my cadets to apply. Earning their commercial license will help them achieve an ROTC college scholarship.

I keep peanut butter, jelly, and bread for kids in the supply closet of my office. They don't always eat well. One girl comes in a couple times a week between classes. Even when I don't have classes, she's in my classroom—studying, chatting, or whatever. It's the one place she feels she belongs and excels. A lot of my cadets are like that. It's not uncommon for me to arrive at work to find up to twenty kids hanging out. At the end of the school day, I practically have to kick them out so I can go home.

Yesterday, I took my students to a regional drill competition. There were seven events. I'd seen them perform better, and I wasn't happy with how they were doing. Even so, all my teams finished first and second place. We took the first-place cup overall. They were happy and got all emotional. Their hard work paid off.

Many of my students don't join the military, and I'm okay with that. We train our cadets to become good citizens and leaders. As I write this, I'm in my fifth year of teaching, and I'm really happy for my students who have a plan and are able to act on it—especially those who come from tough situations and are in danger of falling under bad influences. They make me want to keep doing what I'm doing. I'm looking forward to helping the next students who're in need of that little bit of guidance and that extra push to make their lives better. They can do so much more than they think. I can too.

I think Nate, Tom, and Dave would want me to be happy and move on with my life. It's okay to miss them and hurt from time to time, but it's best to keep moving forward. Life isn't always about riding unicorns and shitting rainbows. It's bittersweet. Sometimes it doesn't make sense—maybe it never will—but that's okay. Suck it up when it's bitter and savor it when it's sweet.

EPILOGUE

IEDs CAUSED 63 PERCENT OF US deaths in Iraq. As early as 2006, Iran began to employ the more sophisticated and deadly explosively formed penetrators (EFPs) as part of its puppet war to attack US troops and their allies. A year later, one of these EFPs was struck by Nate, Tom, and Dave. The Iranian puppet master who pulled the strings of evil men in Iraq like Captain al-Hakim and Moped was General Qasem Soleimani.

Over the years, OSI and an alphabet soup of intelligence agencies used confidential informants, surveillance, and other intelligence sources to track General Soleimani and his activities. He was second in power in Iran and the most powerful terrorist in the world. He commanded Iran's Islamic Revolutionary Guard Corps (IRGC) and its Special Operations Quds force to cause bloodshed around the globe. His goal was to destabilize foreign governments and establish Iranian control in those countries.

On the evening of January 3, 2020, General Soleimani and four of his IRGC officers flew into Baghdad International Airport. Five of his puppets in the Iraqi Shia militia of the Popular Mobilization Front (PMF) rolled up to the general's plane in two vehicles and parked at the bottom of the plane's stairs. General Soleimani and his four officers loaded into the two vehicles. A half-moon shone on them as they sped onto Airport Street and headed for Baghdad.

Under direction of President Donald Trump, above General Soleimani's sight and beyond his hearing, flew an air force MQ-9 Reaper and other aircraft. The Reaper launched several missiles that blasted the two vehicles. In an ironic twist of fate, General Soleimani, his four officers, and five Iraqi militiamen were devoured by flames. The puppet master's strings were permanently severed.

When evil raises its ugly head again, and it will, good men and women like those in the air force's OSI will visit violence. Most of their operations remain classified, but their triumphs will continue to allow us to sleep safe at night.